A
SHORT HISTORY
OF THE
BAPTISTS

A
SHORT HISTORY
OF THE
BAPTISTS

HENRY C. VEDDER

JUDSON PRESS ®
VALLEY FORGE

PREFACE

As this preface was being written news was received of the tragic death of Kenneth Scott Latourette, "dean of American church historians" and loyal Baptist churchman, at eighty-four years of age. A no more appropriate time could have been chosen, therefore, than the departure of this devoted scholar, for Judson Press to republish a work of another Baptist historian, the late Henry Clay Vedder. It is an undeserved but cherished honor to write this preface for *A Short History of the Baptists*, for it combines features in both quality of workmanship and content which make its publication both justifiable and desirable.

It is not that Baptists have not been writing more about themselves in the last two decades; to the contrary. All such books are useful; however, some deal with special groups, areas, periods, or aspects of Baptist history; others are written in a "popular" style, and are not suitable for texts. The most important one-volume history of the Baptists is that of Robert G. Torbet, *A History of the Baptists*, published by Judson in 1950 and revised in 1963. Thorough and scholarly, it has attained wide acceptance, but the continued popularity of Vedder reflects a need for a briefer authoritative account of the people called Baptists. Since the introduction of the revised publication of *A Short History of the Baptists*, it has passed through seventeen printings. For a half a century it was the undisputed and standard textbook for Baptist history in colleges and seminaries.

When Dr. Vedder decided in 1897 to revise and enlarge his book, originally published in 1892, an entire decade was required for its completion. He made a thorough restudy of the whole field, including months of travel, collection of new materials, and "the careful rewriting of the entire work and the addition of much new matter." Although he added more than twice as much material as the original, he still felt justified in retaining the original title. Therefore, the present volume remains what it was in 1907, a careful, scholarly, concise study of the history of Baptist principles (Part I) and the growth and expansion of the modern Baptist movement from the seventeenth through the nineteenth centuries (Part II).

In fact, this presentation in some detail of the historical development of Baptist principles constitutes one of the important contributions of the book. In both content and approach it provides a unique approach to Baptist historiography and interpretation. On the one hand, it is a sharp corrective to Landmarkism, a nineteenth century Baptist movement of extreme sectarianism committed to a Baptist "successionism" back to apostolic days which is still found in stubborn pockets in the South and Southwest. Instead, Vedder interprets the struggles of earlier groups holding certain principles common to modern Baptists as the gradual renascence of evangelical Christianity after its early suppression, but set in the general context of Christian history. He blends an appreciation for the contributions of these early "protestants" with historical objectivity, with no attempt to "maintain a thesis or minister to denominational vanity." On the other hand, his inclusion of this material, which Dr. Torbet was compelled to cut drastically in his revised edition to include contemporary material, is a wholesome reminder to some current Baptists, who tend to ignore all tradition and deny any rootage, that our denomination does share a heritage of "radical reformation." Indeed, the final chapter of the book on the progress of Baptist principles reads with the relevance of tomorrow's newspaper on the nature of the church, religious liberty, and separation of church and state.

Perhaps the most striking evidence of Dr. Vedder's scholarship and "up-to-date" material is his analysis of the Anabaptist movement. Although written over sixty years ago, without the benefit of the veritable avalanche of material available during the past quarter century, his account is remarkably accurate, contemporary, and incisive. His unerring historical sense is seen in beginning that story in Zurich with the Swiss Brethren, rather than south Germany (Chapter X) with the Zwickau prophets. His major conclusions on the entire movement have been vindicated by modern scholarship.

The second part of the book, of the same high quality, assumes a similar importance. The Baptists have experienced tremendous growth, especially in America, and have been a significant influence in the Free Church movement. Dr. Vedder in his most optimistic moment could not have dreamed his denomination today would number thirty million in a worldwide fellowship; some today could not dream it was ever otherwise. The reader will find here an inspiring and succinct record of the earlier struggles for recognition and freedom, the evangelistic and missionary spirit which has been the cause of its phenomenal growth and the genius of its unity.

Its brevity and balance, accurate scholarship and historical objectivity, as well as the importance of its subject matter, all combine to give the book a wide appeal to interested Baptists North and South as well as overseas, and to non-Baptists who desire to know more about us. This book should indeed receive a response "commensurate with the favor that has been shown its predecessors." In a time of reevaluation of denominational traditions and perspectives this book will help the reader to understand the particular contributions that Baptists make to the total Christian fellowship.

James D. Mosteller
Professor of Church History
New Orleans Baptist Theological Seminary

New Orleans, Louisiana
February, 1969

CONTENTS

PART II

A HISTORY OF BAPTIST CHURCHES

ILLUSTRATIONS

xiii

INTRODUCTION

INTRODUCTION

THE word Baptists, as the descriptive name of a body of Christians, was first used in English literature, so far as is now known, in the year 1644. The name was not chosen by themselves, but was applied to them by their opponents. In the first Confession of Faith issued by the Particular Baptists in 1644, the churches that published the document described themselves " as commonly (but unjustly) called Anabaptists." While they repudiated the name Anabaptist, they did not for some time claim the new name of Baptists, seeming to prefer "Baptized believers," or, as in the Assembly's Confession of 1654, "Christians baptized upon profession of their faith." These names were, however, too cumbrous, and they finally fell in with the growing popular usage. The name Baptists seems to have been first publicly used by one of the body in 1654, when Mr. William Britten published "The Moderate Baptist." The first official use of the name is in " The Baptist Catechism " issued by the authority of the Assembly. The surviving copies of this document are undated, and we only know that it was prepared and printed " some years " after the Assembly's Confession.

For the fact that the name Baptist comes into use at this time and in this way, but one satisfactory explanation has been proposed: it was at this time that English churches first held, practised, and avowed those principles ever since associated with that name. There had been no such churches before, and hence there was no need of the name. The name Anabaptist had been well known, and it described not unfairly from the point of

3

view of those who invented it, the principles and practices of a body that, under various names, had existed
from the eleventh century. The Anabaptists denied the
scripturalness of infant baptism, and insisted on a baptism upon profession of faith. But the Anabaptists, for
the most part, were content to practise the rite of baptism as they saw it in vogue about them; that is to say,
sprinkling or pouring. They gave little attention to the
act of baptism, regarding the subjects of baptism as a
matter of far greater importance, as indeed it is. The
English Anabaptists seem, at the beginning of their history, to have differed not at all from the other branches
of the party in this respect; but about the year 1640 the
attention of some among them was called to the question
of the fitting act of baptism according to the Scriptures,
and the introduction of immersion soon after followed.
The name Baptists came to be applied to them almost
at once as descriptive of their new practice.

The history of Baptist churches cannot be carried, by
the scientific method, farther back than the year 1611,
when the first Anabaptist church consisting wholly of
Englishmen was founded in Amsterdam by John Smyth,
the Se-Baptist. This was not, strictly speaking, a Baptist church, but it was the direct progenitor of churches
in England that a few years later became Baptist, and
therefore the history begins there. There were before
this time, it is true, here and there churches that might
fairly be described as Baptist. Such was the church at
Augsburg about 1525, commonly called Anabaptist, but
practising the immersion of believers on profession of
faith; such were some of the Swiss Anabaptist churches,
apparently; such were some of the Anabaptist churches
of Poland. But we find such churches only here and
there, with no ascertainable connection existing between
them. Further research may establish such connection,

or may bring to light additional instances; but it must be confessed that there is no great probability of such result. At any rate, there are no materials for a history in such facts as are now known. A history of Baptist churches going farther back than the early years of the seventeenth century would, therefore, in the present state of knowledge, be in the highest degree unscientific. The very attempt to write such a history now would be a confession of crass ignorance, either of the facts as known, or of the methods of historical research and the principles of historical criticism, or of both.

"Thou art Peter, and upon this rock I will build my church, and the gates of hades shall not prevail against it." Such was the reply of our Lord when his ever-confident disciple answered the question, "Who say ye that I am?" in the memorable words, then for the first time uttered, "Thou art the Christ, the Son of the living God." The Church of Rome points to this text as conclusive proof of her claims to be God's vicegerent on earth, the true church, against which the gates of hades shall not prevail. It further points to its unbroken succession, and a history which, if dim and uncertain at the first, since the fourth century at least has not a break, and not improbably extends back to the apostolic era, if not to Peter himself. It challenges any of the bodies that dispute its claim to show an equal antiquity and a succession from the days of the apostles as little open to serious question. Those that accept this test and fail to meet it must confess themselves schismatics and heretics, resisters of God, and doomed to overthrow here as well as condemnation hereafter.

Many Protestants make haste to accept Rome's challenge to battle on her chosen ground. Certain Anglican divines have great faith in a pleasing tradition that the Church of England was founded by the Apostle Paul during a third missionary tour hinted at in the New Testament but not described; and they flatter themselves that they thus establish an antiquity not second to that of Rome. Some Baptists have been betrayed into a similar search for proofs of antiquity, misled by the idea that such proof is necessitated by the promise that "the gates of hades shall not prevail" against the true church. If then, they reason, Baptist churches are true apostolic churches, they must have existed from the days of the apostles until now without break of historic continuity. This exaggerated notion of the worth of antiquity as a note of the true church is strengthened by the theory of baptism held by some; namely, that no one is baptized unless he is immersed by one who has himself been immersed. This is to substitute for the apostolic succession of "orders," which the Roman Church boasts, an apostolic succession of baptism. The theory compels its advocates to trace a visible succession of Baptist churches from the days of the apostles to our own, or to confess that proof is lacking of the valid baptism of any living man.

But it is plain that in thus accepting the challenge of Rome Protestants in general, the Baptists in particular, commit as great an error in tactics as in exegesis. To assume the necessity of an outward continuity in the life of the church is gratuitously to read into the words of our Lord what he carefully refrained from saying. Rome, for her own purposes, assumes the only possible import of the words to be that Christ's church will have a historic continuity that can be proved by documentary and other evidence. But this is by no means the necessary meaning of Christ's promise. The church that he said he would build on the rock, to which he guaranteed victory against the gates of hades itself, is not a visible body—that is the great falsehood of Rome—

but the assembly of those in all the ages who truly love God and keep the commandments of Christ. Of these there has been an unbroken line, and here is the true apostolic succession—there is no other. Through the continuous presence of this church and not along any chain of visible churches, the truth has descended to our days. Christ's promise would not be broken though at some period of history we should find his visible churches apparently overcome by Satan, and suppressed; though no trace of them should be left in literature; though no organized bodies of Christians holding the faith in apostolic simplicity could be found anywhere in the world. The truth would still be, as he had promised, witnessed somewhere, somehow, by somebody. The church does not cease to be because it is driven into the wilderness.

To Baptists, indeed, of all people, the question of tracing their history to remote antiquity should appear nothing more than an interesting study. Our theory of the church as deduced from the Scriptures requires no outward and visible succession from the apostles. If every church of Christ were to-day to become apostate, it would be possible and right for any true believers to organize to-morrow another church on the apostolic model of faith and practice, and that church would have the only apostolic succession worth having—a succession of faith in the Lord Christ and obedience to him. Baptists have not the slightest interest therefore in wresting the facts of history from their true significance; our reliance is on the New Testament, and not on antiquity; on present conformance to Christ's teachings, not on an ecclesiastical pedigree, for the validity of our church organization, our ordinances, and our ministry.

By some who have failed to grasp this principle, there has been a distressful effort to show a succession of

Baptist churches from the apostolic age until now. It is certain, as impartial historians and critics allow, that the early churches, including the first century after the New Testament period, were organized as Baptist churches are now organized and professed the faith that Baptist churches now profess. It is also beyond question that for fully four centuries before the Reformation there were bodies of Christians under various names, who professed nearly—sometimes identically—the faith and practice of modern Baptists. But a period of a thousand years intervenes, in which the only visible church of unbroken continuity was the Roman Church, which had far departed from the early faith.

The attempt has been made, at one time or another, to identify as Baptists nearly every sect that separated from the Roman Church. It will not suffice to prove that most of these sects held certain doctrines from which the great body of Christians had departed—doctrines that Baptists now hold, and that are believed by them to be clearly taught in the New Testament—or that the so-called heretics were often more pure in doctrine and practice than the body that assumed to be the only orthodox and Catholic Church. This is quite different from proving the substantial identity of these sects with modern Baptists. Just as, for example, it is easily shown that Methodists and Presbyterians hold a more biblical theology and approach nearer to apostolic practice than the Roman or Greek churches; while yet all know that a considerable interval separates them from Baptists. It is one thing to prove that the various heretical sects bore testimony, now one, now another, to this or that truth held by a modern denomination; and quite another thing to identify all or any of these sects with any one modern body. This is equally true, whether the investigation be confined to polity or to the substance of doctrine.

In thus emphasizing the divergences of the early and medieval sects from the teaching of the Bible, as Baptists have always understood that teaching, no denial is implied of the excellent Christian character manifested by the adherents of these erroneous views. In many instances the purest life of an age is to be found, not in the bosom of the Catholic Church, but among these despised and persecuted sectaries. Not one of them failed to hold and emphasize some vital truth that was either rejected or practically passed by in the church that called itself orthodox. God did not leave his truth without witnesses at any time. Now a sect, now an individual believer, like Arnold of Brescia or Savonarola, boldly proclaimed some precious teaching, perhaps along with what we must regard as pernicious error. But it is impossible to show that any one person, or any one sect, for a period of more than a thousand years, consistently and continuously held the entire body of truth that Baptists believe the Scriptures to teach, or even all its vital parts. It is possible that with further research such proof may be brought to light: one cannot affirm that there was not a continuity in the outward and visible life of the churches founded by the apostles down to the time of the Reformation. To affirm such a negative would be foolish, and such an affirmation, from the nature of the case, could not be proved. What one may say, with some confidence, is that in the present state of knowledge no such continuity can be shown by evidence that will bear the usual historic tests. Indeed, the more carefully one examines such literature of the early and medieval church as relates to the various heretical sects, the stronger becomes his conviction that it is a hopeless task to trace the history of the apostolic churches by means of an unbroken outward succession. A succession of the true faith may indeed be traced, in faint lines at times, but never entirely disappearing; but a succession of churches, substantially like those of our own faith and order in doctrine and polity—that is a will-o'-the-wisp, likely to lead the student into a morass of errors, a quagmire of unscholarly perversions of fact.

The special feature of this history is that it attempts frankly to recognize facts, instead of trying to maintain a thesis or minister to denominational vanity. Beginning with a survey of the history and constitution of the New Testament churches, in which all Baptists profess to recognize the norm of doctrine and polity, the process by which these churches were perverted into the Holy Catholic Church of the succeeding centuries is quite fully traced. The story of the gradual suppression of evangelical Christianity having thus been told, the next step is to show the reverse process—the gradual renascence of evangelical Christianity. This is the sum of Part I., the history of Baptist principles. The second Part is devoted to the history of actual visible Baptist churches, and every statement of fact made is carefully based on documentary sources. For the important question is, not how much may be guessed or surmised or hoped about our history as Baptists, but how much may be known.

PART I

HISTORY OF BAPTIST PRINCIPLES

CHAPTER I

"GO ye therefore, and make disciples of all the nations, baptizing them into the name of the Father, and of the Son, and of the Holy Ghost; teaching them to observe all things whatsoever I commanded you; and lo, I am with you alway, even unto the end of the world." In this parting injunction of the risen Lord to his disciples, which the Duke of Wellington aptly called the marching orders of the ministry, we have the office of the Christian Church for the first time defined. In obedience to this command the early Christians preached the gospel, founded churches, and taught obedience to Christ as the fundamental principle of the Christian life. And though many of them could say with Paul that they spent their days "in labor and travail, in watchings often, in hunger and thirst, in fastings often, in cold and nakedness," they found it a faithful saying that their Lord was with them alway. In so far as the church in all ages has been obedient to Christ's command it has experienced the truth of this promise.

It is significant that in his teaching Jesus mentioned the church but twice, and then only toward the close of his ministry. The distinctive feature of his teaching is the setting up among men of the kingdom of God—a kingdom not of this world, but spiritual, into which he only can enter who has been born from above, who is meek, childlike, spiritually minded. Being spiritual, this kingdom is invisible, but it has an outward, bodily manifestation, an institutional as well as an incorporeal existence. That manifestation is the church, the *ecclesia,* those "called out" from the world and gathered into a society whose aim is the extension of the kingdom.

This church potentially existed from the day when two disciples of John the Baptist followed Jesus and believed on him as the Messiah (John 1: 35-40); but of actual existence as an organized society of believers during the life of Jesus no trace appears in the four Gospels. The day of Pentecost marks the beginning of the definite, organic life of the followers of Christ. The descent of the Holy Spirit, according to the promise of the Lord, was the preparation for the great missionary advance, of which the conversion of three thousand on that one day was the first fruits. Not only did this multitude hear the word and believe, but on the same day they were "added to the church," which can only mean that they were baptized. It was once urged, as an objection to the teaching and practice of Baptists regarding baptism, that the immersion of so many people on a single day is physically impossible. The missionary history of our own time has silenced this objection forever, by giving us a nearly parallel case. In 1879, at Ongole, India, two thousand two hundred and twenty-two Telugu converts were baptized on a single day by six ministers, two administering the ordinance at a time; the services being conducted with all due solemnity, and occupying in all nine hours.

The baptism of this great multitude on the day of Pentecost was not only their public confession of faith in Jesus as the Messiah, and their formal induction into the company of believers, but the beginning of a new life of Christian fellowship. For a time at least, this fellowship took among the saints at Jerusalem the form of virtual community of goods, and this so-called "Christian communism" is often held up as a model for the life of Christians in all ages. "And the multitude of them that believed," says the record, "were of one heart and soul; and not one of them said that aught of the things which he possessed was his own; but they had all things in common. . . For neither was there among them any that lacked, for as many as were possessed of lands or houses sold them, and brought the price of the things that were sold, and laid them at the apostles' feet; and distribution was made unto each according as any one had need." It is evident to one who reads the entire account that this was a purely voluntary act on the part of the richer believers, prompted by a desire to relieve those whom the peculiar emergency had made specially needy. The optional nature of the sales and gifts is evident from the words of Peter to Ananias, who with Sapphira conspired to lie to the Holy Spirit— "Whiles it [the property Ananias had sold] remained, did it not remain thine own? And after it was sold, was it not in thy power?" To sell all one's goods and distribute unto the poor, though proposed by Jesus to the rich young ruler as a test of his desire for eternal life, was not a general condition of discipleship, even at this time and place. But there is no reason to suppose that after the temporary stress had been relieved, this community of goods continued among even the Jerusalem brethren, while there is every reason to believe that no other church in the apostolic age practised anything of the kind. There is entire silence on the subject in the Epistles and the remainder of the Acts—a thing inconceivable if Christian communism had been a fundamental principle of the apostolic churches. It is not wise or fair to draw a sweeping conclusion as to present duty from premises so narrow and uncertain.

The saints at Jerusalem had all been born and bred as Jews, and they had no idea that by becoming followers of Christ they had ceased to be Jews. They were daily in the temple, and scrupulously fulfilled all the duties prescribed by the law of Moses. Nor did the Jewish authorities regard them as adherents of a different religion; they were rather a sect or party among the Jews than a separate body. This is not to say that they were approved by the priests and the Sanhedrin; on the contrary, very soon persecution of them began. The Sadducees were the first to proceed against them, on the avowed ground that the apostles "proclaimed in Jesus the resurrection of the dead." The result of this persecution was a fresh outpouring of the Holy Spirit and a new advance; a multitude of believers were added, until the number of men alone became five thousand. The Sadducees had the experience of persecutors in all ages, that "heresy" is like a firebrand, and he who attempts to stamp out either by violence only scatters the sparks, until the little fire becomes a great conflagration.

About four years after Pentecost a fresh persecution was begun. The stoning of Stephen was its first act, and this was followed by a systematic and determined effort to extirpate this new heresy. This time it was the Pharisees who led the persecution, and prominent among them was Saul of Tarsus. The disciples at Jerusalem were dispersed, but they became preachers of the gospel wherever they went. They had come to Jerusalem from distant places, and had tarried there; now they would naturally return to their homes and carry with them their glad tidings of salvation through Jesus, the Christ. Thus a persecution that at first seemed likely to be fatal to the church at Jerusalem really ensured the perpetuity of Christ's religion by scattering its adherents throughout Asia Minor.

Shortly after this occurred an event, improbable, incredible even. if it were not certain, fraught with consequences most profound and far-reaching to Christianity, nothing less than the sudden conversion of its bitterest opponent. Saul, brought up at the feet of Gamaliel and learned in the law, renowned for his zeal in persecuting the church of God—in which, like so many other persecutors since, he verily believed he was doing God a service—was stricken down and blinded on his way to harry the saints at Damascus, by the appearance in the heavens at midday of the Christ whom he persecuted. Three days later, with sight miraculously restored, he was baptized into the fellowship of Christ's followers, and soon was as zealous in preaching the truth about the Messiah to the Jews as he had formerly been in opposing those who held it. Persecuted by the Jews, distrusted by the Christians, he had to pass through a long and painful ordeal before he became fitted for the work to which God had separated him from birth. Three years were spent in seclusion in Arabia, and several other years in obscure labors, before his fitness for a larger service was recognized by his brethren.

In the meantime, Philip, one of the deacons of the church at Jerusalem, seems for a time to have stepped into the place made vacant by the death of Stephen. He preached the gospel in Samaria, and wrought miracles; many believed and were baptized, both men and women. None of these converts, so far as appears, was a Gentile; and the eunuch shortly afterward baptized by Philip was doubtless a Jewish proselyte. Slow of heart, indeed, were the followers of Christ to admit that any but a Jew could be saved through Christ. They still regarded themselves as Jews; the gospel was a gospel for Jews; salvation was for Jews.

The first recorded case of preaching the gospel to a Gentile is that of the centurion, Cornelius, of Cæsarea, When Peter had gone to him in obedience to a vision;

when he had preached Christ to him and his friends
and they all believed; when the Holy Spirit fell upon
them, so that they spoke with tongues and glorified God;
the apostle felt that he had but one course, and he un-
hesitatingly baptized them. " Who was I that I could
hinder God," he said, in recounting the affair to the
church at Jerusalem on his return; and they, though they
had at first doubted and criticised, were in turn convinced
that this was the work of God, and glorified him, saying:
" So then, to the Gentiles also God has given repentance
unto life." The conversion of Cornelius therefore marks
an era in the history of Christianity, since it was never
after questioned that the gospel was to be preached to
Gentile as well as to Jew; the religion of Christ was
not to be a mere Jewish cult, but one of the great
missionary religions of the world—the greatest of
them all.

This characteristic alone discriminates Christianity
from the Judaism whence it sprung. Judaism was essentially narrow, exclusive, non-missionary; not in the purpose of God, but as the religion was actually held and
practised. It was God's plan, indeed, that in Abraham
and his seed all the nations of the earth should be
blessed, but the Jews never took kindly to that idea.
The fundamental notion in their minds was separation
from the nations; God had chosen them from all others
and made them his peculiar people. Power and dominion were to be given them, according to the promises of prophets, a kingdom more glorious than Sol-
omon's; and that others should share in these privileges was a thought as bitter as wormwood to a Jew.
Though the Jews made proselytes of individuals from
time to time, the number of those thus added to them
was relatively insignificant, and of any general attempt
to convert the world to Judaism there is no trace in the

Jewish literature of any age. If all the world were Jews, where would be the special privilege and glory of the Jew? But Christianity is nothing if not missionary. It exists because its Founder said to his followers, " Go, disciple," and it exists for no other purpose than this. From the day of Pentecost until the day of Christ's second coming, the history of Christianity has been—will be—a history of missionary advance.

But when the world-wide scope of the gospel was admitted, there was still much question as to the status of Gentiles when they had been converted and baptized. The old notion that the Christian was also a Jew was slow in giving way, and with great diligence the task was continued of sewing the new patch of Christianity on the old, worn-out garment of Judaism, notwithstanding Jesus' had declared it to be impossible and foolish. Still in bondage to the law of Moses, many were unwilling that others should enjoy the liberty wherewith Christ has made men free. They demanded that every Gentile convert should become not only a Christian, but a Jew, and insisted that he should be circumcised and become a debtor to the whole law. But there were men like Paul, who, though bred as Jews, when they had become converts to Christianity, comprehended its significance. He, a Pharisee of the Pharisees, glorying in his servitude to the law and his scrupulous observance of all its requirements, strove long and violently against the new faith and its adherents. But when he was enlightened by the Spirit of God, there fell, as it were, scales from his eyes; thenceforth he discerned clearly that Christianity differed profoundly from Judaism, in that it was a religion of the spirit, not of the flesh. He saw that in Christ the whole law had been fulfilled, and that the believer in him is delivered from its bondage; that a religion of types and external rites was now an anachronism, and must soon die out among those who accepted Jesus as the Messiah. Therefore, to bind the Gentile converts with this moribund law, to require spiritual believers to live after fleshly ordinances, was not only ridiculous and unjust, but was in fact to nullify the preaching of the gospel to the Gentiles.

The crisis in this " irrepressible conflict " was reached at Antioch about fourteen years after Pentecost. Paul had preached for some years in Asia Minor, especially at his native city of Tarsus, and at the invitation of Barnabas he went to Antioch to take part in a promising work there. For a year they preached and taught, and there the disciples were first called Christians. At the instance of the Holy Spirit, Barnabas and Saul were set apart for a special work of preaching in the regions beyond, and the second great step forward was taken in the history of Christianity. They made a tour of Asia Minor, and the island of Cyprus, in which they probably spent two years, and on their return to Antioch again abode there a long time. It was at this juncture that certain men from Judea endeavored to persuade the Antioch church that unless Gentiles were circumcised after the custom of Moses, they could not be saved. No little dissension followed, and it was finally decided that " Paul and Barnabas and certain others of them should go up to Jerusalem to the apostles and elders about this question." The proceedings and decision of this " council " at Jerusalem are given fully in the fifteenth chapter of the Acts of the Apostles. The meeting was the Gettysburg of the Judaizing party; the Gentiles were not required to be circumcised and to live as Jews; and although the struggle continued for some time, and once again at Antioch became violent, these were only the expiring throes of error. From this time onward Christianity assumed a distinct character, and was no

longer confounded with Judaism.   The settlement of this
question not only determined for that age the character
of Christ's religion, but prepared the churches for a
larger advance in missionary effort.

The details of the evangelization of the Roman empire
are only imperfectly known to us, though the fact of
such evangelization is amply attested by the New Testament documents, as well as by uniform Christian tradition.   We have a fairly complete account of the labors
of Paul, especially up to his imprisonment at Rome, closing about the year A. D. 63.   Three missionary journeys
of his are described with considerable fulness of detail.
The first has already been mentioned; in its course the
gospel was preached in Salamis and Paphos, at Antioch
of Pisidia, Iconium, Lystra, and Derbe, perhaps in other
places.   Not less than three years must be allotted to
the second journey, during which the apostle preached
in Galatia, at Philippi, Thessalonica, Berea, Athens, and
Corinth, staying in the last-named city a year and a
half.   The third journey occupied about four years, of
which over two were spent at Ephesus, and the rest in
Galatia and Phrygia, Greece (probably at Corinth), and
Troas.   The story of these twelve years of Paul's life
is practically all that we know in any detail of the apostolic labors through the Roman empire.   For the rest
we must depend on vague hints and uncertain traditions.
It appears probable, however, that after A. D. 63 Paul
was acquitted and released, and labored four or five years
more, visiting Crete and Macedonia, Troas and Miletus,
and perhaps also Spain, before his final arrest, imprisonment, and martyrdom.   This conclusion best explains
many passages in the so-called pastoral Epistles that are
otherwise puzzling, not to say inexplicable.

Regarding the labors of the other apostles, our information is even more scanty and less trustworthy.

Had John Mark performed for Barnabas and Peter the service that Luke rendered to Paul; had some disciple of John made a record of his labors, our knowledge of the apostolic era would have been vastly increased. We know that the First Epistle of Peter was written from Babylon and addressed to the Christians of five Asiatic provinces; from this it is perhaps a fair inference that Peter had previously preached in those provinces. That he was ever in Rome does not appear from the New Testament, but tradition is well-nigh unanimous that he suffered martyrdom there. That he was bishop of the Roman church for twenty-five years, according to Roman claims, is a later and manifestly absurd invention. There is no reason to doubt the tradition that John lived to an advanced age and died at Ephesus. The fourth Gospel shows traces of Alexandrine thought that makes probable a period of residence in the greatest of the Eastern cities of the empire. All that we definitely know of him is that for a time he was in banishment on the Isle of Patmos; whether he had any personal connection with the seven churches that he addresses in the Revelation can only be conjectured.

Some few scattered traditions embody the beliefs that were prevalent in the third century regarding the labors of the other apostles. Andrew is said to have preached in Scythia, Bartholomew in India, Thomas to have evangelized Parthia, and Mark to have founded the church at Alexandria. It is impossible to decide whether tales like these are lingering echoes of the truth or the mere inventions of a later time. Even regarding them as inventions, however, they have this significance: they testify to a general belief in the third century that the labors of all the apostles were abounding and fruitful. There is no doubt that the new leaven spread with a rapidity truly wonderful throughout the Roman empire. In the earliest records of Christian literature in the second century we find Christians literally everywhere.   The well-known letter of Pliny to the Emperor Trajan, written about A. D. III, says that this "superstition" pervades not only the cities of his province (Pontus and Bithynia), but villages and even farms, so that the temples were almost deserted, the sacred rites intermitted, and fodder was no longer purchased for the animals to be sacrificed, at which the farmers complained bitterly.   Heathen and Christian writers alike bear witness to the rapid spread of Christianity throughout the empire.   To account for this phenomenon something more is necessary than what we are told in the New Testament records; there is a large amount of unwritten history of the apostolic period, that must forever remain unwritten, but whose general outlines we can vaguely see.   It has been estimated, though this must necessarily be pure guesswork, that when John, the last of the apostles, passed away, near the close of the first century, the number of Christians in the Roman empire could not have been less than one hundred thousand.   In so brief a time the grain of mustard seed had become a tree.

CHAPTER II

"THE church of the living God, the pillar and ground of the truth," writes the Apostle Paul to Timothy, his beloved son in the faith. Though in the Gospels we find little about the church, as has already been noted, in the other New Testament writings we find much. The word *ecclesia* (assembly, church) is used in these documents one hundred and fourteen times, and in three different senses as applied to Christians: once to denote the assembly of the saints in heaven (Heb. 12: 23); often to describe the one assembly of the saints, the church universal, composed of all followers of Christ; but in the great majority of cases (eighty-five) to denote a local assembly or congregation of the followers of Christ. The church universal is not regarded in the Epistles as a visible and organized body, but is wholly spiritual, incorporeal, corresponding essentially to the idea of the kingdom of God taught in the Gospels. The only visible and organized body of Christians recognized by the New Testament writers was the local assembly or congregation. In other words, the apostles knew nothing of a Church; they knew only churches.

These churches, though visible and organized, were also spiritual. They were the outward embodiment of the kingdom of God among men, and the means by which that kingdom was to be extended. But the kingdom of God is before all things spiritual. "Except a man be born anew (*anôthen,* from above) he cannot see the kingdom of God," said our Lord to Nicodemus. And again he states the truth yet more emphatically, this time with a reference to baptism, the symbol of the new birth: " Verily, verily, I say unto thee, except a man be born of water and the Spirit he cannot enter into the kingdom of God" (John 3: 1-21). This new birth, the work of the Holy Spirit, is conjoined to " faith," " belief " in Christ on the part of man, and as its result man is justified in the sight of God (1 Peter 1: 5, 9; Rom. 5: 1; Gal. 2: 20; Heb. 10: 38; 11: 6). The necessity of a new birth through faith in Christ is everywhere assumed in the Epistles as a truth too familiar to be formally stated. It is the postulate, without which the apostolic writings cannot possibly be understood.

Hence the New Testament churches consisted only of those who were believed to be regenerated by the Spirit of God, and had been baptized on a personal confession of faith in Christ. What was done on the day of Pentecost seems to have been the rule throughout the apostolic period: the baptism of the convert immediately followed his conversion. It is a distinct departure from New Testament precedent to require converts to postpone their baptism. It is true, that these converts were Jews, that they only needed to be convinced that Jesus was the promised Messiah, and to submit to him as Lord, to make them fit subjects for baptism; as it is also true that, with the prospect of persecution and even death before them, there was no temptation to make a false profession. This made possible and prudent a haste that in our day might be dangerous; but the principle should be recognized and admitted, as taught by all New Testament precedent, that no more time should separate baptism from conversion than is necessary to ensure credible evidence of a genuine change of heart.

That all those added to the church at Jerusalem on the day of Pentecost were capable of making, and did make, intelligent personal confession of faith, is as certain as words can make anything. Nor is there the slightest indication in the New Testament writings that, during the apostolic age, any were received into the church save those who had come to years of personal responsibility and understanding. No scholar pretends that the baptism of infants is taught in the Scriptures; they are absolutely silent on the subject; yet from this silence certain inferences have been made. It is sometimes assumed that a continuity of life unites the Old Dispensation and the New. As children were by birth heirs of the promise through Abraham, so they are assumed to be by birth heirs of promise through Christ. In this view the New Dispensation is organically one with the Old; baptism merely replaces circumcision, the church replaces the synagogue and temple, the ministry replaces the priesthood, while the spirit of all continues unchanged. It appears to Baptists, on the other hand, to be clearly taught in Scripture that the New Dispensation, though a fulfilling and completion of the Old, is radically different from it. Under the Old Dispensation a child was an heir of promise according to the flesh, but under the New Dispensation natural birth does not make him a member of the kingdom of God; he must be born from above, born of the Spirit. The church has for its foundation principle a personal relation of each soul to Christ, and not a bond of blood; a child might be born a Jew, but he must be born again to become a Christian.

The more this silence of the Scriptures regarding the baptism of infants is considered, the more significant it becomes. Jesus took little children in his arms and declared that of the childlike is the kingdom of God (Matt. 19: 14), but he nowhere authorized baptism save when preceded by faith. The cases where whole households were baptized do not fairly warrant the inference that they contained infants, as is now frankly admitted by all scholars. Either they afford no positive ground for inference of any kind (as in the case of Stephanas, 1 Cor. 1 : 16; 16: 15), or they absolutely forbid the inference that infants were among the baptized (as in the case of the jailer at Philippi, where all who were baptized first had the gospel preached to them, Acts 16 : 32, 33). The case of Lydia and her household is often cited as one that proves infant baptism, but it is impossible to infer from the narrative (Acts 16 : 14, 15), anything certain, or even probable, regarding Lydia's family. Whether she was ever married, or whether she ever had children, or whether her children were not all dead or grown up are matters of pure conjecture. It is possible to guess any of these things, and a dozen besides, but guesses are not fair inferences, still less proofs.

Those who believe in a mixed church-membership, including unregenerate and regenerate, often cite the parable of the Tares (Matt. 13: 24-30). The field, they say, represents the church, and as the tares and wheat were to be suffered to grow together till the harvest, so the regenerate and unregenerate are to be intermingled in the church. It is a decisive objection to this plausible theory that our Lord himself interpreted this parable to his disciples (Matt. 13: 36-43), and declared that the field represents, not the church, but the world; the tares being separated from the wheat in the final judgment of mankind.

If the church "consists of all those throughout the world that profess the true religion, together with their children," as the Westminster Confession declares, does it not necessarily follow that children are equally entitled with their parents to all the privileges of the church? If they are fit subjects for baptism, they are fit subjects for the Lord's Supper. Whoso denies this certainly assumes the burden of proving the reasonableness of his position. There is nowhere in Scripture any authority to give the former ordinance, and to withhold the latter. The Greek Church recognizes the fact that infant baptism logically requires infant communion, and has the courage of its logic; but other Pedobaptist bodies save part of the truth, at the expense of consistency, by denying participation in the Lord's Supper to those baptized in infancy until these have reached years of understanding, and have made a public profession of faith.

The church at Jerusalem, composed of believers baptized on profession of personal faith in Jesus Christ, " continued steadfastly in the apostles' teaching and fellowship, in the breaking of bread and the prayers." There is no record in the New Testament that any joined in the breaking of bread, which is the usual term for the celebration of the Lord's Supper, without first having been baptized. What is stigmatized, therefore, as " close " communion is simply strict adherence to scriptural order—an order that bodies forth the spiritual significance of the two ordinances delivered to his church by Christ: baptism, as the emblem of the new birth, following immediately upon that birth, and being administered but once; the Lord's Supper, the emblem of union with Christ, and spiritual partaking of his nature, coming later and being often repeated. In coming to the table of the Lord, who shall venture to add or to take from the terms prescribed by himself and by apostolic example? Precisely because the table is the Lord's, and not theirs, his obedient followers are constrained to yield to his will.

Such was the first Christian church, as to constitution and ordinances; and such, in these particulars, the churches of Christ continued to be to the close of the apostolic era. There were no other ordinances in those churches, for to constitute an ordinance three things are needful: it must be a command of Christ himself; addressed not to individuals, but to Christians at large, and obviously intended to be obeyed for all time; and there must be evidence that the command was so understood and obeyed generally in the apostolic churches. Only baptism and the communion meet these conditions. The laying on of hands after baptism, and in ordination, is supported by Scripture precedent, but it is not an ordinance, for it was not commanded by Christ. Washing the feet of disciples is a command of Christ, but lacks the element of universality, and was evidently not practised as a rite in the apostolic churches. On the other hand, the commands to baptize and to break bread are accompanied by words indicating that these things were to be observed perpetually by the followers of Christ.

Of organization there was at first none in the church at Jerusalem. The apostles naturally took the lead and oversight of the flock, and for a time the need of officers was not felt. The first step was the appointment of deacons, in order to relieve the apostles from the labor and responsibility of distributing alms. These officers were chosen by the entire church, which is thus seen to be a democracy from the first, and set apart to their work by prayer and laying on of hands—an apostolic precedent that Baptists have not always been careful to follow. The appointment of pastors to have oversight of the churches, as their numbers increased, was the next step, so that the apostles might be free to give themselves to their specific work of evangelization.

We first learn definitely of this office some fourteen years later, when Barnabas and Paul were returning to Antioch from their first missionary journey, visiting the churches they had founded: We read, "And when they [Barnabas and Paul] had appointed for them elders in every church, and had prayed with fasting, they com-

mended them to the Lord, on whom they had believed."
The word translated " appoint " is conceded by all scholars to signify " to stretch forth the hand," probably for
the purpose of voting. This is held to indicate that the
congregations chose each its own pastor, the apostles setting apart the chosen ones with prayer, and, as is implied
in other passages, with the laying on of hands. With
the election of pastors, the organization of the church
became complete, and in the New Testament there is no
evidence of any further ecclesiastical machinery.

The chief officer of a New Testament church is called
by various titles, "bishop," " elder," " teacher," " pastor."
The latter two seem to describe functions rather than an
office, and the former two are interchangeable but not
synonymous. " Bishop " (*episcopus*) is a term of Greek
origin, and means overseer, president. It indicates the
duties of the office, which were executive. " Elder "
(*presbuteros*) is of Hebrew origin, and refers to the
honor paid this officer, as in the Jewish synagogue, an
honor that was doubtless originally due to the selection of
the older and wiser members for the office. It is admitted
by all scholars that in the apostolic times " bishop " and
" elder " were the same; but some advocates of episcopacy hold the later bishops to have been the successors
of the apostles. Of this, however, there is no evidence,
either in the writings of the apostles themselves or in the
literature of the second century.

Not only was the New Testament bishop chosen by his
flock, and the officer of the single congregation, but he is
regarded as one of them and one with them. No idea of
a division into " clergy " and " laity " appears in the New
Testament. No priestly character or function is ascribed to either bishop or deacon, but the universal
priesthood of believers is unmistakably taught. Sacerdotal ideas are not found in the generation immediately

succeeding the apostles, but are distinctly of a later development, and are unmistakable marks of the degeneracy and corruption of the churches.

In the churches of Asia Minor, if not generally in the New Testament churches, there was a plurality of elders in each church. This may have been due to the fact that the churches of which we read most were in cities, and soon became too large for the oversight of one man. It is possible that in some cases, as at Jerusalem, they became too large to assemble in any one place, and met in separate congregations, each with its own elder. If this conjecture is sound, it still remains unquestionable that the several congregations were regarded as one, the division being merely for convenience; for while we read of " the churches " of a province like Galatia, we always read of " the church " at Corinth or Ephesus or Antioch or Jerusalem.

Simple in organization and democratic in government, the New Testament churches were independent of each other in their internal affairs. There is no instance of a single church, or of any body of churches, undertaking to control the action of another, or of a church being overruled by superior ecclesiastical authority. To the teaching of apostles guided by the Spirit of God, they did, indeed, defer much, and rightly; but not so much to the apostolic office as to the Spirit of God speaking through the apostle. The so-called council of Jerusalem, the nearest approach to the control of local churches by exterior authority (presbytery), had an authority rather moral than ecclesiastical, and its decision was final rather because it was felt to be the wisest solution of a grave question than because it was imposed by ecclesiastical powers and enforced by ecclesiastical discipline.

But though independent of external authority, the churches were not independent of external obligations.

The church, in the broadest sense of the term, in the New Testament, includes all the regenerate living in obedience to Christ. Hence, though for convenience of administration divided into local congregations, independent of each other as to internal management, it is still the one body of Christ. The several churches owed to their fellow-Christians, both as individuals and as Christians, whatever of loving service it was in their power to render. They were bound to give counsel and help to sister churches that had need of either, and frequent records in the New Testament show that this obligation has been acknowledged and fulfilled. The interdependence and fraternity of the churches is a broader and more precious truth than their independence. If the former, when abused, leads to centralization and prelacy, the latter, pushed to extremes, leads to disintegration, discord, and weakness. The apostles urged upon churches as well as upon individuals the duty of bearing one another's burdens, comforting each other in trouble, assisting each other in need, and generally co-operating to further the interests of the kingdom of God.

The worship of the early Christians was simple and spiritual. The public services consisted of prayer, praise, and the preaching of the word, probably with reading of the Old Testament writings, and of the New Testament writings as they appeared and were circulated through copies. In these respects the first churches, as was natural, no doubt followed the custom of the Jewish synagogues, to which their members had been accustomed from infancy. Music filled an important place in this worship, as we may infer from the apostle's reference to the " psalms and hymns and spiritual songs " as in common use. The chanting of psalms, antiphonal and otherwise, was no doubt a marked feature of Christian worship from the first, especially among those educated as Jews.

Traces of ritual are found in the New Testament, not only in the Lord's Prayer and the doxologies, but in rhythmical passages in the apostolic writings. But this ritual was simple, plastic, voluntary; not a rigid and required service. Nothing is more marked in the spiritual life of the early church, so far as it is disclosed in the Acts and Epistles, than its spontaneity and freedom from the bondage of formalism. This is, of course, more markedly manifest in the informal gatherings, closely resembling the modern prayer-meeting, that supplemented the more public and general assemblies of the Lord's Day. These, however, like the *agapæ*, or love feasts, that for a time accompanied the celebration of the Supper, were liable to abuse, and against disorderly proceedings in them we find the Apostle Paul warning the Corinthian church.

The distinctive day of worship among apostolic Christians was the first day of the week, the Lord's Day. The disciples met on the evening of this day, on which the risen Christ had manifested himself to some of them, and he met with them. A week later they again assembled, and again he met them. There is no reason to doubt that the observance continued thereafter without a break. Thus, while there is no definite precept for the observance of the Lord's Day, there is definite precedent, and the example of the apostles, where it is clear and explicit, is tantamount to command. By the year A. D. 55 this first-day meeting of Christians seems to have become a recognized custom (Acts 20 : 7; I Cor. 16 : 2); yet it is not until the second century that we have positive proof that the Lord's Day was universally observed among Christians. For some time those who had been bred Jews continued to observe the Sabbath in their usual manner, and the matter even became a subject of contention between Jew and Gentile (Rom. 16 : 5, 6; Col. 2 : 16); but in the second century sabbatizing was condemned by

Christian writers. Neither in the New Testament nor in the Christian literature of the first three centuries is there any confounding of the Sabbath and the Lord's Day, or any intimation that the fourth commandment has anything to do with the observance of the Lord's Day. On the contrary, the Sabbath is treated as typical and temporary, like circumcision, and done away with as were all the ordinances of the law.

There were doubtless other times of meeting in the apostolic churches, besides the first day of the week. For a brief time after the day of Pentecost, every day appears to have been a day of worship, as it even now is with churches during a season of special revival; and the Lord's Supper was at this time celebrated daily. At a later period it was celebrated, apparently, every Lord's Day, though there is nothing to indicate that this was regarded as obligatory. Any Baptist church, however, that should choose to spread the table of the Lord every Lord's Day would have sufficient Scripture precedent to justify it in so doing. The one thing for which no New Testament precedent can be pleaded is the letting of months go by without a celebration of the Communion.

CHAPTER III

BEFORE the end of the apostolic age the followers of Christ suffered severe persecution at the hands of the Roman emperors. The first great persecution, that of Nero, probably had no other origin than the capricious cruelty of that infamous ruler. The persecutions of his immediate successors were prompted by passion rather than by principle; it is not till the reign of Trajan that we find persecution for the first time adopted intelligently and deliberately as a fixed imperial policy. This emperor, in his letter to Pliny, governor of Bithynia from 109 to 111, directed that Christians should not be sought out nor proceeded against on anonymous accusations; but when accused by a responsible person they should be tried, and on conviction should be put to death.

To understand these persecutions by the better of the Roman emperors—and, as a rule, the higher an emperor's character the more severely he persecuted the Christians—we must look at the Roman laws. Religion was from the earliest times a matter of statecraft in Rome. There was a State religion, and public worship of the State deities was conducted by the magistrates. The worship of foreign gods was prohibited on pain of death by the Twelve Tables, the earliest code of laws among the Romans, and for a time this prohibition seems to have been absolute; but as other nations were conquered and absorbed a liberal policy was shown toward the religions of the conquered peoples. By act of the Senate these national deities were given recognition; temples in their honor could be established in Rome, and their devotees had equal rights with Romans, but were forbidden to make proselytes. Until a religion was thus formally recognized, it was forbidden (*religio illicita*), but on such recognition it became a tolerated religion (*religio licita*). Christianity was at first supposed to be a form of Judaism, which as a national religion was tolerated and even protected by the emperors; and accordingly it was at first treated as *religio licita*. Soon, however, its real nature came to be known. It was found to be exclusive of all other religions; it not only made proselytes, but by its rapid progress it threatened the overthrow of the State religion. It was, therefore, *religio illicita,* and to embrace it was a capital offense.

Moreover, Christians were suspected of disloyalty. They avoided military service. Their conscientious refusal to offer divine honors to the emperor—which was done by throwing a little incense on the fire burning before his statue, to the Roman an act like the taking of the oath of allegiance among us—was misconstrued into political hostility. There were severe laws in the empire against clubs, secret societies and the like; no association was lawful unless specially licensed, and the emperors were so jealous of these clubs, as affording opportunities for conspiracy, that Trajan actually refused to sanction a company of firemen in Nicomedia. The Christian church was constructively an illegal secret society, since it was an organization not sanctioned by the emperor, that held frequent private meetings; and in order to protect themselves, the Christians held these meetings with great secrecy.

It was not mere wanton cruelty, therefore, that led the emperors to persecute the Christians, but a fixed

State policy. But nevertheless, popular hatred at times waxed hot against the Christians, and emperors occasionally persecuted to gratify this hatred, based on ignorance and slander. Public opinion is not without influence, even in a despotic government. A saying that passed into a proverb was: *Deus non pluit—duc ad Christianos* (the heavens do not rain—lead us against the Christians). Tertullian probably exaggerates little when he says: " If the Tiber overflow its banks, if the Nile do not water the fields, if the clouds refuse rain, if the earth shake, if famine or storms prevail, the cry always is, ' Throw the Christians to the lions ! ' "

Ten persecutions are mentioned by the Christians of this period and by many historians, of which three are specially remarkable for bitterness and general prevalence through the empire. In the second century persecution was spasmodic and unmethodical, nevertheless the reign of Marcus Aurelius is remembered as one of great suffering by the Christians. It is not certain that he ordered persecutions or sympathized with them, but thousands became martyrs. The first general and systematic persecution throughout the empire was that begun by Decius Trajan (249-251). The authorities were especially severe with the bishops, and Fabian of Rome, Alexander of Jerusalem, and Cyprian of Carthage, are some of those who perished in this persecution. Diocletian began the last great persecution, which raged during the years 303-311. His edicts required that all Christian churches should be destroyed; all copies of the Bible were to be burned; Christians were to be deprived of public office and civil rights, and must sacrifice to the gods on pain of death.

The Christian literature of the first three centuries records the heroic death of many devout believers, but no story is more touching than the martyrdom of Per-

petua and her companion Felicitas, as told by Tertullian.
Vivia Perpetua was a matron of Carthage, about twenty-
two years of age, and had an infant son. She was well-
born and well-educated. Of her husband the narrative
tells us nothing, but we may infer that he was, like her
father, a heathen. After being apprehended, her father
and brother used all their arts of persuasion to induce
her to recant, but in vain. When brought before the
procurator, he besought her thus: " Spare the gray hairs
of your father, spare the infancy of your boy, offer sacrifice for the well-being of the emperor." She replied:
" I will not do so." The procurator said: "Are you a
Christian?" She replied: " I am a Christian." The
procurator then delivered judgment on the accused, Perpetua among them, and condemned them to the wild
beasts. The story of the martyrdom, somewhat abridged,
follows in Tertullian's words:

" The day of their victory shone forth, and they proceeded from the prison into the amphitheater, as if to
an assembly, joyous and of brilliant countenances. For
the young women the devil prepared a very fierce cow.
Perpetua is first led in. She was tossed and fell on her
loins; and when she saw her tunic torn she drew it over
her as a veil, rather mindful of her modesty than her
suffering. So she rose up; and when she saw Felicitas
crushed, she approached and gave her her hand, and
lifted her up; and the brutality of the populace being
appeased, they were recalled to the gate. And when
the populace called for them into the midst, they first
kissed one another, that they might consummate their
martyrdom with a kiss of peace. The rest indeed immovable and in silence received the sword-thrust; but
Perpetua, being pierced between the ribs, cried out loudly,
and she herself placed the wavering right hand of the
youthful gladiator to her throat. Possibly such a woman

could not have been slain unless she herself had willed it, because she was feared by the impure spirit. O most brave and blessed martyrs! O truly called and chosen unto the glory of our Lord Jesus Christ!"

Early in the fourth century it became apparent that Christianity was stronger than the Cæsars, and could not be destroyed. The long contest ended with the surrender of the emperors. In 311, an edict of toleration was published, confirmed in 313, and with the triumph of Constantine in 323 as sole emperor, Christianity became practically the established religion of the empire. In spite of the persecutions to which they had been subjected, the Christians had come to number, according to the most trustworthy estimates, about ten millions in the Roman empire; or one-tenth of the entire population. It was no empty boast of a rhetorician when Tertullian wrote, a century before toleration was won: " We are a people of yesterday, and yet we have filled every place belonging to you—cities, islands, castles, towns, assemblies, your very camp, your tribes, companies, palace, senate, forum! We leave you your temples only. We count your armies; our numbers in a single province will be greater."

While the Christian faith was thus engaged in a life-and-death contest with the imperial power, it was compelled to defend itself against the hardly less dangerous attacks of heathen adversaries. The emperors threatened with destruction the external organization; heathen philosophers threatened to undermine the very foundations of the faith. Pagan men of letters undertook to bring to pass what imperial power had failed to do. The terrors of the prison and the sword had proved of little avail to hinder the progress of Christianity; the question was now to be tested whether the pen could cut deeper than the sword, whether logic and rhetoric could overcome an obstinacy proof against death itself. The attacks made upon the religion of Christ in the first three centuries have never been surpassed in ability and force. No keener-witted, no more learned, no more bitterly hostile critics have searched the Scriptures with intent to overthrow them than were found in these days. We are authorized in saying this, though their works are known to us only through the references made to them by their Christian antagonists. Not only is this the general repute of these critics, but the profuse quotations from their words in the answers to them show the scope and cogency of their arguments. Nearly all the latter-day skeptical objections to Christianity are to be found in these early anti-Christian writings. The new light that modern opponents of evangelical religion profess to have discovered is only the old darkness.

There were then, as now, two stock objections to the religion of Christ—first, the incredibility of the Scriptures as history; second, the absurdity of the doctrines taught in the Scriptures. Then, as now, skeptics objected to the miraculous element in the Bible, and sought to overthrow men's belief in the book as inspired by pointing out its alleged contradictions. Then, as now, men could not reconcile their human systems of philosophy with the biblical teaching regarding the inherent sinfulness of man, the vicarious atonement, regeneration, union with Christ, sanctification, and a resurrection unto eternal life. But it was paganism, not Christianity, that proved incredible when subjected to searching examination. The worship of the gods declined, while the worship of God and his Son, Jesus Christ, spread rapidly through the Roman world. The attacks of the pagan scholars and philosophers hardly retarded the process perceptibly, though for a time they seemed to constitute a serious danger.

These attacks were answered by Christian writers, so completely, so conclusively, that later defenders of the faith have had little to do but repeat, amplify, and re-state their arguments. Among the ablest were Justin, Tertullian, and Origen. Justin, the earliest, was a Platonist, and in his writings stood mainly on the defensive. His two apologies, addressed to the Roman emperors, were largely devoted to showing that Christians were falsely accused by their enemies, that they were not to be blamed for public calamities, and that in all things they were good Romans and loyal subjects of the emperor. In addition he maintained that the Scriptures are the only source of truth, the pagan mythologies abounding in falsehoods and contradictions. In his dialogue with Trypho, Justin attempts to answer the usual objections of the Jews to the Christian faith, and to prove the Messiahship of Jesus from the Old Testament. This is almost the only trace, outside of the New Testament, of controversy between Jews and Christians. Tertullian defended the supernatural element in Christianity with great skill. He is the most finished rhetorician among the early Christian apologists, and seldom stood on the defensive, but boldly carried the war into Africa. He was a man of genius, but there was a strain of enthusiasm or fanaticism in him that made him an unsafe guide; nevertheless, his services as a defender of the faith were great.

The culmination of this series of apologies was the treatise of Origen against Celsus. He was born of Christian parents at Alexandria, in 185. The statement will be found in many books of reference that he was baptized in infancy, but as there is no record of his baptism the statement can be nothing more than an inference from the fact that he advocated infant baptism in later years. It is more probable that he was not baptized in infancy, since the custom was far from general when he was born. He received a careful education and as a boy knew whole sections of the Bible perfectly. During the greater part of his life he was a teacher at Alexandria—though he was at one time deposed from the office of presbyter, excommunicated and exiled—and was in high repute as a scholar and writer.

Origen labored to reconcile Greek philosophy with biblical theology, not with entire success, since his teachings afforded some ground for the charges of heresy brought against him. His doctrine concerning Christ was the precursor of the later Arianism, and his denial of eternal punishment has had a great influence on the church in every succeeding century. His great work against Celsus, valuable as it was in its time, had not the same worth for the church of all time as his exegetical studies. He was the first commentator on the Scriptures who seriously set himself, by grammatical and historical study of the text, to ascertain what the word of God really means. This was, in truth, his greatest contribution to apologetics, though in form it was not a defense of Christianity. Has it not been true in all the ages since, that the religion of Christ has been most successfully defended by those who have best set forth its teachings to the world, not by those who have ostensibly, not to say ostentatiously, gone about the task of formal defense? The most effective refutation of error is to teach the truth.

The victory of Christianity was no less complete in controversy than in the civil conflict. About the time the emperors were convinced that persecution was futile, the philosophers saw the uselessness of criticism. The triumph of Christianity was the survival of the fittest. It won because truth must win when pitted against error, since it has behind it all the power of God. In these ages, as in many others, we can now see that the opposition of pagan writers was a blessing to the church. It compelled Christians to examine well the foundations of their faith, to study the Bible and systematize its teachings, to recognize the discrepancies and apparent contradictions of the Scriptures and inquire how and how far these might be harmonized. The result was that Christianity emerged from its conflict with paganism rejoicing in a faith greatly strengthened, and above all more intelligent. The faith of the church in its Scriptures as a divine revelation could never be seriously shaken after the searching tests they had so triumphantly encountered.

But the victory was in part a defeat also; as often happens, the conquered overcame the conquerors. Christianity apparently vanquished heathenism, but heathenism succeeded in injecting much of its superstition and ritual into Christianity. In the long struggle with the Cæsars, Christianity had apparently won; but while appearing to gain all, by obtaining the patronage of Constantine, it was in danger of losing all. The process of degeneracy and corruption—in polity, in doctrine, in spiritual life—had begun long before, but adversity had kept the church comparatively pure. Now it became rapidly assimilated to the world, and the increase of the church in wealth, in numbers, and in worldly power was accompanied by an equally marked decadence of spiritual life, and a departure from the simplicity of the apostolic doctrine and practice.

CHAPTER IV

BEFORE the last of the apostles had passed away, there were unmistakable signs of degeneracy and corruption in the Christian churches. Warnings against heresies and false teachers, not as future dangers but as present, are found in all of the later New Testament writings. From the very first, the preaching of the cross was to the Jews a stumbling-block and to the Greeks foolishness; and even when Jews and Greeks were converted they endeavored to amalgamate the old religion with the new. In spite of our Lord's assurance that the new wine could not be put into the old bottles without the loss of both, this attempt went on. Profoundly as the religion of the Jews differed from that of the Greeks and of other heathen nations, yet all pre-Christian religions had one element in common—they promised salvation to those who would attain the scrupulous observance of ecclesiastical rites. The note of all religions before Christianity was salvation by works; Christianity alone taught salvation by faith.

The efforts of converts imperfectly converted to assimilate Christianity to their former faith were only too successful. They failed to grasp the fundamental principles of the new religion, that each soul's destiny is the result of a personal relation to Jesus Christ, that eternal life is not the mere escape from retribution hereafter, but that it begins here in an intimate and vital union with the Son of God. They imagined that eternal destiny is settled by outward act, that the wrath of God may be averted by rites and ceremonies. The natural result was the substitution of formalism for spirituality, devotion to the externals of religion taking the place of living faith. To this one root may be traced in turn every one of the corruptions of the church, all of its aberrations of doctrine and practice. So soon as the churches founded by the apostles lost sight of the truth that man must be born again, and that this new birth is always associated with personal faith in Christ, the way was prepared for all that followed.

In the earliest Christian literature, after the apostolic period, we may trace three tendencies toward degeneration, all proceeding from this common cause, developing along lines parallel at first, yet distinct, afterward converging, and at length constituting a logical, consistent whole. These are: the idea of a Holy Catholic Church, the ministry a priesthood, and sacramental grace.

Jesus prayed that his disciples might be one, and his apostles taught that the church is the temple of the Holy Ghost, and therefore both one and holy. Early in the second century, however, these ideas assumed a different form from that of the New Testament. The churches were conceived of as forming together one Church, not spiritual merely, but visible, extending throughout the world, and therefore catholic (i. e., universal). Persecution doubtless had much to do with emphasizing in the minds of Christians their unity, but an exaggerated notion of the value of formal oneness came to prevail, until schism was reckoned the deadliest of sins a Christian could commit. The preservation of outward unity thus becoming the paramount consideration, it followed that whatever error a majority in the church might come to hold, the minority must accept it, rather than be guilty of this deadly sin of schism. This ideal of a Holy Catholic Church, outside of which was no salvation, unity with which was necessary to unity with Christ, prepared the way for all the corruptions that were introduced.

Another parallel development downward in the second century was the attribution of some mystical or magical power to baptism. It must be confessed that there are a few passages in the New Testament writings which, if they stood alone, would favor this view. " Except a man be born of water and the Spirit, he cannot enter into the kingdom of God " (John 3 : 3). " Which also after a true likeness doth now save you, even baptism " (1 Peter 3 : 14). " Arise and be baptized, and wash away thy sins " (Acts 22 : 16): If passages like these stood alone, unmodified, we should be compelled to the conclusion that faith alone, without baptism, does not avail to save. By ignoring to a great degree those other and relatively numerous passages in which the spirit is exalted above the letter, and faith is made the vital principle of the Christian life instead of ritual, the churches soon made outward rites of more significance than inward state. Baptism was regarded, not perhaps as absolutely necessary to salvation, but as so necessary an act that if it could not be performed precisely in accordance with Christ's command and apostolic precedent, some simulacrum of it must be substituted.

The Christians of that age were indeed justified in laying great stress on the importance of obeying Christ in baptism. It never seems to have occurred to them, as it has occurred to Christians of recent times, to evade this command, because to obey was inconvenient or distasteful; or on the avowed ground that something else might be substituted for the act commanded that would be more accordant with the delicate sensibilities of cultivated and refined people. Their obedience was implicit, ready, complete. Its one fault was an excess of virtue— an attempt to obey in cases where obedience was impossible. When water in sufficient quantities for immersion was wanting, there could be no proper baptism; but, as baptism was now conceived to be so very important, something must be done, and water was in such cases poured upon the head thrice, in quantities as profuse as possible, no doubt, thus counterfeiting immersion as nearly as might be. The true principle was missed— that where obedience is impossible God accepts the willingness to obey for obedience itself; and the wrong principle was adopted—that God can be obeyed by doing something other than what he commands.

We see the first step in this process in the document known as " The Teaching of the Twelve Apostles," which scholars assign to the first half of the second century. The injunction regarding baptism is: " Now concerning baptism, thus baptize ye: having first uttered all these things, baptize into the name of the Father, and of the Son, and of the Holy Spirit, in running water. But if thou hast not running water, baptize in other water; and if thou canst not in cold, then in warm. But if thou hast neither, pour water upon the head thrice, into the name of the Father, and Son, and Holy Spirit. But before the baptism let the baptizer and the baptized fast, and whatsoever others can; but the baptized thou shalt command to fast for two or three days before." There is only a bare hint here of a sacramental idea, but by the time of Justin Martyr (about A. D. 150) the process of identifying the sign with the thing signified had made no little progress. He calls baptism " the water-bath of regeneration." " Those who believe our doctrine," he says, " are led by us to a place where there is water, and in this way they are regenerated." By the time of Tertullian (200) the idea of baptismal regeneration is firmly established. That is to say, baptism is no longer regarded as merely a type or symbol of regeneration, but the means by which the Spirit of God effected regeneration. In the writings of the Ante-Nicene church Fathers, the use of " regenerate " to mean " baptize " is so common as to be almost the rule. For a time, doubtless, the usage was figurative, but the figure was soon lost sight of, and baptism was accepted as a literal means of regeneration.

One of the first practical consequences of this doctrine regarding baptism was the usage known as " clinic " baptism (from *klinê*, a couch), or the baptism of those supposably sick unto death. The first recorded case of this kind, though others may have occurred before, is that of Novatian (sometime before 250). Being very ill, and supposed to be near death, yet desiring to be baptized and wash away his sins, water was brought and poured about him as he lay on his couch, immersion being thus simulated as closely as possible under the circumstances. Novatian recovered, however, or we should probably never have heard of this case, and afterward entered the ministry, but the sufficiency of his clinic baptism was from the first disputed. The question of the validity of such baptisms was submitted to Cyprian, bishop of Africa, and in one of the letters of that ecclesiastic we have an elaborate discussion of the matter. He was asked, he tells us, " of those who obtain God's grace in sickness and weakness, whether they are to be accounted legitimate Christians, for that they are not to be washed, but affused (*non loti sunt, sed perfusi*) with the saving waters." His chief argument was one since common among mutilators of the ordinance, that a little water would answer as well as much. His conclusion was that " the sprinkling of water (*aspersio*), prevails equally with the washing of salvation; and that when this is done in the church, when the faith both of receiver and giver is sound, all things hold and may be

THE MAMERTINE PRISON, ROME

The Three Fountains

THE EMPEROR NERO

THE EMPEROR TRAJAN

THE BAPTISTERY OF ST. JOHN LATERAN

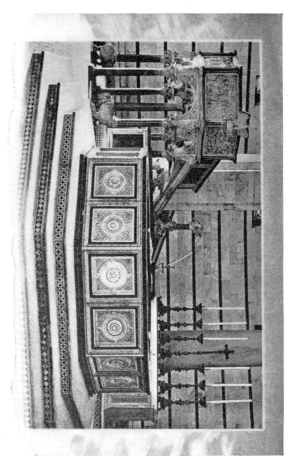

THE BAPTISTERY AT PISA

THE OLD CATHEDRAL AT BRESCIA

STATUE OF ARNOLD

consummated and perfected by the majesty of the Lord, and by the truth of faith."

It will be noted by the attentive reader of these words that the decision rests wholly on the sacramental notion that baptism conveys God's saving grace. It was a natural conclusion by those who held this view that God's grace could work with a little water as well as with more. But it was long before Cyprian's view fully prevailed in the church. It was agreed, to be sure, that clinic baptism would suffice for salvation, but it was felt to be an incomplete and unsatisfactory form, and ordination was long refused those who had been subjects of this mutilated ceremony. The idea that affusion would serve as baptism in other than cases of extreme necessity made its way very slowly in the church, and that form of administration had no official sanction until the Synod of Ravenna, in 1311, decided that "baptism is to be administered by trine aspersion or immersion."

The first clinic baptisms, as we have seen, were performed by so surrounding the body of the sick person with water that he might be said to be immersed in water. It was, however, a short and easy step to diminish the quantity of water, and then to apply it to other than sick persons. The practice of perfusion and affusion gradually increased from the time of Novatian, though for several centuries immersion continued to be the prevailing administration of the ordinance.

Another consequence of the idea of baptismal regeneration was the baptism of infants. It logically followed, if those unbaptized were unregenerate, that all who died in infancy were unsaved. This was a conclusion from which the Christian consciousness of the early centuries revolted as strongly as that of our own day, which utterly rejects the Westminster declaration that "elect infants" are saved, with its logical corollary that non-elect infants are lost. The true solution of the difficulty would have been found in a return to apostolic ideas of the nature and function of baptism; but a contrary idea having become too deeply settled in the church for such a return, the only alternative solution was to baptize infants, so that they might be regenerated and saved if they died before reaching the years in which personal faith is possible.

Just when infant baptism began is uncertain; scholars have disputed long over the question without arriving at any decisive proof. The passages often quoted from the writings of Justin and Irenæus are admitted by candid Pedobaptist scholars to fall far short of proof that infants were baptized in their times. It is tolerably certain, however, that by the time of Tertullian the practice was common, though by no means universal. We know, for example, that Augustine, though the son of the godly Monica, was not baptized in infancy, but on personal profession of faith at the age of thirty-three. Gregory of Nazianzum and Chrysostom are two others. Similar cases were frequent without a doubt, though from this time on they became more rare, until after the sixth century the practice of infant baptism was universal, or nearly so. Nothing in the history of the church did so much as this departure from apostolic precedent to prepare the way for papacy. It introduced into the church a multitude whose hearts were unchanged by the Spirit of God, who were worldly in aims and in life, and who sought for the worldly advancement of the church that thus their own power and importance might be magnified. This consummation was doubtless aided and hastened by the rapid contemporary growth of the church in numbers and its increase in worldly prosperity.

In the section concerning baptism, already quoted from "The Teaching of the Twelve Apostles," the catechumenate is already recognized, at least in germ. Baptism was no longer to be administered upon the mere confession of faith, but was to be preceded by a somewhat elaborate instruction, for which the first six chapters of the " Teaching " were originally devised. The catechumenate was not in itself a departure from the fundamental principles of the primitive churches. There was a necessity, such as is felt by the missionaries in heathen lands at this day, of instructing converts in the first principles of the Christian faith. It is true now in heathendom as it was then, that a sufficient knowledge of the Christian faith for salvation may be gained in a comparatively brief time, while the convert is in a dense state of ignorance regarding all else that separates Christianity from his heathen faith. Accordingly, our own missionaries are compelled in some cases, perhaps in all, to exercise caution in the reception of those heathen who profess conversion, and to give them such preliminary instruction in Christian doctrine as will enable them intelligently to become disciples of Christ and members of a Christian church. But it is evident that instruction of this kind, prior to baptism, should be extremely simple and elementary, and need not be greatly protracted. So soon as the catechumenate was an established institution in the Catholic Church, its system of instruction became elaborate and prolonged, and candidates were delayed in these schools of instruction for many months, even for several years, before they were allowed to be baptized. The tendency of such an institution was to foster the idea that men might be educated into Christianity, and to decrease the reliance of the church upon the agency of the Holy Spirit in the conversion of men. The practical result was to introduce many into the church who had never been subjects of the regenerating grace of God, but had simply been instructed in Christianity as a system of theology or philosophy, and their intellectual assent to its teachings was accepted as equivalent to saving faith. What might have been and doubtless was at first an effective agency for good, became an instrument for the corruption of the church. While it endured and flourished, however (from the second to the fifth centuries), the catechumenate was an evidence not to be controverted of the general prevalence of adult baptism. Its decline and the growth of infant baptism were synchronous.

The idea of sacramental grace did not stop with the corruption of the doctrine of baptism, but extended to the Communion, or Eucharist, as it came to be generally called from the second century onward. There are passages in the early Fathers that amply justify the later doctrine known as the real presence and consubstantiation, if they do not go to the extreme length of transubstantiation. With the decrease of vital faith the increase of formalism kept pace, and the administration of the Lord's Supper, from being a simple and spiritual ceremony, became surrounded by a cloud of ritual and finally developed into the mass of the Roman Church. Laying as great a stress as Luther did later upon the mere letter of Scripture, the church of the third and fourth centuries insisted that the words " This is my body " were to be accepted by all faithful Christians as a literal statement of truth, and that Paul's words when he says that the broken bread is the body of Christ do not indicate a spiritual partaking of Christ's nature, but a literal and materialistic reception of it and through the bread and wine.

The development of the sacerdotal idea was an equally powerful agency in corrupting the church. Though the idea of a priesthood, other than the priesthood of all believers, is not found in the New Testament, we find it very early in the post-apostolic literature. Both Jews and pagans were familiar with this idea of a priesthood, and they naturally, almost inevitably, carried their old religious ideas over into the religion that they had adopted in their adult years. For a time the Fathers seem to have used sacerdotal terms as they used sacramental terms, with a figurative rather than a literal meaning. When they speak of " sanctuary " and "altar," of " priest " and " sacrifice," they do not at first mean all that those words literally imply; but it was not long before the figure of speech disappeared and the literal meaning only remained. Clement of Rome was the first writer to draw a parallel between the Christian ministry and the Levitical priesthood, and is the first to speak of the " laity " as distinct from the clergy. In Tertullian and Cyprian we may trace the completion of the process, and by the end of the third century or early in the fourth, the idea was generally accepted that the clergy formed an ecclesiastical or sacerdotal order, a priestly caste completely separate from the laity.

So great a corruption in the idea of the functions of the ministry could hardly be unaccompanied by a change in its form; and the degeneration we have traced in the practices of the church would naturally affect its polity. What we might reasonably expect to happen did in fact come to pass. In the New Testament we find presbyter-bishops, one office with two interchangeable titles, but early in the second century we find bishops and presbyters, two offices, not one, the bishop being superior to the presbyters. Just how this happened is not known, but it is supposed that in churches where a plurality of elders was found, one of the presbyters became the leader or president—whether by seniority, force of character or election can only be conjectured, and is unimportant. To him the title of bishop was gradually appropriated, so that from being at first only *primus inter pares* he came, after a generation or two, to be regarded as superior to the presbyters. This is the state of things that we find in the letters of Ignatius, written about the year A. D. 115. But the bishop was as yet bishop of a single church, though there may have been several congregations, each with its presbyters. The state of things was not unlike that which we find now in some of our large cities, where a church has a pastor and several assistants, ministers like himself, who have charge of mission stations in various parts of the city. If, now, we were to give to such a pastor the exclusive title of bishop, and regard his assistants as presbyters only, we should almost exactly reproduce the polity that we find in Ignatius.

How and when this episcopate became diocesan we do not exactly know. As the churches of the great cities in the empire sent out preachers into the suburbs and adjacent towns, and new churches were formed, they would not unnaturally come under the authority of this bishop. We find from Irenæus onward his jurisdiction, originally described as his parish (*paroikia*), gradually enlarging, until the third century sees the diocesan system quite fully established. Cyprian goes so far as to call the bishop the vicegerent of Christ in things spiritual, and almost to make him the church itself: " The church is in the bishop, and the bishop is in the church, and if any one is not with the bishop he is not in the church."

We may also trace in these early centuries the beginnings of the characteristic doctrines and practices that we associate with Romanism. " The church of the first four centuries " is the shibboleth of many High Churchmen, but they who adopt this motto must assuredly be wofully ignorant of the Fathers about whom they talk so much. If all roads do not lead to Rome this one certainly does. Make antiquity the test of truth and Rome has the argument—if by " antiquity " is meant as is usually the case, the first four centuries of Christianity, exclusive of the evidence of the New Testament. In those centuries we find the full doctrine of the mass, the doctrine of penance, confession and priestly absolution, purgatory, the invocation of saints and the use of images in worship. In short, we find all of Romanism but its name and the pope.

We find another thing, not alone characteristic of Romanism, though most prominent in that system, a growth of asceticism resulting in the practice of clerical celibacy and monachism. This likewise may be traced to the root-idea of salvation by works. The Gnostic and Manichæan heresies, though nominally rejected by the Church, were in part accepted. Teaching an eternal conflict between spirit and matter, and that the latter is the source of all evil, this philosophy was easily reconciled with the idea of salvation by works. Sin was held to be the result of the union of man's spirit with a body, and only by keeping the body under, mortifying the flesh by fasting and maceration, could sin be overcome. The contempt for marriage and the undue exaltation of virginity that appears in the Fathers, notably in Jerome, not only gave impetus to monachism and the celibacy of the clergy, with their vast train of evils, but laid the foundation for the exaltation of Mary above her Son, and the idolatries and blasphemies of Roman Catholicism.

It would be unprofitable to go further into the details of this doctrinal and moral corruption of Christianity. All its ramifications sprang from the one idea that salvation is not the free gift of God through Christ, but something to be earned by human effort or purchased from a store of merits laid up by the saints. But it is worth our while to note, in conclusion, that the rapidity with which the doctrine, ritual, and polity of the early church degenerated, was directly proportioned to its growth in wealth and worldly prosperity. There is no lesson taught by the first centuries that needs to be learned now by Baptists more than this. So long as the church was feeble, persecuted, and poor, though in some things it departed from the standard of the New Testament, it was comparatively pure in both doctrine and life. Adversity refined and strengthened it; prosperity weakened and corrupted it. What the persecutions of Nero and Domitian were powerless to accomplish, the patronage of Constantine and his successors did only too well. Baptists have had their period of adversity, when they inherited Christ's promise, " Blessed are ye when men shall reproach you, and persecute you, and say all manner of evil against you falsely, for my sake." Will they endure the harder test of prosperity, when they are great in numbers, in wealth, in influence, so that all men speak well of them?

CHAPTER V

THE STRUGGLE FOR A PURE CHURCH

THIS degeneration in the church, whose stages we traced in the preceding chapter, was a gradual process, whose completion occupied several centuries. It did not occur without resistance, determined, prolonged, and frequently renewed. Many attempts were made at a reformation of the church, a return to the simplicity and purity of the apostolic churches. The truth was not totally eclipsed at first, only obscured; from time to time men taught anew the spiritual nature of Christ's church, the necessity of regeneration in order to membership in a church of Christ, salvation by grace and not by sacraments and penances. At times these reactions promised to be successful, but they all in turn failed to effect their object. Some failed by their own inherent weakness, others were suppressed by force, and in the end the Holy Catholic Church triumphed over them all. It is instructive to consider the causes of the partial success and the final failure of these attempts to restore an evangelical Christianity.

The first of these protests against the corrupt teachings and life that had come to be prevalent in the church, even in the second century, was Montanism. Little is positively known about the origin of the Montanists, and even the existence of their reputed founder has been denied. Montanus is said to have been a native of Phrygia, a converted priest of Cybele, and began his teachings about 150. He soon gathered about him many followers, among whom were two women of rank, Maxi-

57

milla and Priscilla (Prisca), who left their husbands to become evangelists of the new sect, among whom they were soon esteemed prophetesses. The new teaching spread with great rapidity, and for a time met with little opposition. We are more fortunate in regard to the Montanists than in the case of many "heretical" sects, for we are not dependent solely on their Catholic opponents for a knowledge of their teachings; a large part of the writings of Tertullian, their ablest adherent and advocate, are also available for our instruction in this matter. From these and other sources we gather that the characteristic doctrines of Montanism were three.

First, they clearly apprehended the fundamental truth that a church of Christ should consist of the regenerate only. As a result of the doctrine of sacramental grace, large numbers were becoming members of the church who, in the judgment of the most charitable, could not be regarded as regenerate. This was true of the adults baptized on profession of faith, and the case became continually worse as the practice of infant baptism extended. Montanus advocated a return to the principle of the New Testament—a spiritual church. His immediate followers called themselves "spiritual" Christians, as distinguished from the "carnal" who were found in the Catholic Church in great numbers. The Spirit of God has not only regenerated every Christian, they taught, but dwells in an especial manner in every believer, even as Jesus promised the Paraclete (John 16: 13).

So far the Montanists were strictly scriptural. But they went on to teach that by virtue of this indwelling of the Paraclete the "spiritual" not only received an illumination that enabled them to apprehend the truth already revealed, but were given special revelations. The gifts of prophecy and divine inspiration were therefore perpetual in the church. The Montanistic prophets spoke with tongues, with accompaniments of ecstasy and trance. Montanus himself seems to have brought over to his Christian faith not a few of his heathen notions. Soothsaying and divination, accompanied by ecstasy and trance, were characteristic of the Cybele cultus; and though the Montanists rejected the soothsaying and divination as Satanic, they believed the ecstasy and trance to be marks of divine communications. The revelations thus received by these prophets were held to be supplementary, and in a sense superior, to Scripture. A special sanctity was attributed to the sayings of Montanus, Maximilla, and Prisca; but the few examples that have been preserved seem in nowise remarkable.

This was perhaps the gravest departure of Montanism from the model of New Testament Christianity on which it professed to be formed. This single note shows a complete separation in spirit between Montanists and those whose fundamental belief is that in the canon of Scripture we have a complete and authoritative revelation from God, and that whatever contradicts the written word is of necessity to be rejected as untrue. One may trace a curious correspondence in many things between this Montanistic teaching and the doctrine regarding the " inner light " held by the Society of Friends; and an equally curious correspondence between the history of Montanism and the rise in our own day of the sect known as Irvingites, though they prefer to call themselves the Catholic Apostolic Church. It has often happened in the history of Christianity that a sect or party, beginning with the object of restoring the doctrine and practice of apostolic times, has fallen into fanaticism and false teaching, because, like Montanism, it failed to keep closely to the word of God, as the sole and sufficient rule of faith and practice, not to be supplemented by pretended new revelations any more than by the traditions of men. The supreme authority of the New Testament is the only safe principle for a reformation of religion; if the history of the church teaches anything it teaches that.

The second of the chief features in Montanism was a belief in the speedy coming of Christ to reign with his saints a thousand years. The fragmentary sayings of their prophets that have come down to us, the writings of Tertullian, and the testimonies of the Catholic writers against Montanism combine to make this certain. This chiliastic doctrine was then, as often in the later ages of Christianity, tinged with fanaticism. Wherever it has been held by any considerable body of Christians, it has been associated with grave errors and serious disturbances.

This teaching regarding the second coming of Christ doubtless gave a great stimulus to the ascetic spirit among the Montanists, which was their third leading characteristic. Their idea of a regenerate church naturally necessitated a strict discipline, but by no means discipline on an ascetic basis. The Scriptures teach the need of self-control, temperance, subduing the lust of the flesh, keeping the body under; but this victory is to be won by spiritual, not by physical means. Keeping the body under does not mean starving or macerating the body. The New Testament honors the body, and does not teach that it is the essential enemy of the spirit. That is a heathen notion, probably derived from the Manichæans, or possibly from the Gnostics, who also taught the essential evil of matter.

From some such source, certainly not from the Scriptures, the Montanists obtained the notion that to mortify the flesh is the road to heaven; and among them fasts and vigils were commended, if not commanded, as productive of the bodily state most conducive to holiness. In similar spirit they forbade the use of ornaments. They exalted virginity above marriage, as a state of greater purity, and forbade second marriage as equivalent to adultery. Seven sins were regarded as peculiarly deadly or mortal (pride, covetousness, lust, anger, gluttony, envy, sloth), which when committed after baptism, might be forgiven by God, but should forever cut the sinner off from communion with the church.

At first Montanism was rather a party than a sect, an *ecclesiola in ecclesia,* and for a time it was tolerated by the bishop of Rome and seemed likely to prevail in the church. The Roman bishop finally rejected Montanism as a heresy, and his already recognized primacy in the West, at least, caused this decision to be generally accepted. Professor Möller [1] is simply just when he says:

Soon the conflict assumed such a form that the Montanists were compelled to separate from the Catholic Church and form an independent or schismatic church. But Montanism was, nevertheless, not a new form of Christianity; nor were the Montanists a new sect. On the contrary, Montanism was simply a reaction of the old, the primitive church, against the obvious tendency of the church of the day—to strike a bargain with the world, and arrange herself comfortably in it.

Much nonsense has been written by historians about Montanism, because they could not or would not grasp this idea. The Montanists were in general rigidly orthodox, and no serious aberration from the Catholic faith is alleged against them by their opponents. No council formally condemned them, and they were treated as schismatics rather than as heretics. For their schism the Catholic Church was responsible; they did not go out, they were driven out from the church. The church

[1] Schaff-Herzog Encyclopedia, article " Montanism."

at large resisted and rejected the reformation that Montanism attempted, but it adopted precisely those features in Montanism that were least scriptural—namely, its asceticism, and its belief that the written revelation admits of supplementary revelations. There is this difference, however, that Rome makes the Spirit dwell in the church at large, not in each believer, so that his revelations are made through the church, and especially through its head, both church and pope being preserved from error by this indwelling Spirit.

Of course the Montanists immersed—no other baptism, so far as we know, was practised by anybody in the second century. There is no evidence that they baptized infants, and their principle of a regenerate church would naturally require the baptism of believers only. In their polity they seem not to have differed from the Catholics; for, though Tertullian speaks as if the idea of the priesthood of all believers was prevalent among them, he also speaks of "bishop and clergy," and the "ecclesiastical order." The only natural conclusion, from his undoubtedly Montanistic writings, is that the Montanist bishop was like the Catholic, an officer above the presbyter in rank and authority.

Montanism declined rapidly after the fourth century, though traces of it are found as late as the sixth. It has seemed worth while to set down thus fully the ascertained facts concerning this party, because many writers have claimed that the Montanists were Baptists in all but the name. Nothing has been said concerning them except what is abundantly proved by their own literature; and every intelligent reader will be able to judge for himself in what respects they held the views of modern Baptists and how far they diverged from what we hold to be the teachings of the Scriptures.

Another partial reformation of the church was at-

tempted by the Novatians about the middle of the third
century. Novatian was the man whose clinic baptism
has already been described. He recovered from his supposed mortal sickness and was ordained a presbyter by
Fabian, bishop of the church of Rome. When Fabian
died, in 250, there was a vacancy in the office for about
a year. The terrible Decian persecution was then raging, and many Christians, overcome by the prospect of
death, denied the faith and sacrificed to the emperor.
The question soon arose, What should be done with these
faithless Christians (*lapsi*) when they afterward professed penitence, and desired to be readmitted into the
church?

Two views prevailed, and soon two rival parties in
the church advocated them. One party favored a strict
discipline; those who had lapsed had committed mortal
sin through their idolatry and should remain perpetually
excluded from the church—though even the stricter party
conceded that if one of the lapsed were sick unto death
he should be absolved. The other party held that perpetual exclusion of the lapsed from the church and its
sacraments—in which alone salvation could be found—
was to anticipate the judgment of God. They, therefore would take a more merciful view of the infirmity
of those who had yielded under the stress of persecution, and would restore the lapsed to the communion of
the church, after a public confession and a period of
probation.

During the vacancy in the Roman episcopate, Novatian was the leading man in the church, and strongly
inclined toward the stricter discipline. The laxer party
seem, however, to have been in the majority, and in 251
they elected Cornelius as bishop. His election appears
to have been entirely regular, but the stricter party would
not acknowledge him, and chose Novatian, who was

consecrated by three obscure Italian bishops. A synod held at Rome, probably in October, 257, excommunicated him and his followers. Thereafter they constituted a separate sect, called by their opponents Novatians, but themselves preferring the title of Cathari (the pure). The Novatians were the earliest Anabaptists; refusing to recognize as valid the ministry and sacraments of their opponents, and claiming to be the true church, they were logically compelled to rebaptize all who came to them from the Catholic Church. The party gained great strength in Asia Minor, where many Montanists joined it, and in spite of persecution, the Novatians survived to the sixth or seventh century. In this case, as generally, persecution stimulated what it would have destroyed.

The Donatist party in Africa, like the Novatians in Rome, seemed to originate in a mere squabble over an office. Two parties were formed in the church of Carthage regarding the treatment of those who had surrendered the sacred books to be burned during the Diocletian persecution (303-311). These *traditores,* as they were called, incurred great odium. When Caecilian was elected bishop of Carthage in 311, it was as the representative of those who favored the readmission of *traditores* to the church on easy terms. He was consecrated bishop by Felix of Aptunga, instead of Secundas of Tigisis, the primate of Numidia. This was irregular, yet not in itself invalid; but the stricter party refused to recognize Caecilian, on the ground that Felix was a *traditor,* and even Caecilian himself was not above suspicion on this score. The real issue at stake was not who should be bishop of Carthage, but what should be the character of that church, and of the Christian churches of Africa generally. Dr. Schaff says of the controversy, writing with a candor and insight not common among church historians:

The Donatist controversy was a conflict between separatism and catholicism; between ecclesiastical purism and ecclesiastical eclecticism; between the idea of the church as an exclusive community of regenerate saints and the idea of the church as the general christendom of State and people. It revolved around the doctrine of the essence of the Christian church, and, in particular, of the predicate of holiness. . . The Donatists . . . laid chief stress on the predicate of the subjective holiness or personal worthiness of the several members, and made the catholicity of the church and the efficacy of the sacraments dependent upon that. The true church, therefore, is not so much a school of holiness, as a society of those who are already holy; or at least of those who appear so; for that there are hypocrites, not even the Donatists could deny, and as little could they in earnest claim infallibility in their own discernment of men. By the toleration of those who are openly sinful, the church loses her holiness, and ceases to be a church.[1]

Unfortunately, the Donatists made one capital error: they appealed to the civil power to decide the question that was in its essence spiritual. Donatus himself, who was chosen bishop of Carthage by the stricter party in 315, seems to have been opposed from the first to the intermeddling of the emperor with religious questions, but his party was not controlled by him in this matter. Constantine referred the dispute first to a select committee of bishops, then to the synod of Arles, and finally decided the question himself on appeal. All these decisions were against the Donatists; and after the case had irrevocably gone against them, they came out as stanch defenders of religious liberty, and denied the right of the civil power to meddle in matters of faith and discipline. Their disinterestedness in taking this stand would have been less open to suspicion if they had professed it in the first instance and abstained from all appeals to the imperial power against their opponents. One who appeals to a court for redress is estopped in

[1] "History of the Christian Church," Vol. III., p. 365.

honor, as well as in law, from afterward denying its jurisdiction.

Like the Novatians, the Donatists were Anabaptists, but their rebaptizing seems to have been based on a false idea, namely, that in baptism the chief thing is not the qualifications of the baptized, but those of the baptizer. The Donatists and Novatians both rebaptized those who came to them from the Catholic Church, not because they did not believe these persons regenerate when baptized, but because they denied the " orders " of the Catholic clergy. These ministers had been ordained by *traditores,* by bishops who were corrupt; they were members of a church that had apostatized from the pure faith, and therefore had no valid ministry or sacraments; and for this reason their baptism could not be accepted.

Neither of these attempted reformations was sufficiently radical. Novatians and Donatists seem to have shared the errors of the Catholic Church regarding sacramental grace; their episcopacy cannot be distinguished from that of the Catholic Church, and was certainly far from the simplicity of apostolic order. The Donatists, at any rate, seem to have practised infant baptism; on any other supposition the arguments of Augustine, in refutation of their errors, are unintelligible. Both sects grasped the great truth of the essentially spiritual nature of the church, the necessity of regeneration and a godly life to membership in it; but they failed to follow this truth to its logical implications and to return to the New Testament faith and practice in all things.

Many writers have treated this period as if the truth were only to be found with the so-called heretics, assuming that the Catholic Church must necessarily be always in the wrong. But such is by no means the case;

we are, on the contrary, often compelled to admit that as between the heretical sects and the Catholic Church the truth was with the latter. Wrong doctrine and practice were by no means uniformly triumphant. This was especially evident in the notable controversies regarding the doctrine of the Person of Christ. Corrupt as Christianity was fast becoming, it had kept close to the Scripture in the fundamentals of Christian theology until the beginning of the fourth century. Then Arius, a presbyter of Alexandria, taught a doctrine, the germs of which may be found in the teachings of his predecessors (notably, Origen), but was first fully elaborated by his logical and acute mind. His teaching was that the Father alone is God, unbegotten, unchangeable. The Son is the first of created beings, who existed before the worlds were and created them; he is the Logos, the perfect image of God, and may be called God in a sense; but he is not eternal, for he had a beginning, and is not of the same substance as the Father. Arius was an adroit, fascinating man, and propagated his doctrine industriously. It obtained great currency in Palestine and Nicomedia, and spread to all parts of the empire, threatening to displace the orthodox faith.

This spread was accompanied by much bitter controversy, and this fact moved Constantine to interfere. He was anxious, for political reasons, to preserve the peace and unity of the church, otherwise its value to him as an instrument of governing was gone. He therefore summoned a council of the bishops of the church, who, to the number of more than 300, assembled at Nicæa in 325. When he accepted Christianity, he made it the religion— or, at least, a religion—of the State. The emperor was the Pontifex Maximus of the old religion, its official head and high priest; and though but a layman in the new faith, he nevertheless aspired to a similar position of authority. Constantine, though at that time not even baptized, presided in his robes of State at the council of Nice, took an influential part in its business and greatly influenced if he did not practically dictate its findings. This council decided against the Arians and adopted the orthodox creed that, with some later changes, still bears its name.

Under Julian the apostate, orthodoxy suffered a reverse and Arianism again seemed about to triumph; but when Theodosius I. became emperor—he having been trained under Nicene influences—he used all his power, and successfully, to suppress the heresy. The conflict was practically ended with the council of Constantinople (381), which readopted the Nicene creed, and from that time Arianism gradually disappears as a dangerous heresy, though it often reappeared in later ages. For a time, indeed, a form of semi-Arianism lingered in the church. The orthodox maintained that the Son is of the same substance with the Father (*homo-ousion*); the Arians that he is of a *different* substance (*hetero-ousion*); the semi-Arians that he is of a *like* substance (*homoi-ousion*). Like most compromises, semi-Arianism could not be permanently acceptable to either party; to the orthodox it seemed as objectionable as Arianism itself, while to the Arians, though they were at first willing to accept it as a compromise (indeed, it came near getting into the Nicene creed), it seemed to concede too much to orthodoxy.

Athanasius, the leader of the orthodox party, in its struggle against Arianism, was born in Alexandria about 298, received a good education and entered the ministry. At the time of the council of Nice he was not more than twenty-seven years of age, and only an archdeacon, but he was one of the most prominent of the orthodox party and had a large share in the definition of the creed adopted. A similar and even more remarkable case of theological precocity is that of Calvin, who published his immortal " Institutes " at the age of twenty-seven. In June, 328, Athanasius was chosen bishop of Alexandria, but was fiercely opposed from the first by the party of Arius. Three times they succeeded in driving him from the city, twice by order of the emperor and once by violence. At one time it seemed a case of *Athanasius contra mundum*—this one man against the world; but with the victory of the orthodox party, he was suffered to return to Alexandria and there to pass his remaining days. He died in May, 373, before the council of Constantinople registered the final triumph of the orthodox faith.

Athanasius saw clearly that a true doctrine of God was the only foundation for the absoluteness of Christianity. He defended Christianity as truly divine, the highest revelation, an absolute and final revelation; clearly seeing that, if the Arian doctrine were true, Christianity could be merely relatively true, and might be superseded by a more perfect revelation, or even by a higher human philosophy. He rightly contended, therefore, that the religion of Christ would be empty and meaningless if he who is set forth in the Scriptures as the one who unites God and man in real unity of being is not the absolute God, but merely the first of created beings. There could be no mediation between God and man by such a being, and the heart is therefore taken out of Christianity by Arianism. Athanasius was a doughty champion of the truth. His exegesis of Scripture is often faulty, but his dialectical skill was great, and in his extant writings he shows the philosophic contradictions and absurdities of the Arian system in a masterly way. Selections from these writings have been translated into English, and may be found in Vol. IV. of the " Nicene and Post-Nicene Fathers" (second series). The so-called Athanasian creed, though long confidently attributed to him, is certainly not his composition, and cannot be positively traced to an earlier period than the eighth century. This creed was expunged from the prayer-book of the Episcopal Church in the United States in 1785, but it is still required to be said or sung thirteen times a year in every parish of the Church of England.

CHAPTER VI

THE ECLIPSE OF EVANGELICAL CHRISTIANITY

FROM the close of the apostolic era, even beginning in the days of the apostles, we have seen two opposing tendencies struggling for the mastery in the churches of Christ, which may be briefly described as the spiritual and the worldly. Jesus and his apostles taught salvation by faith, but almost immediately some Christians taught salvation by works. According to the former teaching, baptism and the Lord's Supper were ordinances to be observed by those regenerated by the Spirit of God; according to the other teaching baptism and the Lord's Supper were sacraments, channels of divine grace, by which men were made regenerate and confirmed in holiness. The administration of such sacraments demanded a priesthood. So step by step, and by an inevitable process of evolution, the doctrine of salvation by works produced what we know to-day as the Roman Catholic Church, at its head an infallible pope, outside of which church salvation is assured to none. Against this process of development various bodies of Christians, as we have seen, contended in vain during the first four centuries. There were similar contentions throughout the process. The truth was never quite crushed to earth; there were always parties or sects, bitterly hated and persecuted by Catholics, that held with more or less consistency to the evangelical religion. These comparatively pure survivals are found latest in the two extreme portions of the then civilized Europe, in Britain and in Bulgaria.

Rome's most audacious theft was when she seized

bodily the Apostle Peter and made him the putative head and founder of her system; but next to that brazen act stands her effrontery when she " annexed " the great missionary preacher of Ireland and enrolled him among her " saints." In order to conceal the true character of the transaction, Romanists have published lying biographies of Patrick without number, until the real man has been quite forgotten. Modern research has, however, brought the truth to light once more.

Patrick was born about 360, probably near what is now Dumbarton, Scotland. His father was a deacon and a Roman civil officer. At the age of sixteen he was carried away captive and sold into slavery in Ireland. Six years after he escaped, and in later life he was moved to become a Christian missionary to the people among whom he had lived as a slave. These facts, and all other trustworthy information about Patrick, we learn from two of his writings that have survived, his " Confession " or " Epistle to the Irish," and an " Epistle to Coroticus." The date of his death is as uncertain as that of his birth, but tradition ascribes to him extreme old age.

From these writings of Patrick we learn that his teaching and practice were, in many particulars at least, evangelical. The testimony is ample that he baptized believers only. For example, he writes: " So that even after my death I may leave as legacies to my brethren, and to my sons whom I have baptized in the Lord, so many thousand men." " Perhaps, since I have baptized so many thousand men, I might have expected half a screpall [a coin worth six cents] from some of them; tell it to me and I will restore it to you." Not only is there no mention of infants, but he uniformly speaks of "men," " handmaidens of Christ," " women," and " baptized believers." It is inconceivable that he should not have added " infants " had he baptized such.

Again, from all that we can learn, Patrick's baptism was that of apostolic times, which was still general throughout Europe, immersion.   He does not speak explicitly on this point in his own writings, but the earliest accounts of his labors agree that his converts were baptized in fountains, wells, and streams.   His baptism probably differed from the apostolic in being trine immersion, since that was the form practised in the ancient British church, and in practically the whole Christian world in his day.

Patrick also pays great reverence to Scripture as the supreme authority in religion.   He never appeals to the authority of church, or council, or prelate, or creed, but to the word of God; and in his extant writings, brief as they are, no fewer than one hundred and thirteen passages of Scripture are referred to or quoted.   There is no trace in his letters of purgatory, mariolatry, or submission to the authority of pope.   He did not oppose these things, he was simply ignorant of them, it would appear, though in some parts of the church they were fast gaining ground.

The churches founded by Patrick, and those existing in other parts of Britain, were not according to apostolic pattern in some things.   Patrick was himself a bishop, and the three orders of the ministry seem to have been already developed in the British churches of his day.   Though celibacy of the clergy was not required, there was a strain of asceticism and monasticism in these churches that became very pronounced in succeeding ages. It is probable that few, if any, of these monasteries came into existence during Patrick's life, and in their earlier stages they were valuable educational and missionary centers, not what they afterwards became.

The theology of these churches, up to the ninth century, continued to be remarkably sound and scriptural.   They taught original sin and the impossibility of salvation by human merits or effort, Christ alone being the sinner's righteousness. They taught the vicarious atonement, the agency of the Holy Spirit in the conversion of men, justification by faith, the intercession of Christ alone for the saints, and held firmly to the administration of the Lord's Supper in both kinds. Sacramentalism began to make inroads soon after Patrick's time, however, for we find such phrases as " a sacrificial mystery," " the holy Eucharist," " the mysteries of the sacred Eucharist " and the like used to describe the Supper. This is a long way short of the mass; and so late as the ninth century John Scotus Erigena maintained that the bread and wine are no more than the symbols of the absent body and blood of Christ. These churches too knew nothing of the doctrine of purgatory, but from Patrick onward for centuries taught that the souls of the saints immediately after death enter paradise and are with God.

The progress from the simplicity of the gospel to the corruptions of Romanism was slower in Ireland and Britain than in any other part of Europe. Primitive doctrine and practice survived there, not in absolute but in relative purity, long after they had vanished from the continent. The inevitable end came at last, and these churches also became Romanized; but it was not until the twelfth century that the papacy succeeded in establishing, with tolerable completeness, its jurisdiction over the churches of Great Britain and Ireland.[1]

In the East, as well as in the West, the corrupted form of Christianity did not become supreme without a strenuous and long-continued resistance on the part of a more evangelical religion. This was especially true of the

[1] For a fuller discussion of Patrick and his work see " Ancient British and Irish Churches," Rev. William Cathcart, D. D. Philadelphia, 1894. Also, Bury, " Life of St. Patrick and his Place in History." New York, 1905.

region now known as Bulgaria. From the fourth century onward we find a group of sects in various parts of Europe, having a practical continuity of belief, if not a demonstrable historic connection. They are variously known as Paulicians, Cathari, Albigenses, Bogomils, and by half a score of other names. These sects have one fundamental doctrine in common, derived from the Manichæans. Manichæism is not properly a form of Christianity, but a distinct religion, as distinct as Mohammedanism. It originated in Persia, about A. D. 250, in the teachings of Mani. Its distinctive feature is a theodicy, rather than a theology, an explanation of the moral phenomena of the universe by the hypothesis of the eternal existence of two mutually exclusive principles or forces, one good, and the other evil. These forces, conceived as personal, and corresponding to the God and Satan of the Christian theology, are in everlasting conflict, and neither can ever overcome the other. In Manichæism the good spirit was represented as the creator of the world, but his work was vitiated by the agency of the evil spirit, which introduced sin and death.

The Paulicians, accepting this dualistic system, taught that the world is the creation of the evil spirit, not of the good. Manichæism, as it advanced from Persia through the Roman empire, came into contact with Christianity, and borrowed from it some of the latter's features that lent themselves most easily to such grafting, but it was essentially an alien religion, and not a Christian heresy.

The Bogomils are a typical form of this party, more Christian and less Manichæan than some others, and especially interesting because they survived all persecutions down to the Reformation period. Various explanations have been given of the name; some say it means " friends of God "; others trace the party to a Bulgarian bishop named Bogomil, who lived about the middle of the tenth century. What is certain is that the thing is older than the name; that the party or denomination called Bogomils existed long before this title was given to them. They represented through the medieval period, as compared with Rome, the purer apostolic faith and practice, though mixed with some grotesque notions and a few serious errors.

It ought always to be borne in mind, however, that for the larger part of our information regarding those stigmatized as heretics we are indebted, not to their own writings, but to the works of their opponents. Only the titles remain of the bulk of heretical writings, and of the rest we have, for the most part, only such quotations as prejudiced opponents have chosen to make. That these quotations fairly represent the originals would be too much to assume. With respect to the Bogomils, our knowledge is exclusively gained from their bitter enemies and persecutors. All such testimony is to be received with suspicion, and should be scrupulously weighed and sifted before we accept it. Where these prejudiced opponents did not knowingly misstate the beliefs of "heretics," they often quite misunderstood them, viewing these beliefs as they did through the distorting lenses of Roman or Greek Catholicism.

We get our chief information about Bogomil doctrine from the writings of one Euthymius, a Byzantine monk who died in 1118, who wrote a learned refutation of these and other "heresies" of his time. His account is generally accepted by historians as substantially correct—a most uncritical conclusion. The Bogomil theology as set forth by Euthymius was a fantastic travesty of the gospel, with marked Manichæan elements. God had two sons, the elder of whom, called Satanael, was chief among the hosts of heaven and created the material universe. In consequence of his ambition and rebellion he was driven from heaven with his supporters among the angelic hosts. Then God bestowed power on his younger son, Jesus, who breathed the breath of life into man and he became a living soul. Thenceforth there was constant conflict between Satanael and Jesus, but the former met with signal defeat in the resurrection of Jesus, and is destined ultimately to complete overthrow. There are also traces of the docetic heresy in the theology of the Bogomils; they were said to deny that Jesus took real flesh upon himself, but believed his body to be spiritual.

Euthymius charges the Bogomils with rejecting pretty much everything believed by other Christians. They did not accept the Mosaic wrtings as part of the word of God, though they did accept the Psalms and New Testament; they rejected water-baptism, like the modern Quakers; they declared the Lord's Supper to be the sacrifice of demons, and would have none of it; they thought churches the dwelling-places of demons, and the worship of the images in them to be mere idolatry; the fathers of the church they declared to be the false prophets against whom Jesus gave warning; they forbade marriage and the eating of flesh, and fasted thrice a week.

Some of these charges clearly appear to be misapprehensions. Trine-immersion, the doctrine of baptismal regeneration and infant baptism, were taught by the Catholic Church. Denial of these may have been taken by prejudiced prelates to be denial of baptism itself. There is evidence that the Bogomils practised the single immersion of adult believers. No doubt they did call the mass "the sacrifice of demons," or something to that effect; but only to a bigoted and ignorant Catholic would that imply rejection of the Lord's Supper, scripturally celebrated.

The chief peculiarity of the Bogomils is said to have been the division of their members into two classes: the *credentes,* or believers, and the *perfecti,* or pure ones—a division characteristic of Manichæan sects generally, as well as corresponding to the "novices" and "adepts" of many orders and societies. Before admission among the *perfecti* one must have passed a period of probation and received the *consolamentum,* or rite of initiation, by the laying on of hands. The *perfecti* were celibates— women were admitted to this rank—and lived an ascetic life, devoting themselves to the preaching of the gospel and charitable works. It does not appear that marriage was forbdden to the *credentes.* The *perfecti* received the title of "elders," and were preachers to and pastors of the congregations, as well as missionaries and evangelists. There was a total absence of a hierarchy among them. It is charged against them that they held the *perfecti* to be above the law and incapable of sin— the same error of antinomianism into which some Calvinists, Baptists among them, fell later.

The most prominent man among the Bogomils toward the close of the eleventh century was a venerable physician named Basil. He is sometimes described as their "bishop"; he was really one of the "elders" or *perfecti,* and his preeminence was due to his learning and character, not to his official rank. The emperor Alexander Comnenus I., was a bitter persecutor. He did not hesitate to lay a trap for Basil by inviting him to the imperial table and cabinet, and by pretending a deep interest in the Bogomil's views drew from his victim a full exposition of them. A scribe hidden behind tapestries took it all down, and then the perfidious emperor arrested his venerable guest and put him in prison. Basil was condemned and burned at the stake, to the last steadfast in his faith and meeting his cruel death with unfaltering trust in Christ. No charge was or could be brought against him, but his "heresy." To the elevation of his character and his life of good works even the daughter of the emperor, who recorded her father's shame, bore unwilling witness. We learn from her also that many families of the highest rank had embraced the Bogomil doctrines. At the height of their prosperity the *credentes* are said to have numbered two millions, and the *perfecti* perhaps four thousand.

Through the early medieval times, therefore, down to the eleventh century, we find evangelical Christianity suppressed with virtual completeness throughout Europe. Even those forms of Christianity that may, in comparison with Rome, be called evangelical are far from bearing a close resemblance to the doctrine and practice of the apostles. No other conclusion can be drawn from a careful and impartial survey of all the evidence.

CHAPTER VII

WHEN Hildebrand became Pope Gregory VII., in the eleventh century, the papacy reached a height of pretensions and power of which the earlier pontiffs had scarcely dreamed. His predecessors had claimed supremacy in the church; it remained for him to claim universal supremacy, not merely the guidance of all believers in spiritual affairs, but a moral superintendence of the nations. Temporal interests are confessedly inferior to spiritual; in claiming spiritual supremacy, therefore, Hildebrand held that supremacy in temporal affairs was included. Adopting the principles of feudalism, the papacy henceforth declared that all princes and monarchs held their dominions as feofs of the church. This theory the papacy has never since disclaimed. It is a right in abeyance, and it will be revived and reasserted whenever in the future a pope judges himself to be able to enforce the claim. Claims so extravagant produced revolts, both political and religious; some of these revolts partook of both characters to such an extent that it is difficult to class them. They failed, it is true, for the times were not yet ripe for thorough reformation of the Church or State, but they were foregleams of the dawn that was to break over Europe in the sixteenth century.

About the year 1130 a young priest began to attract much attention by his preaching in Brescia, one of the free cities of Northern Italy, and soon all Lombardy was stirred. He was a native of that city, and we first hear of him as a *lector* in the church there. Then he studied in Paris under Abelard, who was already more than suspected of heresy, and not without reason. The Roman Church was not unjust, from its own point of view, in its subsequent condemnation of Abelard; for, whether he were himself in strictness a heretic, he was certainly the cause of heresy in others. The most serious revolts of the twelfth century against the church are directly traceable to his lecture room.

Abelard's instructions had opened Arnold's eyes, broadened his mind, and sent him to the Scriptures. The result was a deepening of his spiritual life, and disgust with the corrupt state of the church in Italy. He became a reformer, and with fiery eloquence exhorted men to repent and live according to the precepts of Christ. He boldly attacked and unsparingly denounced the vices of the clergy, their luxury and debauchery. From study of the Scriptures he had imbibed the notion of a holy and pure church, and he labored incessantly to restore the church as he found it to the pattern of apostolic times. This was the foundation of all his teachings—the necessity of a spiritual church, composed of true believers living in daily conformity to the teachings of Christ.

This was closely coupled with another principle, which, as we have seen, is a necessary corollary from this fundamental teaching of the Scriptures: the complete separation of church and State. The root of the evils that beset the Church Arnold found in its wealth; and its wealth was the result of an unholy alliance with the civil power. Therefore he demanded that the clergy of his day should imitate the apostles—renounce their worldly possessions and privileges, give up secular business, and set all men an example of holy living and apostolic simplicity. He was himself self-denying to the verge of asceticism, living a life of voluntary poverty and celibacy.

The clergy, he taught, should not depend on tithes, but accept for their support the voluntary offerings of their people; and he conformed to his own teaching.

It does not appear that Arnold attacked directly either the organization or the doctrine of the church, at least, during this period of his life. His mind was severely practical. Abelard had given him a strong spiritual impulse, without imparting to his pupil any ‘of his own genius for speculation. Arnold was no theologian, but a man full of zeal for a reformation of the church in its life, rather than in its doctrine and organization. Accordingly he was not charged with heresy, but with being a disturber of the church. His bishop laid the matter before the Second Lateran council in 1139, and he was condemned, banished from Brescia, and forbidden to preach. He is said to have bound himself by an oath to obey, but it seems certain that the terms were limited, for he is not charged with breaking it in what he afterward did.

Banished from Brescia, Arnold went to France and joined his teacher, Abelard, then at the height of his controversy with St. Bernard. He zealously defended Abelard, and shared with him the condemnation of the synod of Sens, in 1140. His stay in France was but a few months; he then found refuge in Switzerland, but Bernard pursued him from place to place with the implacable hatred of the religious zealot who is also a good man.

Arnold went to Rome after the death of Pope Innocent II., to whom (according to Bernard) he had sworn submission, and about 1145 began to preach there. His views had meanwhile undergone a great alteration. He still preached reform, but now it was a political reform, not a spiritual. This may have been, in part, because he found that the Romans had no affinity for his spiritual teachings; but there was a change in his whole spirit and aim that can only partially be explained in this way.

In his view the State should be, not the empire at that time regarded as the ideal earthly government, but a pure republican democracy. Every city, he taught, should constitute an independent State, in whose government no bishop ought to have the right to interfere; the church should not own any secular dominion, and priests should be excluded from every temporal authority. This teaching differed totally from the then prevailing notion of a universal *sacerdotium* and *imperium,* the one ruling spiritual affairs, the other temporal, the civil ruler receiving his authority from the spiritual, and in turn protecting the latter with his sword and enforcing its decrees.

Under the leadership of Arnold the Roman people denied the pope's supremacy in temporal affairs, and compelled him to withdraw from the city. The people, and Arnold himself, cherished wild dreams of the restoration of ancient splendor and power, when the Roman Senate and people should again rule the world. Attempts were made to realize this dream of a new republic, but it was soon rudely shattered. Pope Adrian IV., from his exile at Orvieto, aimed a blow at Arnold and his nascent republic that proved fatal—he laid the interdict on the city and put the leader under the ban. The blow was all the more effective in that nobody could charge the pope with exceeding his spiritual functions. It is hard for us to realize in this day what the interdict meant to a people who still believed that salvation was assured only in the church, by means of sacraments administered by a duly qualified priesthood. The doors of all churches were closed; no mass was said; the living could not be joined in marriage or shriven of their sins; the dead could be buried only as one would bury a dog, with no priest to say a prayer for him. In addition, when Arnold was put under the ban, anybody who gave him shelter or food thereby made himself liable to the severest censures of the church. The interdict was too much for human nature to endure. By this terrible weapon, when all other means failed them, the medieval popes again and again brought the proudest monarchs of Europe to their knees, to sue for pardon and absolution.

When the Emperor Frederick Barbarossa was persuaded by the pope to undertake his cause and entered Italy, he found it easy to procure Arnold's expulsion from Rome. The fallen leader received protection for a time among the nobility, but he was finally delivered up to the pope, and the prefect of Rome hanged him, burned his body and scattered the ashes in the Tiber. Thus perished one of Italy's noblest martyrs, and with his death ended the first struggle for reform of the church.

Arnold has been claimed as a Baptist; but he is also claimed by others as belonging to them—indeed, two of his latest biographers are Roman Catholics, who hold that he taught nothing inconsistent with the Catholic doctrine of his day, and was never condemned as a heretic. His supposed affinity with Baptists has little evidence in its favor save the statement made by Otto of Freisingen, a contemporary historian, " He is said to have had unsound notions (*non sane dicitur sensisse*) regarding the sacrament of the altar and the baptism of children." This is given as a report merely; Bishop Otto, who says everything unfavorable about Arnold that he can devise, does not venture to state this positively. The only other scrap of evidence that seems to connect him with Baptists is the statement, apparently handed on from writer to writer without re-investigation, that he was condemned by the Lateran Council for his rejection of infant baptism. The Second Lateran Council (1139) condemned all who rejected " the sacrament of the body and blood of the Lord, the baptism of children, priesthood and other ecclesiastical orders, and the bonds of lawful marriage," but nobody is mentioned by name. Some historians infer that this was a condemnation of Arnold, but that begs the very question at issue, namely, how many and which of these errors he taught.

Nobody has summed up the work of Arnold, and indicated its significance, with more eloquence and insight than Bishop Hurst:

To study the career of Arnold and its unhappy end one would conclude that it was simply a revolutionary episode in the turbulent age in which he lived. But we must take a broader view. He greatly weakened the confidence of the people in the strength of the papacy. He proved that it was possible for one man, endowed with energy, to overthrow, at least for a time, the temporal sovereignty of popes, introduce a new political life in Rome itself, and mass the people to support his views. His most bitter enemies could not find any flaw in his moral character. His purity of life was in perfect harmony with the gospel which he preached. His personal worth, and the temporary changes which he wrought, were the great forces which continued to work long after his martyrdom. In every later effort for reform, and even in the Reformation in Germany and other countries, the name of Arnold of Brescia was a mighty factor in aiding towards the breaking of the old bonds. Even in these latest times it has its historical value, for in the struggle of the Protestantism of New Italy for mastery over the thought of the people, that name is a comfort to all who are endeavoring to bring in the new and better day, from the Alps down to Sicily.[1]

It was three centuries before Italy saw another serious attempt to purify the church, and in the meantime the papacy had lost much of its political power and descended to the lowest depths of degradation. All that ancient historians have related of the horrible crimes of Nero and other emperors of Rome, and much besides, may be truthfully told of Alexander VI., the father of Cæsar and Lucretia Borgia. His wickedness was colossal, sim-

[1] " Short History of the Christian Church," p. 152.

ony and murder being the least of his sins, and the worst
unnamable. Under him and his immediate predecessors
the corruption of the church became frightful; if there
were not the fullest proof of the facts they would be
incredible. A man who had murdered his two daughters
was duly condemned to death, but on the very morning of
his execution was set at liberty for the payment of eight
hundred ducats. A high official of the papal court calmly
remarked: " God willeth not the death of a sinner, but
that he shall pay and live." In the monasteries, what
could be expected but notorious and almost universal unfaithfulness to their vows of poverty and chastity?
Among the secular clergy the case was little better. Of
course there were devout and faithful souls in the midst
of all this wickedness, as there have been in every age
of the church, but the fifteenth century was a sink of
corruption. The moral tone of Christendom was never
lower. The rulers were despotic, cruel, oppressive; the
people were brutally selfish; both were dissolute and
knavish. Such is the picture of the times drawn by contemporary writers, loyal sons of the church. Nothing
but a root-and-branch reformation could save church
and society from utter dissolution. Was such a reformation—revolution rather—possible? If so, could it proceed
from within?

About the time Columbus was setting forth on his first
voyage to America the people of Florence discovered that
a young Dominican monk in their city was one of the
great preachers of the age. Girolamo Savonarola was
born in Ferrara in 1452, of noble descent, and was
destined by his parents for the profession of medicine.
In his twenty-third year, becoming greatly anxious about
his soul, he forsook his home and entered a Dominican
monastery—an experience almost exactly duplicated by
Luther a generation later. He became an ardent student

of the Scriptures, of which he is said to have committed nearly the whole to memory. He was a man of somewhat gloomy, melancholy nature, given to fasts and vigils, ascetic in life, and in manner like one of the old prophets. When he first began to preach his success was meager, but suddenly at Brescia he preached as if a new inspiration had come upon him; and from the time he went to Florence (1490) he attracted multitudes. His favorite theme was the exposition of the apocalypse, and in that book he found ample materials for heart-searching sermons, laden with fierce denunciations of the sins of the age. Savonarola began, as so many had begun before him, as Luther was to begin later, with an idea simply of the moral regeneration of the church. He imagined that the rottenness of the church and society about him could be cured by preaching, that the mere proclamation of the truth was enough. He soon came to see, however, that the evils he denounced were inseparably bound up with the political system of his age, and his efforts at reformation took a political turn.

For a time the eloquence of Savonarola seemed to carry all before it. Lorenzo di Medici died, and his incompetent son, Pietro, was soon driven from the city. The government was reorganized on a theocratic basis, with Savonarola as the vicegerent of God. The golden age appeared to have returned to Florence, and, as a contemporary writer said, "the people seemed to have become fools from mere love of Christ." Emboldened by his success, Savonarola attacked the papacy, in which he rightly saw the chief source of the evils of the age. Alexander VI. sought to buy his silence with the archbishopric of Florence and a cardinal's hat, and failed. Then the pope accepted the issue Savonarola had forced upon him, and it became a life and death struggle between these two.

Alexander first summoned the daring preacher to Rome to answer for his alleged errors, but he was not silly enough to comply. He was then forbidden to preach for a time, and respected the prohibition until it was removed. The old jealousy between the Franciscans and Dominicans, however, broke out afresh, and this quarrel was skilfully used by the pope to cause Savonarola's downfall. Alexander excommunicated his antagonist in May, 1497, and later threatened to lay the interdict upon the city if it did not surrender its favorite preacher. But Florence stood by him, and might have continued to do so, though it was wavering, had it not been for an error of Savonarola's that was fatal to his cause. A Franciscan preacher denounced him as a heretic, and challenged the reformer to undergo with him the ordeal by fire. Savonarola did not approve of the ordeal, and refused it for himself, but the pressure of opinion induced him to permit one of his followers to accept the challenge. It was a fatal move. The pyres were lighted, and all Florence had assembled to see the trial. The Franciscans managed to get up a bitter quarrel with the Dominicans over the question whether the cross or the host was to be carried through the flames; and while they contended a rainstorm came on and put out the fires. The people, disappointed of their expected spectacle, with the usual fickleness of the mob, visited all their displeasure upon Savonarola, and from that day his influence declined so rapidly that he soon fell into the power of Alexander's agents. Under torture he was said to have confessed everything that his enemies desired, but the reports are so garbled as to be utterly unworthy of trust; and it is certain that afterward he retracted all that he had confessed. Not even torture and garbling could make him out a heretic or guilty of any capital offense, and he was finally condemned in defiance of both law and justice. He was first hanged and then burned, with two of his chief adherents, " in order that," so ran the sentence, " their souls may be entirely sep‹ arated from their bodies." The sentence was duly executed, in the presence of a vast multitude. Savonarola bore himself with composure and fortitude, and his last words were, " O Florence, what hast thou done to-day? " What, indeed! Nothing but postpone for almost four centuries Italy's deliverance from the papal yoke.

Few men have been more variously estimated than Savonarola. By one party he has been represented as an inspired prophet, a saint, a miracle-worker; by another as ambitious, fanatical, even hypocritical. By one he is called a patriot, by another a demagogue. He was not a heretic; to the last he believed in all the dogmas of the Roman Catholic Church. Rome never condemned his teachings as heresy, and though he has not yet been canonized, there is no obstacle to his canonization at any time, as his admirers in the church, in increasing numbers, demand. He resisted the pope politically, but acknowledged him as the head of the church. Nevertheless, he had adopted principles that, if they had been given an opportunity to work themselves out, would have compelled his separation from Rome. The pope was wiser in his generation than the reformer.

The next serious revolt against the papal supremacy was in Bohemia. Early in the fifteenth century, that kingdom was greatly stirred by the preaching of a Czech scholar. John Hus (so he wrote the name, it being an abbreviation of Hussinetz) was educated at the Uni‹ versity of Prag, and after taking his Master's degree in 1396, began to lecture, with such success that in 1401 he was made dean of the philosophical faculty, and in 1403 rector of the university. In 1402 he was also made pastor of the Bethlehem Chapel, where he preached in the Czech language. He was a diligent student of the Scriptures, but his theology was not mainly derived from that source—or, rather, the writings of another had first opened his eyes to the meaning of Scripture.

In the middle of the fourteenth century a professor at Oxford had attracted much attention by the boldness and novelty of his teaching. John Wiclif was a Protestant before Protestantism, condemning and opposing in his writings nearly every distinctive doctrine of Rome—a man far more radical than Luther, though less violent in his manner of utterance. Among his plain teachings, all of which proceeded from the root-principle of the supreme authority of the Scriptures, were these: No writing, not even a papal decree, has any authority, save as it is founded on the Scriptures; transubstantiation is not taught in the Bible, but by the popes; in the primitive church there were but two orders in the ministry, bishops and deacons; there is not good scriptural warrant for confirmation and extreme unction; the clergy should not interfere in civil affairs. In addition to this already long list of heresies, Wiclif opposed the doctrine of indulgences, the mendicant orders and monks of all sorts, the use of images and pictures in churches, canonization, pilgrimages, auricular confession, and celibacy of the clergy! But though he disowned and combated every distinctive feature in the Roman Church of his day, Wiclif was not condemned, and at length died peacefully in his bed. This was due partly to his distance from Rome, and partly to the powerful protection he received from English kings and nobles. His followers (Lollards) were severely persecuted, but not exterminated, and his teachings prepared England for a subsequent reformation. Especially did his translation of the Scriptures, which was widely circulated, leave an indelible impression on the English mind and character.

Hus adopted nearly all of Wiclif's views, and may fairly be called the disciple and follower of the great English reformer. It need not surprise us that Wiclif's doctrines thus found an acceptance in Bohemia hardly obtained in England. His writings were chiefly in Latin, then the common language of educated men everywhere; so that ideas then passed from England to Bohemia far more easily than they do in the twentieth century. It was, moreover, the custom of medieval students to migrate from university to university, in order to hear some renowned lecturer; and students from Oxford brought Wiclif's writings to Prag and made them known to Hus. But though a disciple, Hus was more than a mere echo of Wiclif. He was content to follow where Wiclif led the way—possibly because Wiclif's was the stronger, more independent, more original mind—but he had gifts of eloquence that his master seems never to have possessed. Wiclif was the scholar, the teacher, the retiring thinker, while Hus was not merely scholar and teacher, but apostle.

At first Hus undoubtedly believed in the possibility of reforming the church from within. He had apparently the confidence of his ecclesiastical superiors, and hoped to accomplish great things. Not only did he industriously spread abroad the doctrines of Wiclif, but as a synodical preacher he exposed and denounced the sins of the clergy with great faithfulness. Appointed to investigate some of the alleged miracles of the church, he did not hesitate to pronounce them spurious—and he bade all believers cease looking for signs and miracles and search the Scriptures. In 1409, the pope forbade the use of Wiclif's writings, which precipitated a conflict between Hus and his archbishop, the latter burning Wiclif's books wherever he could find them, and Hus continuing to preach with increasing boldness. In March, 1411, he was excommunicated by the archbishop and Prag was laid under the interdict, but Hus had the university and the city with him so completely that no attention was paid to the sentences. Hus and his sympathizers now went much further; they declared that neither pope nor bishop has the right to draw the sword; that indulgences are worthless, since not money but true repentance is the condition of forgiveness; that the doctrine of the pope's infallibility is blasphemous.

This was one of the questions that the Council of Constance was expected to decide, and Hus had agreed to submit himself and his teachings to the decision of a general council. When the body met, in November, 1414, great things in the way of reform were expected from it, and at first it seemed likely to realize at least a part of the expectations. Pope John XXIII., one of the worst scoundrels that ever disgraced the See of Rome— and that is saying much—was deposed, and committees were considering carefully liberal propositions concerning the improvement of the church constitution, the reformation of abuses and extortions, and the eradication of simony. The future of the church turned on one point; whether the reformation or the election of a pope should first be set about. The great mistake was made of electing a pope first, and when Martin V. found himself in the papal chair, he was astute enough to frustrate all attempts at reform and bring the council to a close with nothing accomplished. The abuses for which reform was demanded were the very sources from which pope and cardinals drew the greater part of their revenues; and it was absurd to expect reform under such circumstances if they were able to prevent it. The sequel proved that they were able.

One of the things to which the Council of Constance speedily devoted its attention was the agitation in

Bohemia, which had now become a matter of European notoriety. Hus had never denied, but rather affirmed, the authority of an ecumenical council. King Sigismund, of Hungary (who was also the emperor), summoned Hus to appear before the council and gave the reformer a safe conduct. In June, 1415, he had his first public hearing, and two other hearings followed; in all of them he stood manfully by his teachings and defended them as in accord with Scripture. During the rest of the month frequent attempts were made to induce him to retract, but he stood firmly by his faith. On July 6th condemnation was finally pronounced, and it is said that, on this occasion, the emperor had the grace actually to blush when reminded of the safe conduct he had given. Hus was then publicly degraded from the priesthood with every mark of ignominy, and delivered, with Rome's customary hypocrisy, to the civil power for execution. Thus the church could say that she never put heretics to death! When being tied to the stake he preached and exhorted until the fire was kindled, when he began singing with a loud voice, " Jesus, Son of the living God, have mercy on me." This he continued until his voice was stifled by smoke and flame, but his lips were seen to move for a long time, as in prayer. When his body was consumed, the ashes were cast into the Rhine, that the earth might no more be polluted by him.

Never was it more clearly demonstrated that the blood of the martyrs is in the seed of the church. The legitimate development of Hus' teachings was not through the so-called Hussites, but through the Unitas Fratrum, anciently known as the Bohemian Brethren, and in later times as Moravians. Their organization began in a secluded nook in Bohemia in 1457. The principles of Hus were avowed in their confessions, and their growth was rapid. By the beginning of the Lutheran Reformation they numbered four hundred parishes, with two hundred thousand members, but by persecution and absorption they almost disappeared. A remnant, however, was preserved, a " hidden seed," and the order of bishops, originally derived from the Waldensians, was continued in secret but regular succession. Finally the survivors settled, in 1722, and the following seven years, on the estate of Count Zinzendorf, in Saxony, and there built a town called Herrnhut ("watch of the Lord"). March 13, 1735, David Nitschmann was consecrated the first bishop of this revived Moravian Church, and a new era in its history began. Few things in the history of Christianity are more full of romance and of encouragement to faith than this story of the Moravians, their providential preservation for over a century, after their existence was supposed to be ended, and their almost miraculous emergence into a new life, to become the leaders of Christendom in missionary enterprise.

How came it about that not only these attempts at reform, but others that are still to be recounted, failed?— failed in spite of being founded on the Scriptures and having the favor of the people. To tell that story is the object of the next chapter.

CHAPTER VIII

THE WRATH OF THE DRAGON

UNTIL Christianity conquered the Cæsars and became the religion of the Roman State, it had been often persecuted, but never a persecutor. As if to show that this was merely because it had lacked the power, as if to prove that in this respect the religion of the Christ was no better than the religions of the gods that it displaced, the Holy Catholic Church almost immediately began to persecute, thereby affording a convincing demonstration that it was neither catholic nor holy. Indeed, persecution was an inevitable consequence of the union of Church and State under Constantine; no other result could reasonably have been looked for, with the confusion of civil and ecclesiastical rights that followed the promotion of Christianity to be a State religion.

Let us strive to be just to Constantine, while true to the facts of history. Let us remember that he was of heathen birth and training; that he was never a Christian, in any proper sense of the term; that he delayed his baptism until his death-bed, in the vain hope of thus washing away all his sins at one fell swoop, and entering the new life regenerate and holy; that during his lifetime he never quite learned the difference between Christianity and heathenism, or that there was any fundamental difference. How, indeed, should he suspect such a thing, in view of the conduct and doctrines of the churchmen of his day? Let us remember, furthermore, that as Imperator Constantine was Pontifex Maximus of the old religion, and that he naturally imported into his newly professed faith this same idea of imperial headship.

And finally, let us take his point of view. Constantine was not a religious man, but he was a statesman, the greatest of the Cæsars after the greater Julius. He saw in Christianity a marvelous force of conviction that had made it triumph over the most cruel and persistent persecutions. He saw in the church, spread throughout the Roman empire, the greatest unifying agency of his day, a society of men bound together in a solidarity to which no other institution could compare. Upon his mind broke the truth that here he had an instrument ready to his hand by which he might consolidate his empire as no predecessor had been able to do—that the civil machinery might be duplicated by the ecclesiastical in every province and town of his domains. A beautiful dream, do you say? But Constantine made it real, and by doing it proved himself one of the great creative statesmen of the world—a man who ranks with Cæsar and Charlemagne and Napoleon.

But it was essential to the realization of this dream that the church should remain a unit. Heresy and schism could not be tolerated, and accordingly Constantine did not tolerate them. He persecuted, not as a bigot, but as a ruler; not for religious, but for civil reasons. At first he personally inclined towards Arius and his followers, but he saw that the orthodox doctrine would finally prevail in the church. He had no narrow prejudices about such matters—orthodoxy and heresy were all one to him—so he at once became the supporter of orthodoxy and threw the whole weight of the imperial power into the scale at the Council of Nice to secure a condemnation of Arianism and a definition of the doctrine of the Trinity as the only orthodox Christian teaching. He was successful, and then set himself the task of

persecuting the Arians out of existence; and though some
of his successors in part undid his work, his policy was
crowned with ultimate success, a century or more after
his death.

Persecution therefore was introduced into the church
of Christ by a man who seems in reality to have been a
heathen, in accordance with a heathen theory of imperial
functions, and for purposes of State. The Holy Catholic Church did not scruple to profit by the policy of
Constantine and even to give him sly encouragement,
but it did not at first dogmatically defend persecution.
Indeed, the reputable Fathers of the Nicene Church
shrank from the idea that one Christian should persecute
another. So late as 385, when the Spanish bishop Pris-
cillian and six of his adherents (accused of Manichæism)
were tortured and beheaded at the instigation of Ithacus,
another bishop, Ambrose of Milan and Martin of Tours
made a memorable protest against this perfidious act and
broke off all communion with Ithacus. The church was
not yet ripe for the proclamation of the doctrine that
Christians were to slay one another for the glory of God.

But a distinguished convert whom Ambrose baptized,
Augustine of Hippo, did not shrink from giving a dog-
matic basis to what had come to be the practice of the
church, and even professed to find warrant for it in Scripture. " It is, indeed, better that men should be brought
to serve God by instruction than by fear of punishment,
or by pain. But because the former means are better,
the latter must not therefore be neglected. Many must
often be brought back to their Lord, like wicked servants,
by the rod of temporal suffering, before they attain the
highest grade of religious development. . . The Lord
himself orders that guests be first invited, then compelled, to his great supper." And Augustine argues that
if the State has not the power to punish religious error,

neither should it punish a crime like murder. Rightly did Neander say of Augustine's teaching, that it "contains the germ of the whole system of spiritual despotism, intolerance, and persecution, even to the court of the Inquisition." Nor was it long before the final step was taken in the church doctrine of persecution. Leo the Great, the first of the popes, in a strict sense of that term, drew the logical inference from the premises already provided for him by the Fathers of the church, when he declared that death is the appropriate penalty for heresy.

Once more, let us be just: the Roman Church is right in this conclusion if we grant its first premise, that salvation depends not on personal faith in the Lord Jesus Christ, as a result of which or in connection with which the Holy Spirit regenerates the soul immediately, but is to be attained only through the church and its sacraments—baptism accomplishing the soul's regeneration, and this new life being nourished and preserved through the Eucharist and other sacraments. Granting this doctrine of sacramental grace, not only is Rome justified in persecuting, but all who believe in sacramental grace are wrong not to persecute. For if salvation is impossible except through the church and its sacraments, every heretic is, as Rome charges, a murderer of souls. Is it not right to restrain and punish a murderer? From this point of view it becomes the duty of the church to root out heresy at all cost of human life—to make the world a desert, if need be, but at any rate to ensure peace. And all persecutors have been half-hearted in the work except only Rome; she has had the courage of her accursed convictions. She alone has recognized that if you say A you must say B, and so on, to the end of the alphabet; that if you once begin to persecute you must not tremble at blood and tears, nor shrink from sending men to the rack, the gibbet, and the stake. The Inquisition is the perfectly logical, the inevitable outcome of Roman doctrine, and the entire system of persecution is rooted in this idea of sacramental grace.

After the theory of persecution was thus fully developed, it remained to put it consistently into practice. This the Roman Church was slow in doing, partly for lack of power, partly because the pressure of need was not strongly felt until the twelfth century. Toward the close of that century these causes of delay no longer existed. During the pontificate of Innocent III. (1198-1216) the papacy rose to the zenith of its baleful authority. This greatest of all the popes, save Hildebrand, blasphemously appropriated to himself, as the pretended vicar of Christ, the words of the risen Jesus, " All power is given unto me in heaven and earth," and strove to realize them in Europe. To King John, of England, he said, " Jesus Christ wills that the kingdom should be priestly, and the priesthood kingly. Over all, he set me as his vicar upon earth, so that, as before Jesus ' every knee shall bow,' in like manner to his vicar all shall be obedient, and there shall be one flock and one shepherd. Pondering this truth, thou, as a secular prince, hast subjected thy realm to Him to whom all is spiritually subject." This claim Innocent made good throughout the greater part of Europe, here by skilful diplomacy, there by aid of the sword, elsewhere by the spiritual censures of the church. He humbled the pride of the kings of France and Spain, made and unmade emperors, and compelled England's most despotic monarch to bow the knee, surrender his realms " to God and the pope," and receive them back as a feudatory.

But while the pope was thus successfully asserting his claim to be supreme, the dispenser and withholder of all temporal sovereignty, the church was menaced by an internal danger that threatened not merely its supremacy, but its very existence. The twelfth century saw the beginning of that tremendous uprising of the human spirit, in its aspiration after greater freedom, which a few centuries later produced the Renaissance, the Reformation, and the Revolution. A reaction began against the despotism that had so long bound the spirit of man in the fetters of absolute dogma. While the popes were triumphing over emperors and kings, heresy was undermining the very foundations of the church. The teachings of Arnold, of Savonarola, of Hus, though more than once the church had believed these detested heresies finally extirpated, had showed an astonishing persistence and fruitfulness. The growth of these heretical sects was doubtless due in part to the simplicity and scripturalness of their teachings, but it is quite as much to be ascribed to the scandalous lives and corrupt practices of the clergy. Men loathed a church in which the cure of souls, from parish priest to pope, was bought and sold as merchandise, when the highest ecclesiastics bartered benefices with almost as little secrecy and quite as little shame as a huckster displays in crying oranges or green peas in our streets. Men instinctively rejected the ministrations of priests known to be depraved in life, and more than suspected to be unbelievers in the saving sacraments they pretended to dispense. Language is inadequate to describe the iniquity of a system in which the very popes swore by the heathen gods and were atheists at heart, in which monastic institutions were brothels, in which the parish priests, though feared, were also hated and despised for their ignorance, their pride, their avarice, and their unclean lives. There is little danger that one who attempts to paint the manners and morals of the medieval clergy will overcharge his brush with dark color. Words that a self-respecting man can address to men who respect themselves are impotent to convey more than tame and feeble hints of that monstrous, that horrible, that unspeakable sink of iniquity, that abomination of putrescence, that quintessence of all infamies thinkable and unthinkable, known as the Holy Roman Catholic Church of the Middle Ages.

In sharp contrast with such a church, these heretical teachers preached the simple faith and practice of the apostolic churches, and illustrated by the purity of their lives the beauty of the gospel they taught. True, their savage persecutors did not hesitate to charge upon these sects horrible immoralities, but these transparent calumnies never deceived anybody—unless we except a few modern historians who ardently desired to be deceived. What gave these heretics favor with the people was not vices, in which they might have rivaled, but could not hope to excel the priesthood, but virtues in which they had few competitors among the clergy. The common people of the Middle Ages were not much given to subtlety of reasoning, but they judged the two trees by their fruits. They looked at the church and beheld rapacity, oppression, wickedness, from highest to lowest in the hierarchy; they looked at these heretical teachers and saw them to be such as Jesus was when upon earth—poor, humble, meek, pure, counting not life itself dear unto them if they might by any means win some. And by thousands and tens of thousands, men turned their backs upon such a church and accepted the teachings of such heretics.

And these teachings were nothing less than revolutionary. They denied that tradition has any authority, they flung aside as rubbish all the writings of the Fathers, all the decrees of councils, all the bulls of popes, and taught that only the Scriptures, and especially the Scriptures of the New Testament, are authoritative in questions of religion, whether of faith or of practice. They denied the efficacy of the sacraments, maintaining that that which is born of the flesh is flesh, and that which is born of the Spirit is spirit; and therefore denying that an inward spiritual change can by any possibility be produced by an outward physical act. They were Lutherans before Luther, in teaching justification by faith and not by works; and more radical and consistent than Luther in accepting the legitimate consequences of their doctrine; for they rejected the baptism of infants as alike unwarranted by Scripture, and absurd in itself, if sacramental grace be denied. These are the distinctive teachings of Baptists to-day, and the men who held these truths from the twelfth century onward, under what various nicknames it pleased their persecutors to give them, were our spiritual ancestry, our brethren in the faith.

But, alongside of these evangelical heresies of the twelfth century was another type of heresy, as widespread, as large in numbers, as threatening to the church, yet widely different in fundamental ideas. This was the sect known to the early church as Manichæans, one of the first forms of heresy and the most persistent of all, which under various names had endured from the age immediately succeeding the apostles. In the East they were long known as Paulicians, in Italy as the Paterines, in Bulgaria as Bogomils, in Southern France as Albigenses, and in all these places as Cathari. This last was their own preferred name, and designated them as Puritans—or those who, both in doctrine and in life, were purer than the so-called Catholic Church. In this claim they were doubtless justified, for, although they are charged with gross immoralities, there is only too good reason to reject the testimony against them; and their doctrinal vagaries, opposed though they were to the gospel, were less gross than Rome's idolatrous worship of the saints, the Host, the images.

Both classes of these heretics flourished during the twelfth century in Southern France. The church was not at all careful to distinguish between them, and they were often included under the name of Albigenses in one sweeping general condemnation. That name, however, does not properly denote the evangelical heretics, who never confounded themselves with these dualistic heretics, and indeed sympathized with them as little as they did with Rome. But Rome hated both with an impartial and undying hatred; and good reason she had for her hatred, for toward the close of the twelfth century it became a life-and-death struggle between the church and these rapidly spreading heresies. In 1167 an Albigensian synod was held at Toulouse. Little is known of its proceedings, but the very fact that such an assemblage could be held shows how powerless the church had become in that region, and how imperative the need was, from the Roman point of view, for active and effectual measures of repression. Before this, recourse had been had to mild measures without effect. Bernard, one of the most eloquent men of his time, and a man of saintly character, had gone on a mission among them. He reports in his letters that the churches were deserted, the altars falling into decay, and the priests starving. He laments that the whole of Southern France seems given over to heresy, and no doubt his grief was genuine.

In the year 1215 Innocent III. summoned the Fourth Lateran Council. The power of the papacy was shown then as never before or since in the history of Europe. Emperors, kings, and princes sent plenipotentiaries as to the court of a more powerful monarch. The pope did not content himself with merely controlling the council; he dominated it. There was no pretense of debate. The pope prepared and handed down such decrees as he wished passed and the council obediently registered his will. Among the decrees thus incorporated into the canon law of the church were three relating to the treatment of heretics: first, that all rulers should be exhorted to tolerate no heretics in their domains; second, if a ruler refused to clear his land of heretics at the demand of the church, he should be deprived of his authority, his subjects should be released from their allegiance, and if necessary, he should be driven from his land by force; third, to every one who joined in an armed expedition against heretics the same indulgences and privileges should be granted as to crusaders. These are still the canon laws of the Holy Roman Catholic Church. They have never been repealed, and if they are not executed to-day it is because Rome lacks the power or thinks it not expedient to use it. The claim is there, ready to be exercised whenever in the opinion of the infallible pontiff the right moment has arrived. And yet Roman priests in America would fain persuade us that Rome is really in favor of liberty and tolerance, that the leopard has changed his spots and the Ethiopian his skin.

Raymond of Toulouse, sixth of the name, at the close of the twelfth century was the most powerful feudatory of France, almost an independent sovereign, allied by marriage and blood to the royal houses of Castile, Aragon, Navarre, France, and England. Most of his barons and the great majority of his people were heretics; and, though he was nominally loyal to the church, his indifference to the suppression of heresy was bitterly resented by the pope. After many warnings, he was excommunicated, and finally a crusade was declared against him. Leaders were found, first in Simon de Montfort, Earl of Leicester, and later in Louis of France; the power of Raymond was broken and the Albigenses were crushed.

The war was carried on for twenty years; town after town was captured; the inhabitants were massacred or sold into slavery. A large part of the most fertile region of France was left a smoking waste, without a green thing or a human being in sight. That is Romanism in its bright flower and full consummation: better desolation and death than heresy.

But even then heresy was not suppressed—the snake was scotched, but not killed. The " crusaders " could not find and slay all the heretics, though they tried faithfully to do it. Some fled to other parts, others dissembled or recanted and saved their lives. After the crusade was over, it was found that heresy persisted in secret, that the heroic remedies of fire and sword were not sufficiently drastic to accomplish the desired result. Organized and armed heresy had indeed ceased to show its head, but a mailed knight on horseback could not cope with secret heresy—that required the subtle ingenuity and devilish malignity of a priest. This necessity produced, by a natural evolution, the Holy Office of the Inquisition. (One notes in passing the tendency in the medieval church, wherever any institution or practice arose, more than usually satanic in spirit and administration, to dignify it by the epithet " holy.")

There was already in existence a system of episcopal courts for the discovery and punishment of heresy. The effectiveness of these courts depended on the intelligence and energy of the bishop. Generally they were not very effective, since the bishop would usually await popular rumor or definite accusation before proceeding against any one. This regular church machinery having proved clumsy and ineffective, it remained to devise a better. Precedent for this already existed in a custom, dating from Charlemagne, of occasionally appointing papal commissioners for a special emergency in a particular locality. It needed only to make such a commission per-manent and to enlarge the scope of its labors until it was co-extensive with the church. What the necessities of the time demanded was a continuous process against heresy directed by one mind.

An institution peculiar to the medieval church nat-urally suggested the fitting agents for this work—the mendicant orders, scattered over the whole of Europe, not under the control of the bishops, independent of the secular clergy, responsible only to the pope. Accord-ingly, on April 20, 1233, Gregory IX. issued two bulls making the prosecution of heresy the special function of the Dominican order. From this time on the institution rapidly developed, and by the close of the thirteenth cen-tury had become the most terrible engine of oppression that the mind of man or devil ever conceived, before which kings on their thrones and prelates in their palaces trembled. Inquisitors could not be excommunicated while in the discharge of their duties, nor could any legate of the pope interfere with them or suspend them from office. While performing their duties they were freed from all obligations of obedience to their own generals, as well as to the bishops. Their jurisdiction was universal, and any one who refused obedience to their summons or opposed them became *ipso facto* excommunicated.

What hope was there for one who, charged with heresy, fell into the clutches of judges such as this sys-tem provided? The arrest was usually secret; all that the friends of the accused ever knew, in most cases, was that he had disappeared. It was not considered con-ducive to health to make any open inquiries about his whereabouts; it having been observed that such inquiries were followed by the disappearance of the too curious inquirer also. The accused was never permitted to have counsel; he was confronted by no accuser; he was not required to plead to any precise indictment. He could call no witnesses in defense; he was himself usually the chief witness for the prosecution—all principles of jurisprudence and all natural equity being set at naught by requiring him to testify against himself. Everything that human—no, everything that diabolical—ingenuity could do to entrap him into damaging admissions and to extract from him a confession of guilt was done. The inquisitor played on the conscience, on the affections, on the hopes and fears of his victim, with cynical disregard of every moral law and inflicting the most exquisite mental tortures, in the hope of securing a confession.

Finally, if all other means failed, the inquisitors had another device for encouraging (such was their grim word) the accused to confess. That was physical torture—the rack, the thumbscrew, the boot, cautery in various forms, every infernal machine that could be devised to produce the most excruciating agony without unduly maiming or killing. Sometimes solitary confinement in a dungeon was tried, as a means more effective than pain of breaking a stubborn will. Months lengthened into years and years into decades, and still the Inquisition's victim might find himself unconvicted, but with no better prospect of liberty than on the first day. The Inquisition had all the time there was and was willing to wait; its patience never wearied. If a prisoner's resolution gave way under torture or imprisonment, he had to sign a statement that his confession was not made because of love, fear or hatred of any one, but of his own free will. If he subsequently recanted, the confession was to be regarded as true, and the retraction as the perjury of an impenitent and relapsed heretic, who received condign punishment without further trial.

Though no effort was spared to obtain a written confession of heresy, the accused might in the last resort be condemned without it. Only in one way could he be certain of saving his life, and that was by a full confession at once, accompanied by a recantation of his errors and abject submission to the church. Then his life would be spared, but more likely than not it would be spent in some dungeon; only in rare cases was one who once fell into the clutches of the Inquisition suffered to return to his home and estate; and in those rare cases he was subject to life-long espionage and harassment.

When the process was completed and the accused was found guilty of heresy—which was the normal ending of a case—the inquisitors handed the heretic over to the civil power for punishment, with a hypocritical recommendation to mercy. But woe to the secular authority that heeded the recommendation! If a magistrate failed for twelve months to put to death a condemned heretic, the refusal itself constituted heresy, and he became subject to the kind offices of the Inquisition. Even if he were excommunicated, the magistrate must do his duty. The church, with characteristic evasion of the truth, claims to this day that it has never put a heretic to death. The claim is technically correct, if we except those who died in its dungeons and torture-chambers; but the church coerced the civil power into becoming its executioner, and therefore its moral responsibility is the same. When the heretic was dead, the vengeance of the church was not sated. All his lands and goods were confiscated, his blood was attainted, his family were beggared, if they did not share his fate, and his name was blotted out of existence—life, property, titles, all disappeared.

We must not think of the Inquisition as the instrument of wicked men solely, or even mainly, though its satanic origin seems to be stamped all over it. But saintly Bernard was a more bitter persecutor than the infamous Borgias; Innocent III., the purest of the medieval popes, must be called the father of the Inquisition. In fact, the more pious a medieval Catholic was, the more he believed with all his heart and soul in the church and her sacraments, the more he was impelled to persecute. Such men hunted down heresy, not because they hated the heretic, but because they loved the souls of men, whose eternal salvation they believed to be endangered. It is an awful warning to all the succeeding ages of the fathomless iniquity into which a perverted conscience may lead men whose greatest desire is the glory of God.

The names of few of these martyrs have been preserved, but the complaints of their obstinacy and obduracy that abound in the Catholic writings of the period are the convincing testimony to their heroic constancy. They saw the truth clearly and were loyal to it at every cost. They were slain by tens of thousands; a remnant of them were driven into inaccessible mountain fastnesses, where they maintained themselves and their faith for centuries; they became a " hidden seed " in many parts of Europe. By her system of vigor and rigor the Roman Church won a temporary triumph: heresy was apparently suppressed; the reformation of the church was postponed for three centuries.

CHAPTER IX

THERE were protestants before Protestantism, reformers before the Reformation—not only individual protestants, as we have already seen, but protestant bodies. The corruption of the primitive churches and the development of Roman Catholicism was a logical process that extended over a period of centuries. As the church diverged more and more widely from the faith once delivered to the saints, as the papacy gradually extended its power over all Europe, except where the Greek Church successfully resisted its claims, it was inevitable that this tyranny should, from time to time, provoke revolts; that against this apostasy there should be periodic reactions toward a purer faith. From the beginning of the twelfth century these uprisings within the church became more numerous, until the various protests combined their forces, in large part unconsciously, to form the movement since known as the Reformation. It is a curious fact that each of these revolts against the corrupt doctrine and life of the church had an independent origin within the church itself. There may have been, there doubtless was, some connection between these various revolts, some connection also between them and the earlier heresies and schisms, so called, in the church. Though one may feel morally certain of this fact, actual proof of it is not possible; all trace of the connection has disappeared, and there is little reason to hope that proofs will ever be recovered.

But if we may not trace, by unbroken historical

descent, a line of sects protesting against the corruptions and usurpations of the Roman Catholic Church, and so establish the antiquity of any one modern Protestant denomination, it still remains an unquestioned historic fact that these successive revolts constituted a gradual and effective preparation for the general movement known as the Reformation, and for the rise of modern evangelical bodies. So convinced are some modern investigators (not Baptists) of the substantial identity of these various attempts at a reformation, from the twelfth century onward, that they treat these attempts as one continuous movement. Dr. Ludwig Keller, formerly State archivist at Münster, gives to the various phases of this revolt against Rome, the title of " The Old Evangelical Party," and asserts its substantial unity and identity for several centuries before the Lutheran Reformation. By ingenious conjecture, rather than by valid historic proofs, he makes out a plausible case, which further research may, perhaps, fully confirm. An identity of spirit, a substantial unanimity of teaching, he has shown, and this is a fact of great significance.

The earliest of these protests that took definite form grew out of the work of Peter of Bruys. Not much is known of the life of this teacher. It is said by some that, like Arnold of Brescia, he was a pupil of Abelard, but this is doubtful. He is found preaching in Southern France soon after the beginning of the twelfth century, where he labored for twenty years, and he was burned as a heretic in the year 1126. His doctrines are known to us chiefly through his bitter enemy and persecutor, Peter the Venerable, Abbot of Clugny, who wrote a book against the heresy of the Petrobrusians. With due allowance for the mistakes honestly made by this prelate, we may deduce approximately the teachings of this body. We find their fundamental principle to be the rejection

of tradition and an appeal to Scripture as the sole authority in religion. The abbot complains in his treatise
that these heretics will not yield to tradition or the authority of the church, but demand Scripture proof for
everything; because it would have been easy for him to
confute them by quoting any quantity of passages from
the Fathers, only these obstinate heretics would have
none of the Fathers.

In the preface to his treatise, the abbot sums up the
errors of the Petrobrusians under five heads, which he
then proceeds to answer at length. The first error is
their denial " that children, before the age of understanding, can be saved by the baptism of Christ, or that
another's faith avails those who cannot exercise faith
since, according to them [the Petrobrusians] not
another's, but one's own faith, together with baptism,
saves, as the Lord says, ' He who will believe and be
baptized shall be saved, but he who will not believe shall
be condemned.' " " Infants, though baptized by you
[Romanists], because by reason of age they nevertheless cannot believe, are by no means saved; [that is to
say, are not saved by baptism; this is evidently what the
Petrobrusians taught, not a denial of the salvation of
infants; to a Romanist, denial of baptism was a denial
of salvation, but not so to the Petrobrusians] ; hence it
is idle and vain at that time to wet men with water,
by which ye may wash away the filth of the body after
the manner of men, but ye can by no means cleanse the
soul from sin. But we wait for the proper time, and
after a man is prepared to know his God and believe in
him, we do not (as you accuse us) rebaptize him, but
we baptize him who can be said never to have been
baptized—washed with the baptism by which sins are
washed away."

The second error charged was that these heretics said,

" Edifices for temples and churches should not be erected; that those erected should be pulled down; that places sacred to prayer are unnecessary for Christians, since equally in the inn and the church, in forum or temple, before the altar or stable, if God is invoked he hears and answers those who deserve it." Again, they are quoted as saying, " It is superfluous to build temples, since the church of God does not consist in a multitude of stones joined together, but in the unity of the believers assembled."

The third shocking error enumerated by the abbot is that the Petrobrusians " command the sacred crosses to be broken in pieces and burned, because that form or instrument by which Christ was so dreadfully tortured, so cruelly slain, is not worthy of any adoration, or veneration or supplication, but for the avenging of his torments and death it should be treated with unseemly dishonor, cut in pieces with swords, burnt in fire."

The fourth error, according to the same authority, was that the Petrobrusians denied sacramental grace, especially the doctrine of transubstantiation, the keystone of the sacramental system: " They deny, not only the truth of the body and blood of the Lord, daily and constantly offered in the church through the sacrament, but declare that it is nothing at all, and ought not to be offered to God." They say, " Oh, people, do not believe the bishops, priests, or clergy who seduce you; who, as in many things, so in the office of the altar, deceive you when they falsely profess to make the body of Christ, and give it to you for the salvation of your souls. They clearly lie. For the body of Christ was made only once by Christ himself in the supper before his passion, and once for all at this time only was given to his disciples. Hence it is neither made by any one nor given to any one." These words convey an utter absurdity, that

Christ, while still in the flesh, made and gave his body to his disciples; but the absurdity is doubtless one of the abbot's blunders. What is certain is the repudiation by the Petrobrusians of the sacrifice of the mass.

The fifth error is that " they deride sacrifices, prayers, alms, and other good works by the faithful living for the faithful dead, and say that these things cannot aid any of the dead even in the least." Again: " The good deeds of the living cannot profit the dead, because translated from this life their merits cannot be increased or diminished, for beyond this life there is no longer place for merits, only for retribution. Nor can a dead man hope from anybody that which while alive in the world he did not obtain. Therefore those things are vain that are done by the living for the dead, because since they are mortal they passed by death over the way for all flesh to the state of the future world, and took with them all their merit, to which nothing can be added."

From these statements of Peter the Venerable it is plain that the Petrobrusians held that a true church is composed only of believers; that faith should precede baptism, and therefore the baptism of infants is a meaningless ceremony. They held these things because they found them taught in the Scriptures, and rejected the authority of the church and of the Fathers to impose terms of salvation on them beyond those imposed by Christ and the apostles. Their apparent denial of the salvation of infants is probably a misconception of the abbot's, as was also his attributing to them the notion that man may merit the favor of God by good works in this life. The good Peter was so fully imbued with Catholic ideas that he was incapable of comprehending fully the teachings of the Petrobrusians, though he seems to have tried to do it.

What shall we say to the opposition of the Petrobrusians to church buildings, crosses, the singing of hymns—which the abbot mentions in the body of his treatise—and the like? This merely: they had become so accustomed to the misuse of these things, to seeing them the concomitants of an idolatrous worship, that they became unwise, extreme, fanatical, in their opposition to them. It was a quite natural result of the vigor of their reaction from the false teaching and false practice that they found in the Catholic churches of their day.

It is evident that the "errors" of the Petrobrusians were what Baptists have always maintained to be the fundamental truths of the Scriptures. Any body of Christians that holds to the supremacy of the Scriptures, a church of the regenerate only, and believers' baptism, is fundamentally one with the Baptist churches of to-day, whatever else it may add to or omit from its statement of beliefs. Contemporary records have been sought in vain to establish any essential doctrine taught by this condemned sect that is inconsistent either with the teaching of Scripture or with the beliefs avowed in recent times by Baptists. With regard to the act of baptism contemporary record says nothing. There was no reason why it should, unless there was some peculiarity in the administration of baptism among the Petrobrusians. It cannot be positively affirmed that they were exclusively immersionists; but if they were, the fact would call for no special mention by contemporary writers, since immersion was still the common practice of the church in the twelfth century.

There were other preachers of a pure gospel, nearly contemporary with Peter of Bruys and more or less closely connected with him. Like him they came forth from the Roman Church. The monastery of Clugny, in Burgundy, was the most famous cloister of medieval times. Founded early in the tenth century, it enforced

the rule of Benedict with rigor, and was famous for the
piety and scholarship of its abbots and monks. At the
beginning of the twelfth century its discipline had been
greatly relaxed, and its internal management had become
scandalous. Chastity, sobriety, and piety were unmeaning words; they represented nothing in the life of the
inmates. Later, under the rule of Peter the Venerable,
the discipline was reformed and the ancient glories of
the cloister were more than equaled.

At a time when things were at their worst, a monk
named Henry became an inmate of Clugny. His birthplace and date of birth are not certainly known; both
Switzerland and Italy are given for the former, and of the
latter all that can be said is that he was probably born
toward the close of the eleventh century. We know that
he was a man of earnest soul, to whom religion was not
a mere mockery, and that he was so disgusted with the
immoral lives of the Clugny monks that he could no
longer stay there. Renouncing his cowl and the cloister
life, he began to preach the gospel from place to place.
He never ceased to denounce the monks, and they, in
turn, followed him with calumnies. Even the saintly
Bernard speaks of Henry's shameless mode of life, but
gives no proofs; and his letter is so tinged with bitterness
as to make his charges of no weight.

Henry is a somewhat vague figure. We can only
catch glimpses of him going up and down France, like
a flaming fire, rousing the people to detestation of the
monks, and to some degree of the secular clergy also.
He is described as a man of imposing appearance, whose
fiery eye, thundering voice, and great knowledge of the
Scriptures made him a preacher who swayed at will the
multitudes that listened to him. He does not appear to
have been a heretic, at least in the earlier part of his
career, but a would-be reformer. In 1116 he created a

great commotion in the diocese of Mans, denouncing the corruption of the clergy and preaching the truths of Scripture until the bishop drove him away. Soon after this he met Peter of Bruys and accompanied him in his labors. It does not appear that at this time he avowed sympathy with the doctrines of Peter, for when he was arrested in 1134 by the bishop of Arles and brought before the Council of Pisa he was not condemned, as an adherent of Peter would certainly have been, but soon after released. No doubt he was considered indiscreet in the things he had been saying about the clergy, but evidently no ground was then discovered for treating him as a heretic.

After this he repaired to Southern France, and continued his preaching. From this time there is good reason to suppose that he adopted, in part at least, the opinions of Peter of Bruys, especially the denial that infants are scripturally baptized. One of Bernard's letters seems to be conclusive on this point. Writing to the Count of Toulouse, to warn him against this ravening wolf masquerading in sheep's clothing, he thus bears testimony to the extent of Henry's influence and speaks of his teachings:

The churches are without congregations, congregations without priests, priests without their due reverence, and, worst of all, Christians without Christ. Churches are regarded as synagogues, the sanctuary of God is said to have no sanctity, the sacraments are not thought to be sacred, feast days are deprived of their wonted solemnities. Men are dying in their sins, souls are being dragged everywhere before the dread Tribunal, neither being reconciled by repentance nor fortified by Holy Communion. The way of Christ is shut to the children of Christians, and they are not allowed to enter the way of salvation, although the Saviour lovingly calls on their behalf, "Suffer little children to come unto me." Does God, then, who, as he has multiplied his mercy, has saved both man and beast, debar innocent little children from this his so great mercy? Why, I ask, why does he begrudge to little ones their Infant Saviour, who was born for them? This envy is of the devil. By this envy death entered into the whole world. Or does he suppose that little children have no need of a Saviour, because they are children?

It does not seem open to reasonable doubt, therefore, that Henry of Lausanne, like Peter of Bruys and the Waldenses, taught that only believers should be baptized, and that the baptism of unconscious babes is a travesty upon the baptism of the New Testament.

The end of Henry is sad. He was again arrested and arraigned before the Synod of Rheims in 1148, by which body he was condemned to perpetual imprisonment. It is not definitely known whether he was convicted of heresy, probably not, or immediate death would have been his portion. It is possible that under torture some kind of retraction was wrung from him; and when a heretic thus confessed, the church would sometimes mercifully (?) spare his life and let him drag out a miserable existence in her dungeons. Nothing more is known of his fate. From the oubliettes of the church none ever returned, and the day of their death was never known. We may hope, in the absence of all information, that Henry of Lausanne continued to the last the faithful confessor of the truth he had preached. He left behind him numerous followers, who took the name of Henricians and were little other than Petrobrusians under a different name. Like the Petrobrusians, they seem to have been absorbed into the body known as Waldenses, and do not long maintain a separate name and existence.

In the latter part of the twelfth century Southern France was the scene of a still more energetic reaction from the Church of Rome, which is remarkable in that it was not at first a reform movement, and was not hostile to the church until driven by it into hostility. The new party was called Poor Men of Lyons, Leonists, and Waldenses, the last being perhaps their best-known name. The origin alike of name and party is obscure, but both seem to have originated with a citizen of Lyons named Peter Waldo, or, more properly, Valdez (Latin, Valdesius). This name probably indicates the place of his birth—in the Canton of Vaud perhaps; and as Peter of the Valley he was distinguished from the numerous other Peters of his day. We first gain sight of him about the year 1150 when, already past middle life, he was a rich merchant of Lyons, who had not been over-particular, it is said, about the means by which he had acquired his fortune. One day a friend fell dead at his side. Waldo said to himself: If death had stricken me, what would have become of my soul? Other circumstances increased his burden of mind, until he sought a master of theology for the consolation that he was unable to find in the round of fasts and penances prescribed by the church. The theologian talked learnedly, and the more he talked the greater became Waldo's perplexity. Finally he asked, " Of all the roads that lead to heaven, which is the surest? I desire to follow the perfect way." "Ah!" answered the theologian, " that being the case, here is Christ's precept: ' If thou wilt be perfect, go sell that thou hast and give to the poor, and thou shalt have treasure in heaven; and come take up thy cross and follow me.' "

Waldo returned home pondering these words. Had he been a learned theologian he would at once have understood that the words were not to be understood literally, but contained some mystical or allegorical meaning; he was a plain man and knew no better than to obey. First of all, he told his resolution to his wife. She being of a worldly turn, and by no means alarmed about her soul's salvation, was much vexed. At length

Waldo said to her, " I am possessed of personal property and real estate, take your choice." The real estate was of no small value: including houses, meadows, vineyards, woods, bake-houses, and mills, the rents of which brought in a goodly income. The wife's choice was quickly made; she chose the real estate, leaving to Waldo the business and ready money. Closing out his business, Waldo devoted a portion of his money to providing a dowry for his daughters; and with other sums he made reparation to such as he had treated unjustly in business.

Considerable money yet remained to him, and he devoted it to the relief of the poor in Lyons, where a famine was then raging. He had been a man of business, and his charity was managed in a business-like way. He planned a distribution of bread, meat, and other provisions, three times a week, beginning at Pentecost and continuing until mid-August. Thus he did until his money was exhausted, and he was fain to ask food of a friend for himself. His wife heard of this and was very angry. She appealed to the archbishop, and besought Waldo himself in these words: " Husband, listen; if any one is to redeem his soul by the alms he gives you, is it not best that it should be your wife rather than such as are not of our household? " The archbishop delivered a homily on his extravagance and formally forbade him, when he was in the city, ever to take food anywhere but at his wife's table.

In the meantime, Waldo had been studying the Scriptures. Finding the Latin hard to understand, he sought out two ecclesiastics who were willing to translate it into his vernacular, for a consideration. One wrote while the other dictated, and in this way they made a translation of the Gospels, selections from the Epistles, and a collection of maxims from the Fathers of the church. This translation Waldo read and studied until it was indelibly engraved on mind and heart, and flowed spontaneously from his lips. From meditating on it himself he began to repeat it to others. The wandering ballad-singer was a popular institution in his time and country, and he had little difficulty in persuading people to listen to his stories from the Gospels, instead of a secular ballad. And so Waldo became a preacher of the gospel, little more than a reciter of its precepts at first, and with no intention of revolting against Rome, wishing only the privilege of telling to others the good news of salvation that had been so precious to his own troubled heart. Soon he gained disciples. These he taught assiduously, until they too could tell the simple gospel story, and as they gained skill he sent them forth tŏ the shops and market-places, to visit from house to house, and preach the truth. These preachers literally obeyed the instructions of Christ to the seventy; they went forth in voluntary poverty, anxious only to proclaim the kingdom of God, and accepting such hospitality as was voluntarily offered them.

Such a work as this could not go on long without the cognizance of Roman ecclesiastics. The preachers were becoming numerous and spreading apace. True, they did not oppose the church in any way; they were not known to teach any heresy; but the priesthood was jealous of these unauthorized preachers and demanded that they be silenced. Waldo was banished from the diocese of Archbishop Guichard, and in 1177 he betook himself to Rome to appeal to the pope, Alexander III. But those were the days of triumphant clericalism, and Waldo's appeal was fruitless. The pope received Waldo kindly, as a good son of the church; his vow of poverty was a thing that every ecclesiastic approved. It is even said that Alexander kissed Waldo's cheek, as a sign of recognition of his holy repute. But in the matter of preaching, the pope stood firm; his answer was: " You shall not, under any circumstances, preach except at the express desire and under the authority of the clergy of your country "—the men who had already silenced and banished him.

This hard sentence was the parting of the ways to Waldo and his followers. Should they obey God or man? Should they choose church or Christ? They were not long in making choice, and in making it they became heretics, reformers, for they set themselves against the church that they might have liberty to follow Christ. In this treatment of Waldo, Rome showed herself less wise than afterward, when Francis of Assisi sought similar tolerance for his order of preachers. Had Pope Alexander III. been a little more astute there might have been a new order of lay preachers in the Roman Church, no sect of the Waldenses and, perhaps, no Lutheran Reformation.

But though the Waldenses now became schismatics, and were soon regarded as heretical, they did not cease to multiply. Persecution had no effect in checking their growth, at least for some time. This rapid growth of the body cannot be explained wholly by the general preparedness of the church for the preaching of a more spiritual faith; or, rather, that state of feeling itself requires explanation. In the scattered fragments of preceding sects, notably of the Petrobrusians, soil was found most favorable for the propagation of the teachings of Waldo. The Waldenses, in their earlier history, appear to be little else than Petrobrusians under a different name. For, though there is reason to suppose that Waldo himself owed nothing to Peter of Bruys, but arrived at the truth independently, he at once became the spiritual heir of his predecessor and namesake, and carried on the same work. The doctrines of the early Waldenses are substantially identical with those of the Petrobrusians, the persecutors of both being witnesses. For example, Roman writers before 1350 attribute the following errors to the Waldenses:

1. Regarding the Scriptures. Their enemies charge the Waldenses with holding these errors: " They assert that the doctrine of Christ and the apostles, without the decrees of the church, suffices for salvation. They know by heart the New Testament and most of the Old Testament in the vulgar tongue. They oppose the mystical sense in the Scriptures. They say holy Scripture has the same effect in the vulgar tongue as in the Latin. Everything preached which is not to be proved by the text of the Bible they hold to be fable." " They neither have nor receive the Old Testament, but the Gospels, that by them they may attack us and defend themselves; saying that when the gospel came all old things passed away." But this, if true at all, is true only of some of the Waldenses, for nothing is better established than that they translated the whole Bible and received it all as authoritative.

2. Regarding baptism. " They say that a man is then truly for the first time baptized when he is brought into their heresy. But some say that baptism does not profit little children (*parvulos*), because they are never able actually to believe." " One argument of their error is, that they say baptism does not profit little children to salvation, who have neither the motive nor the act of faith, because, as it is said in the latter part of Mark, ' He who will not believe will be condemned.' " " Concerning baptism they say that the catechism is of no value. . . That the washing given to infants does not profit. . . That the sponsors do not understand what they answer to the priest. They do not regard compaternity." *i. e.*, the relation of sponsors.

3. Concerning the church. " They say that the Roman Church is not the church of Jesus Christ, but is a church of wicked ones, and it [that is, the true church] ceased to exist under Sylvester, when the poison of temporal things was infused into the church. . . All approved customs of the church of which they do not read in the Gospels they despise, as the feast of candles, of palms, the reconciliation of penitents, adoration of the cross, the feast of Easter, and they spurn the feasts of the saints on account of the multiplication of saints. And they say one day is just like another, therefore they secretly work on feast days." " The Roman Church is the harlot of Babylon, and all who obey it are condemned. . . They affirmed that they alone were the church of Christ and the disciples of Christ. That they are the sucessors of the apostles and have apostolic authority." . .

4. Concerning purgatory. " They say there is no purgatory, but all dying immediately go either to heaven or to hell. They assert that prayers offered by the church for the dead do not avail; for those in heaven do not need them, and those in hell are not at all assisted. They say that the saints in heaven do not hear the prayers of the faithful, nor the praises by which we honor them. They argue earnestly that since the bodies of the saints lie here dead, and their spirits are so far removed from us in heaven, they can by no means hear our prayers. They say also that the saints do not pray for us, and therefore we ought not to implore their prayers; because, absorbed in heavenly joy, they cannot take heed of us or care for anything else." " Whenever any sinner repents, however great and many the sins he has committed, if he dies he immediately rises [i. e., to heaven]. . . They assert that there is no purgatorial fire except in the present, nor do the prayers of the church profit the dead nor does anything done for them."

5. Regarding the Mass. "They do not believe it to be really the body and blood of Christ, but only bread blessed, which by a certain figure is said to be the body of Christ; as it is said, ' But the rock was Christ,' and similar passages. But this blessing, some say, can only be performed by the good, but others say by all who know the words of consecration. . . They observe this in their conventicles, reciting those words of the Gospels at their table and participating together as in the supper of Christ." " Concerning the sacrament of the Eucharist they say that priests in mortal sin cannot make [the body of Christ]. They say that transubstantiation does not take place in the hands of the unworthy maker, but in the mouth of the worthy receiver, and can be made on a common table. . . Again they say that transubstantiation takes place by words in the vernacular. . . They say that the holy Scripture has the same effect in the vulgar tongue as in the Latin, whence they make [the body of Christ] in the vulgar tongue and give the sacraments. . . They say that the church singing is infernal clamor."

It seems evident, by comparing these reports, that some of the Roman writers did not clearly comprehend the Waldensian doctrine; according to others, the Waldenses did not believe in transubstantiation at all, but they did believe that the Lord's Supper should be celebrated in the vernacular. As for calling singing " infernal clamor," the reference is evidently to the singing of the mass by the priests, and to the use of Latin hymns, not an objection to singing *per se*. That the latter cannot be meant is proved by the fact that the first literature of the Waldenses took the form of hymns.

Other less serious heresies are alleged: as that the followers of Waldo all preached without ordination; that they declared the pope to be the head of all errors; that

confession was to be made to God alone; that they abhorred the sign of the cross. Also we find attributed
to them certain tenets that were afterward characteristic
of the Anabaptists; such as, " In no case, for any necessity or usefulness must one swear "; and " For no reason
should one slay."

In the face of all but unanimous testimony of Roman
authorities, it has been denied that the early Waldenses
rejected infant baptism. Stress is laid on the fact that in
the earliest of their literature that has come down to us
the Waldensians are Pedobaptists, or at least do not oppose infant baptism. It is also an unquestioned fact that
the later Waldensians—those who found a refuge in the
valleys of Savoy after the crusade of Simon de Montfort
in Southern France—are found to be Pedobaptists at the
earliest authentic period of their history. But all this
is not necessarily inconsistent with the accounts of the
sect as given us by contemporary Romanists. Nearly
three hundred years elapsed between the crusade and the
Reformation, and during these centuries the escaped
Waldenses dwelt among the high valleys of Eastern
France and Savoy, isolated and forgotten. Great ignorance came upon them, as is testified by the literature that
has survived, and in time they so far forgot the doctrines
of their forefathers that many of the writers saw but
little difference between themselves and the Romanists.
Some of the old spirit remained, however, so that when
in 1532 a Pedobaptist creed was adopted at the Synod
of Angrogne, under the guidance of the Swiss reformers,
Farel and Œcolampadius, a large minority refused to be
bound by this new creed, declaring it to be a reversal
of their previous beliefs. That they were correct in this
interpretation is the verdict of modern scholars who have
thoroughly investigated the earlier Waldensian history.

The balance of evidence is therefore clearly in favor

of the conclusion that the early followers of Waldo taught and practised the baptism of believers only. Dr. Keller, the latest and most candid investigator of the subject, holds this view: " Very many Waldenses considered, as we know accurately, the baptism on [profession of] faith to be that form which is conformable with the words and example of Christ. They held this to be the sign of the covenant of a good conscience with God, and it was certain to them that it had value only as such." This belief would logically exclude infant baptism, and accordingly Dr. Keller tells us, " Mostly they let their children be baptized [by Romish priests?], yet with the reservation that this ceremony was null and void." Maintaining these views, they were the spiritual ancestors of the Anabaptist churches that sprang up all over continental Europe in the early years of the Reformation.

The history of the Waldenses is a tale of bitter and almost continuous persecution. Waldo himself is said to have died in or about the year 1217, but if he lived so long he must have seen his followers everywhere proscribed, yet everywhere increasing. In 1183, at the Council of Verone, Pope Lucian III. issued a decree of perpetual anathema against various heretics, including the Poor Men of Lyons. Innocent III., wiser than other popes, attempted to win back the Waldenses. One Durand, who had been, or pretended to have been, a Waldensian preacher, was persuaded at the Disputation of Pâmiers (in the territory of Toulouse) to submit to the church. He and certain others submitted a confession of their faith to the pope, who approved it and authorized them to form a religious order of Catholic poor. The Roman ecclesiastics, in spite of Innocent's repeated admonitions to them, never took kindly to this order, and this reaction did not have the effect anticipated. Innocent himself seems to have at length abandoned hope of reclaiming the Waldenses, and at the Fourth Lateran Council, of 1215, their final condemnation was pronounced. In order to prevent the spread of this and other heresies, the Synod of Toulouse (1229) forbade laymen to read vernacular translations of the Bible, and the Synod of Tarracona (1234) even extended this prohibition to the clergy also.

It does not concern our present purpose to narrate at more length the story of the cruel oppressions to which the Waldenses were thenceforth subjected. Suffice it to say that, except among the valleys of the Alps they were eventually exterminated or driven to a secret life. But in the Alps and Northern Italy they have survived until the present day, and in many parts of Europe they leavened the Roman Church so as effectually to prepare the way for the later Reformation. And it is a curious and instructive fact that the Anabaptist churches of the Reformation period were most numerous precisely where the Waldenses of a century or two previous had most flourished, and where their identity as Waldenses had been lost. That there was an intimate relation between the two movements, few doubt who have studied this period and its literature. The torch of truth was handed on from generation to generation, and though it often smoldered and was even apparently extinguished, it needed but a breath to blaze up again and give light to all mankind.

CHAPTER X

THE origin of the Anabaptists of Switzerland is obscure. The testimony of contemporaries is that
they derived their chief doctrines from sects that ante-
dated the Reformation, and this testimony is confirmed
by so many collateral proofs as to commend itself to
many modern historians. Vadian, the burgomaster of
St. Gall, and brother-in-law to Conrad Grebel, says of
the Anabaptists, " They received the dogma of baptizing
from the suggestions of others." The industrious Füsslin
reached this opinion: " There were before the Reformation people in Zurich who, filled with errors, gave birth
to the Anabaptists. Grebel was taught by them; he did
not discover his own doctrines, but was taught by others."
In our own day impartial German investigators have
reached similar conclusions. Thus Dr. Heberle writes:

In carrying out their fundamental ideas, the party of Grebel
paid less attention to dogmatics than to the direction of church,
civil, and social life. They urged the putting away of all modes
of worship which were unknown to the church of the apostles,
and the restoration of the observance, according to their institution, of the two ceremonies ordained by Christ. They contended
against the Christianity of worldly governments, rejected the
salaries of preachers, the taking of interest and tithes, the
use of the sword, and demanded the return of apostolic
excommunication and primitive community of goods.

It is well known that just these principles are found in the
sects of the Middles Ages. The supposition is therefore very
probable that between these and the rebaptizers of the Reformation there was an external historical connection. The possibility
of this as respects Switzerland is all the greater, since just here

the traces of these sects, especially of the Waldenses, can be followed down to the end of the fifteenth century. But a positive proof in this connection we have not. . . In reality the explanation of this agreement needs no proof of a real historical union between Anabaptists and their predecessors, for the abstract biblical standpoint upon which the one as well as the other place themselves is sufficient of itself to prove a union of the two in the above-mentioned doctrines.[1]

The utmost that can be said in the present state of historical research is that a moral certainty exists of a connection between the Swiss Anabaptists and their Waldensian and Petrobrusian predecessors, sustained by many significant facts, but not absolutely proved by historical evidence. Those who maintain that the Anabaptists originated with the Reformation have some difficult problems to solve, among others the rapidity with which the new leaven spread, and the wide territory that the Anabaptists so soon covered. It is common to regard them as an insignificant handful of fanatics, but abundant documentary proofs exist to show that they were numerous, widespread, and indefatigable; that their chief men were not inferior in learning and eloquence to any of the reformers; that their teachings were scriptural, consistent, and moderate, except where persecution produced the usual result of enthusiasm and vagary.

Another problem demanding solution is furnished by the fact that these Anabaptist churches were not gradually developed, but appear fully formed from the first—complete in polity, sound in doctrine, strict in discipline. It will be found impossible to account for these phenomena without an assumption of a long-existing cause. Though the Anabaptist churches appear suddenly in the records of the time, contemporaneously with the Zwinglian Reformation, their roots are to be sought farther back.

[1] "*Jahrbücher für Deutsche Theologie,*" 1858, p. 276 *seq.*

At the beginning of the sixteenth century, Switzerland was the freest country in Europe—a confederacy of thirteen cantons and free cities, acknowledging no allegiance to emperor or king. These cantons differed greatly in speech, customs, and form of government; their chief bond of union was, in fact, hatred of their common foe, the House of Hapsburg. Zurich was governed by a council of two hundred, and the ultimate power rested with the various guilds to which the burghers belonged. It was, in a word, a commercial oligarchy, maintaining a republican form of government. Little could be undertaken, certainly nothing of moment could be accomplished, without the approval of the council.

The Reformation in Switzerland was quite independent of the Lutheran movement, though it occurred practically at the same time. Reuchlin had given instruction in the classics at the University of Basel; and Erasmus came to that city in 1514, to get his edition of the New Testament printed. The study of the original Scriptures in Hebrew and Greek received a great impetus, and the result could not long be doubtful. The Swiss people had once been devoted adherents of the papacy, but knowledge of the corruption of the church and the unworthy character of prelates had penetrated even there and greatly weakened the hold of the church on the people. The clergy, though not so bad as in some localities, were still far from illustrating the virtues they preached. The Scripture seed fell into soil ready to receive it and give it increase.

The leader in this reformation was Ulric Zwingli, born in 1484, at Wildhaus, in the canton of St. Gall, educated at the University of Vienna, a teacher at Basel and then pastor at Glarus in 1506, later at Einsiedeln, and finally at Zurich. He was during his earlier priesthood unchaste and godless, like many of the clergy, but he was led to the study of the Greek Testament, and God's grace touched his heart and made a new man of him. His preaching became noted for spiritual power and eloquence. As in Luther's case, he was first brought into prominence by opposition to the sale of indulgences. One Samson, a worthy companion to the infamous Tetzel, came to Switzerland hoping to conduct a brisk traffic in indulgences, and was roundly rebuked by Zwingli: " Jesus Christ, the Son of God, has said, ' Come unto me all ye that labor and are heavy laden, and I will give you rest.' Is it not, then, most presumptuous folly and senseless temerity to declare on the contrary—' Buy letters of indulgence, hasten to Rome, give to the monks, sacrifice to the priests, and if thou doest these things I absolve thee from thy sins?' Jesus Christ is the only oblation, the only sacrifice, the only way."

As the Roman Church had been established by law, and its priests were largely paid out of the treasury, it was the most natural thing in the world that, as the reformation continued, the reformed church and ministry should also be an appanage of the State. Zwingli was called to Zurich and was kept in his position there by the council, and as the reform developed that body took into its hands the direction of religious as well as civil affairs. It probably occurred to few of the worthy burghers that there was any impropriety in this. In 1520 the council issued an order that all pastors and preachers should declare the pure word of God, and Zwingli had announced as his principle the rejection of everything in doctrine or practice not warranted by the Scriptures. In a disputation held January 29, 1523, he made his appeal on all points to the Scriptures—copies of which in Hebrew, Greek, and Latin he had on a table before him. He vainly challenged his Catholic adversaries to refute him from the Scriptures, and the council renewed their order that all the preachers in the canton should teach only what was found in the Scriptures.

Up to this time we find no trace of the Anabaptists, as such. The reason evidently is that Zwingli and the Zurich Council were virtually Anabaptists themselves. They had adopted the most radical and revolutionary of Anabaptist principles, that the Scriptures should be the sole rule of faith and practice, and that whatever the Scriptures do not teach must be rejected. Nor was Zwingli unconscious of what he was doing, and he did not at first shrink from the logic of his fundamental principle. As he frankly confesses, he was for a considerable time inclined to reject infant baptism, in obedience to the fundamental principle he had adopted of accepting the Scriptures as the only rule of faith and practice, and rejecting everything that had no clear Scripture warrant. He had but to go on consistently in this way to have made the Zwinglian Reformation an Anabaptist movement. But having put his hand to the plow, he suffered himself to look back. He was in bondage to the idea of a State Church, a reformation that should have back of it the power of the civil magistrate, instead of being a spiritual movement simply. But to fulfil this ideal, infant baptism was a necessity. The moment the church was made a body consisting wholly of the regenerate, it of necessity separated itself from the world. The Zurich Council had supported the reform thus far, but by no means all its members—possibly not the majority—were regenerate men. How far would they support a reform that would, as a first step, unchurch them and deprive their children of the privilege (as they still esteemed it) of baptism? Such a policy of reform seemed to Zwingli suicide at the very beginning, for he could see a possibility of success only through the support of the civil power. In this conviction is to be found, not only his reason for breaking with the Anabaptists, but the secret of his other mistakes and the cause of his untimely death. He gained, it is possible, for his reformation a more immediate and outward success, only to establish it on a foundation of sand.

About the year 1523, therefore, Zwingli and some of his fellow-reformers came to the parting of the ways. Zwingli thenceforth developed conservative tendencies, thought the reform had gone far enough, and endeavored to restrain those who were impatient for more thorough work. A division of sentiment rapidly developed among the hitherto united reformers. A strong minority desired to continue on the line already begun, to carry out consistently the principle already avowed that the Scriptures were to be the sole arbiter in all matters of faith and practice. They pointedly declared that the Bible said no more about infant baptism than it said about the mass, fasts, the invocation of saints, and other popish abominations. The New Testament churches, they said, were composed only of those who gave credible evidence of regeneration.

Up to the time of their separation on this question of infant baptism, those who afterward became Anabaptist leaders were among the most active and trusted of Zwingli's lieutenants. This was particularly true of Conrad Grebel. The son of one of the members of the Zurich Council, he was socially a man of more importance than Zwingli, whose father was a peasant farmer. In eloquence, he appears to have been little the inferior of his leader, and he is described by Zwingli himself as "most studious, most candid, most learned." He was born in the last decade of the fifteenth century, and was educated at the universities of Vienna and Paris. At both institutions he attained high rank among his fellows, but his life was wild and dissipated. Some time before 1522 he was converted, and from this time on his life was one of perfect rectitude and piety. Though not a profound scholar, he was a learned man for his time, and his views regarding the church were derived from careful study of the original Scriptures, especially of the Greek New Testament.

Another of the Anabaptist leaders was Felix Mantz, also a native of Zurich, the natural son of a canon, liberally educated, and especially versed in the Hebrew Scriptures. He was the firm friend and adherent of Zwingli, until the latter gave up his early principle of the supremacy of the Scriptures. Mantz could not chop about so easily. Faithfully following the principle to its necessary conclusions, he became convinced that the baptism of infants is nowhere authorized in Scripture, but is, on the contrary, excluded by the requirement of personal faith as a precedent to baptism.

Other prominent men among the Anabaptists were George Blaurock, a former monk, who for his eloquence and zeal was known as a second Paul; Ludwig Hätzer, a native of the canton of St. Gall, who had studied at Freiburg and acquired a good knowledge of Hebrew, and had the confidence of Zwingli before he became an Anabaptist; and Balthaser Hübmaier, of whose life and labors a more particular account will be given in a subsequent chapter.

By the beginning of 1525 the break between Zwingli and his more radical associates in the work of reform had become marked. Their opposition to infant baptism became so vehement that at length the council appointed a public disputation January 17th. Grebel and Mantz, Hätzer and Blaurock, were present and represented the radical party, but the council decided that the victory was with Zwingli and issued an order that parents should have their children baptized at once, on pain of banishment.

Thus far no reference is made in the contemporary records to Anabaptism. The radicals had begun by simply opposing infant baptism and refusing to have their own children christened. They did not at once see that this contention of theirs invalidated their own baptism. If faith must precede baptism, and for that reason they could not conscientiously permit their infants to be baptized, it necessarily followed that they themselves had not been baptized. They were not long now in seeing this, and from the summer of 1525 we read of rebaptisms. At first affusion was practised, probably according to the common usage of the Swiss churches of that day, but a little later immersion was adopted by some as the baptism prescribed by Scripture. The Swiss Anabaptists did not arrive all at once at a full understanding of New Testament practice, but were led to it gradually, as they were taught by the Spirit of God, and possibly by other Christians.

Anabaptism spread with great rapidity. Zwingli and the Council of Zurich became alarmed, and again hit upon the expedient of a public discussion, on November 6. The Anabaptists came, but it is not likely that they expected a victory, knowing that Zwingli was inflexibly opposed to them, and that his influence was all-powerful with the council. Zwingli brought forward the arguments of which later Pedobaptists have made so free use, that the Abrahamic covenant is continued in the New Dispensation, and that baptism replaces circumcision. The Anabaptists, like Baptists of to-day, argued that there is no command or example for infant baptism in the New Testament, and that instruction and belief are enjoined before baptism. Incidentally, Zwingli reproached the Anabaptists for being separatists; to which they made the unanswerable reply that, if they were such, they had as good a right to separate from him as he had to separate from the pope. The council, however, made an official finding (published under date of November 30), to the effect that " each one of the Anabaptists having expressed his views without hindrance, it was found, by the sure testimonies of holy Scripture, both of the Old and the New Testaments, that Zwingli and his followers had overcome the Anabaptists, annihilated Anabaptism, and established infant baptism." So little confidence had the council in this annihilation of Anabaptism, in spite of their swelling words, that they proceeded to do what they could to annihilate it by means of the civil power. On this occasion they contented themselves with ordering all persons to abstain from Anabaptism, and baptize their young children. They added this grim warning: "Whoever shall act contrary to the order, shall, as often as he disobeys, be punished by the fine of a silver mark; and if any shall prove disobedient, we shall deal with him farther and punish him according to his deserts without further forgiveness."

That this was no light and unmeaning threat, the Anabaptists had immediate reason to know. Grebel, Mantz, Blaurock, and others prominent in the movement, were summoned before the council and commanded to retract their errors; on refusal they were thrown into prison loaded with chains, and kept there several months. Hübmaier, who had been compelled to seek a refuge in the canton, was thrown into prison also; and there sick and weak, he yielded for the moment and consented to make a public recantation. When brought into the pulpit, however, his spirit reasserted itself, and instead of pronouncing his recantation, he made an address declaring his opposition to infant baptism and defending rebaptism. His amazed and disappointed hearers unceremoniously hustled him back to his prison, and by prolonged imprisonment and tortures at length extracted from him a written recantation. This was only a weakness of the flesh, that is no more honorable to Zwingli and his followers than to Hübmaier. On his release, he resumed his Anabaptism and remained faithful to his convictions until his death.

It would be a painful and useless task to detail the cruelties that followed. No persecution was ever more gratuitous and unfounded. Some of its later apologists have alleged that it was more political than religious, that it was a necessary measure to protect the State from seditious persons. It is sufficient to reply that contemporary records make no charge of sedition against the Anabaptists. They were condemned for Anabaptism, and for nothing else; the record stands in black and white for all men to read. The Zwinglians found that having once undertaken to suppress what they declared to be heresy by physical force, more stringent remedies than fines and imprisonments were needed. In short, if persecution is to be efficient and not ridiculous, there is no halting-place this side of the sword and the stake. The Zwinglians did not lack courage to make their repressive measures effectual. On March 7, 1526, it was decreed by the Zurich Council that whosoever rebaptized should be drowned, and this action was confirmed by a second decree of November 19. Felix Mantz, who had been released for a time and had renewed his labors at Schaffhausen and Basel, was rearrested on December 3, found guilty of the heinous crime of Anabaptism, and on January 5 was sentenced to death by drowning.

This barbarous sentence was duly carried out. On the way to the place of execution, says Bullinger (a bitterly hostile historian), " his mother and brother came to him, and exhorted him to be steadfast; and he persevered in his folly, even to the end. When he was bound upon the hurdle and was about to be thrown into the stream by the executioner, he sang with a loud voice, '*In manus tuas, Domine, commendo spiritum meum*' ('into thy hands, O Lord, I commend my spirit') ; and herewith was drawn into the water and drowned." No wonder Capito wrote to Zwingli from Strasburg: " It is reported here that your Felix Mantz has suffered punishment and died gloriously; on which account the cause of truth and piety, which you sustain, is greatly depressed."

If anything could depress the Zwinglian movement, one would think it would be this brutal treatment of those whose only fault was that they had been consistent where Zwingli himself had been inconsistent, in keeping close to New Testament teaching and precedent. About two years later Jacob Faulk and Henry Rieman, having firmly refused to retract, but rather having expressed their determination to preach the gospel and rebaptize converts if released, were sentenced to death, taken to a little fishing-hut in the middle of the river Limat, where, says Bullinger, " they were drawn into the water and drowned."

For these persecutions Zwingli stands condemned before the bar of history. As the burning of Servetus has left an eternal stain on the good name of Calvin, in spite of all attempts to explain away his responsibility for the dark deed, so the drowning of Mantz is a damning blot on Zwingli's career as a reformer. All the perfumes of Arabia will not sweeten the hand that has been stained with the blood of one of Christ's martyrs. If Zwingli did not take an active part in the condemnation of Mantz, if he did not fully approve the savage measures of the council, he did approve of the suppression of Anabaptism by the civil power. There is no record of protest of his, by voice or pen, against the barbarous cruelties inflicted in the name of pure religion on so many of God's people, though his influence would have been all-powerful in restraining the council from passing their persecuting edicts. He cannot be acquitted, therefore, of moral complicity in this judicial murder. Though not personally a persecutor, he stood by, like Saul at the stoning of Stephen, approving by silence all that was done.

Grebel was spared the fate of Mantz by an untimely death. His fiery spirit made him a natural leader of men, and at Schaffhausen, at St. Gall, at Hinwyl, and at many other places, he preached the gospel with great power and gathered large numbers of converts into churches. His labors continued little more than three years, and his name appears in the Zurich records for the last time early in March, 1526. All that we know of him further is that he died, probably soon after, of the pest. Had he lived a few years longer, his fitness for leadership would have given him a large following among his countrymen, the character of the Swiss Reformation might have been radically changed, and the history of Switzerland turned into a new channel for all time. Hübmaier was banished, to meet his martyrdom elsewhere. Blaurock was burned at the stake at Claussen, in the Tyrol, in 1529. Hätzer, driven out of Zurich, went to Strassburg for a time, but being banished thence made his way to Constance, where he was apprehended, imprisoned for four months and then put to death. The formal charge against him was bigamy. He is said in some accounts to have had twenty-four wives, according to others he had nineteen, while some content themselves with saying vaguely " a great many." In the trial record at Constance he is said to have confessed that he married his wife's maid while his wife still lived. There is not a line of confirmatory evidence in the correspondence between Zwingli and his friends at Constance, nor in a contemporary account of Hätzer's last moments by an eye-witness. His death was after a godly manner, and the account says: "A nobler and more manful death was never seen in Constance. He suffered with greater propriety than I had given him credit for. They who knew not that he was a heretic and an Anabaptist could have observed nothing in him. . . May the Almighty, the Eternal God, grant to me and to the servants of his word like mercy in the day when he shall call us home."

This is not the way in which adulterers and vulgar scoundrels die. Dr. Keller pronounces the charge against Hätzer "an unproved and unprovable statement." Resting as it does on an [alleged] confession that is wholly unconfirmed, the official charge is to be regarded as a calumny invented to conceal the fact that there was no fault found in him save that he was an Anabaptist.

Thus one by one the leaders were killed or driven away or died by natural causes. By this means the persecutors at length attained their end. Though persecution at first increased the number of Anabaptists, they were for the most part plain, unlettered folk, rich in nothing else than faith, and little able to hold out unaided and unled against a persecution so bitter and determined. Gradually the Anabaptists disappeared from the annals of Zurich, but not without having left the impress of their character on the people.

While the canton of Zurich was measurably successful in suppressing the Anabaptist movement, it proved to have a greater quality of permanence elsewhere. The Anabaptists of Bern are less prominent during the time of Zwingli than those of Zurich, perhaps because there was no reformer at Bern of the ability and literary activity manifested by Zwingli at Zurich and by Œcolampadius at Basel. There is even better reason than the history of the Zurich movement discloses for supposing that these Anabaptists were the direct descendants of the Waldensian groups that for two or three centuries had leavened parts of Switzerland with their influence.

Except that we have less explicit accounts of the formal organization of the sect, the history of the Bernese Anabaptists is precisely parallel with that of their Zurich brethren, down to the disappearance of the latter. There appears to be no essential difference in doctrine and practice, if we except the fact that no evidence of immersion is found in Bern. There is the same active, relentless persecution by the council, but it does not appear that the death penalty was inflicted in this canton. But the result of these persecutions was very different from what we have found in Zurich. The Bern Anabaptists had less able leaders at first, and consequently may have been less dependent upon leadership. What is certain is that the Bernese authorities themselves regretfully recognized the impotence of their persecuting measures to suppress the movement. Causes for the increase of these people, rather than their diminution, were found by contemporaries in the lax enforcement of the laws by magistrates; in the lack of pious and godly living among the ministers and people of the town; and in the failure of discipline in the churches. The Anabaptists are acknowledged to be more sober, God-fearing, and honest than others, and their preachers expounded the Scriptures more faithfully. Nevertheless, it was believed that such people as these were dangerous and should not be tolerated.

Persecution of the Anabaptists in Bern continued during the seventeenth century, and through the influence of their fellow-believers in Holland, the Mennonites, the Dutch government several times intervened to secure liberty of conscience for these long-suffering people. There were not wanting also Swiss Christians to protest against the inhuman and un-Christian policy of the government. Though these efforts were not immediately successful, the persecutions grew less severe with each successive generation and in the eighteenth century gradually ceased.

In the meantime, however, large numbers of the Bernese Anabaptists had emigrated in order to escape their bitter persecutions. Not a few came to America. The colony that settled in Lancaster County, Pa., from 1715 onward, though commonly called Mennonites, was composed largely of these refugees from Bern. Others settled in the Palatinate and other German States in which some measure of toleration was allowed. But a considerable number refused to leave their native land, endured all the persecutions, and their descendants are found in Bern to this day. Still called *Wiedertäuffer* (Anabaptists) and sometimes simply *Täuffer* (Baptists), they hold the precise doctrines of the medieval evangelicals, and the practices of the sixteenth century Anabaptists. They baptize only believers, but most of them still practise affusion, though the practice of immersion is said to be spreading among them. They refuse to bear arms and prohibit oaths. A part of them formed a separate body in 1830, and are known as New Baptists, because they practise immersion exclusively. Eight of the older congregations are members of a Conference, or Association, which meets semi-annually, but there are some other churches not members of this body. They publish a paper called "Zion's Pilger," and there seems every prospect that they will continue to increase in numbers and influence.

The teachings of the Swiss Anabaptists are accurately known to us from three independent and mutually confirmatory sources: The testimony of their opponents, the fragments of their writings that remain, and their Confession of Faith. The latter is the first document of its kind known to be in existence. It was issued in 1527 by the " brotherly union of certain believing, baptized children of God," assembled at Schleitheim, a little village near Schaffhausen. The author is conjectured to have been Michael Sattler, of whom we know little more than that he was an ex-monk, of highly esteemed character, who suffered martyrdom at Rothenberg in the same year this confession was issued, his tongue being torn out, his body lacerated with red-hot tongs, and then burned.

The Confession is not a complete system of doctrine, but treats the following topics: baptism, excommunication, breaking of bread, separation from abominations, shepherds in the congregation, sword (civil government), oaths. It teaches the baptism of believers only, the breaking of bread by those alone who have been baptized, and inculcates a pure church discipline. It forbids a Christian to be a magistrate, but does not absolve him from obedience to the civil law; it pronounces oaths sinful. With the exception of the last two points—in which the modern Friends have followed the Anabaptists in interpreting the Scriptures—the Schleitheim Confession corresponds with the beliefs avowed by Baptist churches to-day. It is significant that what is opprobriously called " close " communion is found to be the teaching of the oldest Baptist document in existence.

With this Confession agrees the testimony of Zwingli and other bitter opponents of the Anabaptists. The only fault charged against them by their contemporaries, that is supported by evidence, is that they had the courage and honesty to interpret the Scriptures as Baptists to-day interpret them. Of their deep piety there is as little doubt as there is of the cruelty with which that piety was punished as a crime against God and man.

SAVONAROLA

WICLIF

THE MARTYRDOM OF JOHN HUS

Hus

WALDO

HULDREICH ZWINGLI

ZURICH AND THE LIMAT

Balthasar Hubmaier

CHAPTER XI

ANABAPTISM IN GERMANY

THE name Anabaptist stands in the literature of the Lutheran Reformation as a synonym for the extremest errors of doctrine, and the wildest excesses of conduct. The Anabaptists were denounced by their contemporaries, Romanist and Protestant alike, with a rhetoric so sulphurous that an evil odor has clung to the name ever since. If one were to believe the half that he reads about these heretics, he would be compelled to think them the most depraved of mankind. Nothing was too vile to be ascribed to them, nothing was too wicked to be believed about them—nothing, in fact, was incredible, except one had described them as God-fearing, pious folk, studious of the Scriptures, and obedient to the will of their Lord, as that will was made known. The masses of the Anabaptists, as of the Lutherans, were uncultured people; but among their leaders were men unsurpassed in their times for knowledge of the original Scriptures, breadth of mind, and fervidness of eloquence. Historians of their own land and race are beginning to do these men tardy justice. The day is not far distant when historical scholarship will prepare a complete vindication of the men so maligned. In the meantime, enough is already known to set right many erroneous statements that have been handed down from historian to historian for centuries, and accepted as undoubtedly true without re-investigation.

As in Switzerland, so in Germany, hardly had the Reformation begun when we find mention of Anabaptists.

But there is this difference: while the name in Switzerland denoted a party essentially homogeneous in faith and practice, the name Anabaptist is applied in Germany to men of widely divergent views and acts. It was, in fact, a convenient epithet of opprobrium, carelessly bestowed by the dominant party on those who opposed them and so aroused their displeasure. Just as now anybody who holds advanced views about the State and its functions, thereby differing from the orthodox political faith, is called by hasty and superficial people "anarchist" or "socialist" (though he may repudiate both titles), so then anybody who dissented from orthodoxy and would not conform to the State Church was likely to be called "Anabaptist." Many who are called by this title in Reformation literature were never Anabaptists, but practised Pedobaptism as consistently as any Lutheran or Romanist of them all. Others who were so far Anabaptists as to have rejected infant baptism, had not grasped the principle on which rejection of infant baptism properly rests, the spiritual constitution of the church.

Even when the name Anabaptist is properly applied, it does not necessarily connote evangelical beliefs and practice. Any Christians who have re-baptized, for whatever reason, may be called by that title. The Donatists were Anabaptists, but they baptized those who came to them because of a supposed defect in the "orders" of the Catholic priesthood. Baptists have affinity only with such Anabaptists as hold to the theory of a regenerate church, reject infant baptism as a nullity, and re-baptize on profession of faith those baptized in unconscious infancy. These distinctions must be borne in mind by one who would read intelligently about the German Anabaptists.

The seemingly sudden appearance of the Anabaptists

and their rapid growth in Germany is a remarkable phenomenon—one of the strangest things in history if we refuse to look below the surface. Some historians insist that the Anabaptists had no previous existence; that it is in vain to look back of the first mention of them for their origin. But this is to say that an event occurred without an adequate cause. No sect or party in the history of the world ever made such an extraordinary growth as the Anabaptists made during the early years of the Reformation unless it had a previous history.

We have seen in previous chapters how Central Europe was leavened by evangelical teachings. The writings of the medieval Fathers are full of complaints of the extent to which the various heresies had corrupted the people. Making all due allowance for exaggeration (where there was little temptation to exaggerate and nothing whatever to be gained by it) the conclusion cannot be resisted that the persistence of what the Catholic Church pronounced heresy, but what we should call evangelical truth, was complete throughout Central Europe during the three centuries preceding the Reformation. This truth was doubtless mixed with no little error, in some cases, but error less deadly than that taught by the Roman Church. For, with all their deviations from the gospel truth, the heretical sects taught a spiritual religion, not a religion of forms and ceremonies—they were loyal to the idea of salvation by faith, not salvation by works. The *name* Anabaptist we do not meet, as applied to any of these sects before the Reformation; but the Anabaptist party of the Reformation period had its roots in these preëxistent sects, and found in their remnants the materials for its surprising growth. To doubt this is, as before remarked, to assume that so great a result—almost unparalleled in the history of Christianity—had no adequate cause, which is irrational

It is commonly said that the first appearance of Anabaptism in Germany was in 1521, at Zwickau, on the border of Bohemia. Certain "prophets" here made a great stir. These prophets were Nicholas Storch, a weaver, but a man of marked ability and well versed in the Scriptures; Marcus Stübner, who had been a student at Wittenberg; and Marcus Thomä, evidently a man of some learning, since a letter written in Latin is extant, in which he is addressed as "a learned man" (*erudito viro*). Of Thomas Münzer, the writer of the letter, we shall see more hereafter; it suffices the present purpose to say that he joined himself to these prophets for ends of his own, and that though with them for a time, he was never of them.

The prophets being driven out of Zwickau, made their way to Wittenberg, where Carlstadt and Melanchthon received them with favor; but Luther was greatly disturbed by their ascendency, returned from his "captivity" at the Wartburg, and by preaching a series of violent sermons recovered the direction of affairs. The prophets accordingly had to depart, and we hear little more of them. Ever since it has been the fashion among the church historians, following the lead of the Lutherans, to represent the Zwickau Anabaptists as a band of fanatics and disturbers of the peace, misled by a belief in their own prophetic inspiration and believing themselves endowed with a gift of tongues. The contemporary literature, however, gives no support to this view. A strong tinge of mysticism is, indeed, found in their reported teachings, but of fanaticism, or encouragement of civil disorder, there is no trace. These prophets had precisely such visions, opening to them (as they believed) the secrets of the spiritual world, as Swedenborg and George Fox enjoyed. They seem, indeed, to have been the precursors of the modern Friends, so spiritualizing the church as to reject the priesthood, water baptism, and all outward ceremonies of religion. They were not Anabaptists, for they did not baptize, yet they were at one with the Anabaptists in holding that the unregenerate have no place in the church of Christ.

It is difficult, if not impossible, in the present state of research, to set definite bounds for the beginning of Anabaptist churches in Germany. What we know is that two men were influential above others in promoting the Anabaptist movement: Balthasar Hübmaier and John Denck.

Hübmaier was born about the year 1481, in Friedburg, Bavaria. The name of his birthplace (of which the English equivalent would be Peacemont), sometimes done into Latin after the fashion of the learned in those days, furnished a surname often used by him in his writings—Friedburger or Pacimontanus. Nothing definite is known of his family, whose name may be taken to imply that they were small tenant-farmers.[1] The lad was sent at an early age to the Latin school at Augsburg, and thence he went to the University of Freiburg, where he matriculated in 1503. His studies here were diligent and successful, but were interrupted by his going to Schaffhausen as a teacher, to earn means to prosecute his work at the university. He returned and took the master's degree in 1511. So high was his proficiency that he was regarded as a promising young man, and was advised to study medicine, then a profitable career. But he decided to devote himself to theology, saying: " Her alone have I chosen, her before all others have I selected, and for her will I prepare a cell in my heart."

At Freiburg he met two men who had much to do with his subsequent career. John Heigelin, or Faber, and John Meyer, better known as Eck. The former was

[1] Hübmaier-Hübel (provincial for Hügel) meier, " the farmer of the hill."

a fellow-student, the latter his most influential teacher. A dispute arose between Eck and the faculty of the university, and Hübmaier warmly espoused the cause of his teacher and friend, and followed Eck to the University of Ingolstadt on his removal thither. Here Hübmaier's rise was rapid. He was given a chair of theology and appointed university preacher, and finally (1515) vice-rector of the university.

The crisis of his fate was now at hand. In 1516 he was called to be pastor at the cathedral of Ratisbon. This removed him from the overshadowing influence of Eck and gave him chance for independent study and growth of character. He seems, even thus early, to have become an ardent and profound student of the Scriptures. As a scholar he was the equal of Luther, though not the peer perhaps of Melanchthon and Erasmus. He soon became renowned as one of the most eloquent preachers of his time. So far as we can know, he led a pure life and was sincerely pious, though still in error. With such talents there was no position in the church to which he might not aspire. But when the Reformation began, it seems to have appealed at once to his mind, if not to his heart; and it was not long before a brilliant career in the church seemed less attractive than to follow the truth.

Resigning his position, he went to Schaffhausen, where he had formerly made friends, and here he possibly hoped to take an active part in the Swiss Reformation. Soon after we find him pastor at Waldshut, just over the Swiss border in the province of Austria. He did not for a time break with the Church of Rome, and observed all the Catholic forms in his new parish. Whether he had not yet become fully convinced of Romish errors or hesitated to make a breach with the church, in the hope that it was capable of a gradual reformation, it would be profitless to guess. There is a vacillation about his conduct just at this part of his life that is difficult to explain on any theory. He was even recalled to Ratisbon, to a new charge there, and accepted this invitation in November, 1522, but without resigning Waldshut, to which he returned the following March. From this time on he seems definitely to have cast in his lot with the reformers.

In May, 1523, Hübmaier visited Zurich and formed a close connection with Zwingli. The latter was in the beginning of his career as a reformer, and inclined to go to the full lengths demanded by his principle of making the Scriptures the sole rule of faith and practice. Hübmaier clearly perceived that this necessitated the abandonment of infant baptism, and Zwingli assented. In his writings and sermons of this period Zwingli did not hesitate to make the same avowal. It was not, however, for two years thereafter that Hübmaier acted on that conclusion, and by that time Zwingli had begun to draw back from it altogether. At the second Zurich disputation (October 26, 1523), Hübmaier was, next to Zwingli himself, the most prominent disputant; and having thus avowed himself a full believer in the Reformation, he became henceforth its firm and consistent supporter.

Hitherto his acts at Waldshut had been those of a trimmer, or, at least, of one whose course was undecided. On his return, he submitted to the clergy and deanery of Waldshut eighteen articles of religion, in which he upheld justification by faith alone, taught that the mass is not a sacrifice, but simply a memorial of the death of Christ, and denounced images, purgatory, celibacy of the clergy, and other Roman errors. Only three of thirty priests sided with him, but he had better success with the citizens. He gradually began to change the service, first reading the Epistles and Gospels in German, and later giving the cup to all communicants. Some opposition was roused, and just before Whitsunday he resigned his office, but was reëlected pastor by the almost unanimous votes of the parish. The Bishop of Constance, hearing of these acts, summoned Hübmaier before him, but no attention was paid to the summons, the reformer saying, " It would be a little thing for me to stand before that hypocrite." The Austrian Diet, outraged by these proceedings, demanded the surrender of Hübmaier, and though the citizens of Waldshut stoutly refused to give up their pastor, he thought it better to leave the city.

Accordingly, August 16, 1524, he sought refuge at Schaffhausen, where he wrote his tract, " Heretics and those who burn them," but in November he again returned to Waldshut. It was about this time that he became clearly convinced that infant baptism is contrary to the Scriptures, as we learn from a letter written by him to Œcolampadius, written January 16, 1525, in which there is an elaborate argument against the scripturalness of infant baptism.

About this time he married a daughter of a Waldshut citizen, and during Lent he abolished the mass, which up to that time he had celebrated in German, had all pictures and altars removed from the churches, and the priests discarded vestments and wore henceforth ordinary clothing. This was an imprudent step, no doubt, since it was almost sure to rouse Austria to violent measures against Waldshut, but fidelity to the truth seemed to Hübmaier and his followers to demand that it be taken.

A still graver step followed. Up to this time Hübmaier had, indeed, been an Anabaptist in theory, but not in practice. In the spring of 1525 William Reublin, who had been compelled to leave Switzerland, came to Waldshut, and through his instructions Hübmaier became convinced, not only that his baptism in infancy was a nullity, but that he ought to be baptized on personal confession of faith. Others were convinced with him, and at Easter Reublin baptized the Waldshut pastor and others (one authority says sixty, another one hundred and ten). Shortly after the pastor himself baptized three hundred of his flock.

This action not only made Hübmaier's position in Waldshut more difficult, by adding fuel to the flame of Austrian hatred, but speedily embroiled him with the Swiss reformers. The Anabaptists had become very troublesome in Bern, and a public disputation with them was held June 5, 1525. Œcolampadius claimed the victory and published his version of the debate. This did so little justice to the arguments of the Anabaptists that Hübmaier was impelled to enter the lists, which he did by writing two tracts: the first, a dialogue " On the baptism of infants " was not published until some time later, when he had gone to Moravia; but the other, " Concerning the Christian baptism of believers," appeared at once, and had a great effect. Zwingli retorted with great vehemence, not to say bitterness, in his celebrated treatise on " Baptism, Anabaptism, and infant baptism." From this time on the Swiss reformers, who had been so friendly to Hübmaier, became his bitterest opponents.

Affairs in Waldshut grew steadily worse, and a strong Catholic party was formed, which favored surrender of the city to the Austrians. Hübmaier finally saw that his situation was an impossible one, and with forty-five of his adherents sought safety in flight. December 5, 1525, the city was captured by Austrian troops. Hübmaier made his way to Zurich, not fully realizing how implacable an enemy he now had in Zwingli, and soon after his arrival was seized, imprisoned, and treated with great rigor. Grebel, Mantz, and Blaurock had already preceded him to the prison, and it was the evident intention of the authorities to suppress Anabaptism by the most vigorous measures. A show of fairness was, however, still maintained. A public discussion was held December 21, at the close of which Zwingli succeeded in wringing from the ill and enfeebled prisoner a promise to reconsider his views. Ambassadors from Austria demanded the surrender of Hübmaier and, though Zurich refused, a different decision was possible at any time. Besides, it is now certain that torture was applied. At length a written recantation was obtained, and, after a confinement of several months, during which time he was loaded with heavy chains, he was released (June 6, 1526), on condition that he leave Switzerland.

He made his way to Constance, thence to his old residences of Ingoldstadt and Ratisbon, where friends received him kindly. He could not hope for safety in either of these towns, should his presence become generally known, and he determined to seek an asylum in Moravia. About the end of June he arrived at Nikolsburg, in the domains of the lords of Lichtenstein, nobles who were known to be humane and tolerant. Here he began the most fruitful part of his labors. Though they occupied not more than fifteen months, their results were astonishing. He was incessant in his work as evangelist. Lord Leonhard of Lichtenstein himself soon became an Anabaptist, and the sect grew with amazing rapidity. An unfriendly historian estimates their numbers at this time at twelve thousand. Moravia had been well-sown with gospel truth by Waldenses and other evangelical preachers and the field was white to harvest when Hübmaier put in the sickle.

He was equally busy with the pen. Tract after tract, not fewer than fifteen distinct writings in all, was written and printed during this period, and some tracts previously composed now found their way to the public. They were scattered broadcast over Germany and Switzerland, and had an influence that it would not be easy to over-estimate. To this time belong his treatise on the Lord's Supper, his reply to Zwingli, his "Book of the Sword," "Form of Baptism," "Form of the Lord's Supper," "Freedom of the Human Will," etc. These were dedicated to the lords of Lichtenstein and other noble patrons, which certainly did not hinder their circulation.

Though for a time there was no external opposition to this work of Hübmaier, it was not without certain difficulties from within. Hans Hut and Jacob Widemann were to Hübmaier what Hymenæus and Alexander were to Paul—messengers of Satan to buffet him, thorns in the flesh. Hut was the more mischievous of the two. Beginning as a sacristan, then an artisan, afterwards imbued with the spirit and teachings of Münzer, he narrowly escaped from Mühlhausen with his life, to become a "prophet," a fanatic, a preacher of Chiliasm and the gospel of the sword. He proclaimed the speedy end of all mundane things, and first set as the date for this final event the day of the summer feast in 1529. Hübmaier stoutly resisted these men and preached and wrote against their false and demoralizing doctrines. A disputation was held in the castle at Nikolsburg, but the result was not decisive; both sides, as usual, claiming the victory. At length Hut was imprisoned by Lord Lichtenstein in the castle, but made his escape and preached his doctrines in various parts of Germany, especially at Augsburg, where he was put to death in 1529. Not a little of the responsibility for the growth of fanaticism among the Anabaptists must be laid at his door. The unity of the Nikolsburg church was fatally impaired, and the way was prepared for the final catastrophe.

The Anabaptists in Moravia would never have been

unmolested so long, but that the country was in a most disorganized state. The Archduke Ferdinand had succeeded in making good his title as Margrave of Moravia, and now determined to get possession of Hübmaier. Exactly how or when he accomplished his purpose we do not know, but as there is no record that the lords of Lichtenstein suffered any personal inconvenience it has been inferred that they surrendered the Anabaptist preacher to save themselves. Not later than September, 1527, Hübmaier and his devoted wife were taken to Vienna and tried for heresy. During the process he asked for an interview with his old friend Faber, and the latter reported that he had made a partial recantation. On March 10, 1528, he was taken through the streets of the city to the public square, and his body was burned. So died one of the purest spirits of the Reformation. Three days later his wife, who had exhorted him in his last hour to endure steadfastly, was drowned in the Danube.

Hübmaier was one of the Anabaptists against whom his enemies bring no charge of immorality or unchristian conduct. We may be sure they would have found or invented such charges against him had it been possible. He was eloquent, learned, zealous, a man in every way the equal (to say no more) of Luther, Zwingli, and Calvin. His name has been loaded with unjust reproaches; he has been accused of teaching things that his soul abhorred; but in spite of his weakness at Zurich he stands out one of the heroic figures of his age.

Hübmaier was no mystic. He believed in no inner light other than the illumination of the Spirit of God that is given to every believer who walks close with God. His appeal on all disputed points is not to this internal witness of the Spirit, for which other voices might be mistaken, but to the written word of God which cannot err. To the law and the testimony he referred every doubtful question, and by the decision thus reached, he loyally abided.

Another leader of this time, John Denck, was a man of different mental cast. Singularly little is known of his early history: the place and time of his birth are uncertain, and of his parentage and family we can learn as little—we cannot say definitely whether he had brother or sister, wife or child. He is thought to have been a native of Bavaria, about the year 1495. We first get definite knowledge of him as an attendant on the lectures of Œcolampadius at Basel, in 1523, where he took the degree of Master of Arts. Shortly after he became head master of the school of St. Sebald, in the free imperial city of Nuremberg. He had evidently adopted evangelical views before going to Basel, but he was from the first neither a Zwinglian nor a Lutheran, but took a line of his own. Nuremberg had, however, become a Lutheran town under the lead of Osiander, and it was not long before Denck's teachings were found to harmonize ill with those of Luther, especially as to the freedom of the will. He was summoned before the authorities, made a Confession of Faith, and this was adjudged so heretical that he was condemned to banishment.

This Confession has been recently discovered in the archives of the city, and interpreted by Doctor Keller. It plainly appears that Denck held the theological views with which the name of Arminius became later identified. He admits the existence of original or inherited sin, but denies total depravity; on the contrary, he says, a germ of good exists in man. Men are so far from being utterly depraved that every man has in him a ray of the divine light, which he could recognize and follow if he would. To follow this light, to obey the divine will, is the essence of faith, and by such faith alone is one justified. There is a working together of the divine and human in salvation. Faith is not mere belief, but the conformity of our will to the will of God. Scripture is not the sole foundation for faith, for there were men of faith before the Scriptures. Man must first of all believe in God as revealed in his own conscience, and then he will believe in the external revelation, finding the two to harmonize. The witness of the Spirit confirms the witness of the Scriptures—this inner word testifying to the truth of the external word—and only he who has the illumination of the Spirit can understand the Scriptures.

It will be seen from this brief account of his teachings that Denck's theology, as held at this time, was irreconcilable with that of Luther in the fundamental doctrines of human nature, freedom of the will, faith, and justification, to say nothing of the authority of the Scriptures. A city that had declared itself for Luther and his doctrine could hardly be expected, in those times, to tolerate so pronounced dissent from the official faith.

In June, 1525, we find Denck was at St. Gall. He was not yet a professed Anabaptist; possibly up to this time he had not heard of the doctrines of this party. He could hardly fail to hear of them now and to be favorably impressed by them. This would account for his going next to Augsburg, which was already an Anabaptist center. A visit of Hübmaier to the city in the following year decided him to become an Anabaptist, and he was himself baptized by Hübmaier. From this time the Anabaptists in Augsburg grew rapidly, until they are said to have numbered eleven hundred, many of the prominent people of the city joining them. The Augsburg Anabaptists, as we know from a contemporary eye-witness, practised immersion. Their piety was acknowledged even by their opponents and persecutors, though these maintained that it was a work of the devil, and called it " a sort of carnival-play of a holy apostolic life, fitted to make the gospel hateful." At a synod in this city, held in the autumn of 1527, at which Denck presided, it was decided that Christians ought not to obtain power or redress of grievances by unlawful means, that is, by the sword.

Partly urged by his restless spirit, partly compelled by danger of imprisonment and death, Denck spent his last years in rapidly moving from place to place. We find traces of his presence at Strassburg, Worms, Zurich, Schaffhausen, and Constance. His last days were passed at Basel, where he died in the autumn of 1527, of the plague. The exact time of his death and the place of his burial are unknown.

His contemporaries unite in praising Denck's brilliant talents and exemplary life. " In Denck, that distinguished young man," says Vadian, " were all talents so extraordinarily developed that he surpassed his years, and appeared greater than himself." He was of handsome and imposing appearance, and hence was called " the Apollo of the Anabaptists." His eloquence was cele brated, and his learning surpassed his eloquence. His work as translator and author was of high quality. His translation of the Hebrew prophets, made in connection with Hätzer, preceded Luther's by several years, and was freely drawn upon by the latter, which is one testimony among many to its merit. Denck was, however, a mystic ; his mental and spiritual affinities were with such men as Tauler and Thomas à Kempis. He would have hailed George Fox as a brother in the Lord. His belief in the sufficiency and supremacy of the inner light not only led him into some doctrinal vagaries, but had a very mischievous effect upon his followers. The charge that he did not believe in the divinity of Christ, Doctor Keller thinks is unproved; but it is admitted that he believed in the final restoration of mankind. Denck's writings are remarkable for their mild polemics in an age when savage denunciation and personal abuse of opponents too often took the place of argument. He was one of the most influential thinkers in Germany, and probably had in the South and West a greater following than Luther, in recognition of which fact his opponents not infrequently called him " the Anabaptist pope." The influence of his work was felt for many years after his untimely death.

Two views of civil government had been thus far contending for the mastery among the Anabaptists. One is that of the Schleitheim Confession, which defines the sword as " an ordinance of God outside of the perfection of Christ . . . ordained over the wicked for punishment and death," and forbids Christians to serve as magistrates. A very considerable part of the Anabaptists advocated those principles of non-resistance that have been professed by the Friends of later date. Hübmaier and Denck differed from this view in part. They held that the Scriptures direct men to perform their duties as citizens; that Christians may lawfully bear the sword as magistrates, and execute the laws, save in persecution of others. In his tract on the " Christian Baptism of Believers," Hübmaier says: " We confess openly that there should be secular government that should bear the sword. This we are willing and bound to obey in everything that is not against God." In his treatise " On the Sword " he defines and distinguishes civil and religious powers, pointing out the true relations of Church and State, with a clearness that a modern Baptist might well imitate, but could not excel. " In matters of faith," said Denck, " everything must be left free, willing, and unforced." Hübmaier denounced persecution in his " Heretics and Those Who Burn Them," written at Schaffhausen before he had by his rebaptism fully ranged himself with the Anabaptists:

Those who are heretics one should overcome with holy knowledge, not angrily but softly. . . If they will not be taught by strong proofs, or evangelical reasons, let them be mad, that those that are filthy may be more filthy still . . . This is the will of Christ, who said, " Let both grow together till the harvest, lest while ye gather up the tares ye root up also the wheat with them!" . . Hence it follows that the inquisitors are the greatest heretics of all, since they against the doctrine and example of Christ condemn heretics to fire, and before the time of harvest root up the wheat with the tares . . . And now it is clear to every one, even the blind, that a law to burn heretics is an invention of the devil. Truth is immortal.

These disconnected sentences give an idea of the course of thought through his brief tract, which is written with a fire that may well have stirred to wrath the persecutors whom it arraigned.

The Anabaptists of this period were the only men of their time who had grasped the principle of civil and religious liberty. That men ought not to be persecuted on account of their religious beliefs was a necessary corollary from their idea of the nature of the church. A spiritual body, consisting only of the regenerate, could not seek to add to itself by force those who were unregenerate. No Anabaptist could become a persecutor without first surrendering this fundamental conviction; and though a few of them appear to have done this, they ceased to be properly classed as Anabaptists the moment they forgot the saying of Christ, " My kingdom is not of this world."

It remains to tell the disgraceful story of the treatment of the German Anabaptists. Luther began his career as a reformer with brave words in favor of the rights of conscience and religious liberty. At Worms he said: " Unless I am refuted and convicted by testimonies of the Scriptures or by clear arguments (since I believe neither the pope nor councils alone; it being evident that they have often erred and contradicted themselves), I am conquered by the Holy Scriptures quoted by me, and my conscience is bound in the word of God: I cannot and will not recant anything, since it is unsafe and dangerous to do anything against the conscience." But later, when the Anabaptists took precisely this position, Luther assails them with exactly the arguments brought against him at Worms, which he so boldly rejected:

If every one now is allowed to handle the faith so as to introduce into the Scriptures his own fancies, and then expound them according to his own understanding, and cares to find only what flatters the populace and the senses, certainly not a single article of faith could stand. It is dangerous, yes terrible, in the highest degree, to hear or believe anything against the faith and doctrine of the entire Christian church. He who doubts any article that the church has believed from the beginning continually, does not believe in the Christian church, and not only condemns the entire Christian church as an accursed heretic, but condemns even Christ himself, with all the apostles who established that article of the church and corroborated it, and that beyond contradiction.

There was a similar change in Luther's opinions regarding the treatment proper for heretics. In his address to the Christian nobility of Germany (1520) he said: " We should overcome heretics with books, not with fire, as the old Fathers did. If there were any skill in overcoming heretics with fire, the executioner would be the most learned doctor in the world; and there would be no need to study, but he that could get another into his power could burn him." The same ideas are set forth in the tract on Secular Magistracy (1523): "No one can command the soul, or ought to command it, except God, who alone can show it the way to heaven. . . It is futile and impossible to command or by force compel any man's belief. . . Heresy is a spiritual thing that no iron can hew down, no fire burn, no water drown. .

Belief is a free thing that cannot be enforced." Luther even retained these sentiments, at least in the abstract, as late as 1527, for in a treatise written in that year against the Anabaptists, he said: " It is not right, and I am very sorry, that such wretched people should be so miserably murdered, burned, and cruelly killed. Every one should be allowed to believe what he pleases. If his belief is v'rong he will have sufficient penalty in the eternal fire of hell. Why should they be made martyrs in this world also? . . . With the Scripture and God's word we should oppose and resist them; with fire we can accomplish little."

Yet such excellent sentiments as these did not prevent Luther from advising John, Elector of Saxony, to restrain by force the Anabaptists from propagating their doctrines within his domains. A decree issued by that prince in 1528, on the plea that the Anabaptists were seducing simple-minded folk into disobedience to God's word, by preachings and disputations, through books and writings, commanded that " no one—whether noble, burgher, peasant, or of whatever rank he may be, except the regular pastors . . . to whom is committed in every place the care of souls and preaching—is permitted to preach and baptize, or to buy and read forbidden books ; but that every one who learns of such doings shall make them known to the magistrate of the place where they occur, in order that these persons may be brought to prison and justice." It was made the duty of every one to seize and deliver such offenders to the court; and whoever should fail to do so, did it at peril of body and goods. Whoever received such persons into their houses or gave them any assistance, should be treated as abettors and adherents. The Protestants are therefore entitled to the distinction of beginning the persecution of the German Anabaptists.

We cannot wonder that the Catholics followed this example. At the Diet of Speyer, in 1529, when the German princes and representatives of the free cities presented their famous protest, in which, in the name of religious liberty they claimed the right to force the reformed faith upon their unwilling Catholic subjects, while they spoke also a faint-hearted plea for the Zwinglians, they had no good word for the Anabaptists. The Diet at this session passed a stringent decree against these people: "All Anabaptists and rebaptized persons, male or female, of mature age, shall be judged and brought from natural life to death, by fire, or sword or otherwise, as may befit the persons, without preceding trial by spiritual judges. . . Such persons as of themselves, or after instruction, at once confess their error, and are willing to undergo penance and chastisement therefor, and pray for clemency, these may be pardoned by their government as may befit their standing, conduct, youth, and general circumstances. We will also that all of their children according to Christian order, usage, and rite shall be baptized in their youth. Whoever shall despise this, and will not do it, in the belief that there should be no baptism of children, shall, if he persists in that course, be held to be an Anabaptist, and shall be subjected to our above-named constitution."

This decree was formally binding on all the States of the empire, Protestant as well as Catholic, but there was of course great latitude in its practical enforcement. Most of the Protestant princes, like the Elector of Saxony and the Landgrave of Hesse, while greatly desirous of suppressing the Anabaptists, had invincible scruples against persecuting to the death those who, like themselves, claimed to be following conscience and Scripture. In such domains, fines, imprisonment, and banishment were inflicted, but not death. The free cities were still less stringent, and seem to have moved against the Anabaptists only when their numbers became so great as to alarm the authorities. Indeed, these cities became the chief refuge of the Anabaptists in the storm of persecution that raged against them after 1529. In the Catholic States they were pursued with implacable severity, and one chronicler (Sebastian Franck, d. 1542) estimates that two thousand or more were put to death at this time. In the Palatinate the persecution was not less severe than in the Catholic States, for three hundred and fifty are said to have perished there.

Cornelius, though writing as a Roman Catholic, yet also as a conscientious historian, thus sums up the results of these persecutions:

In Tyrol and Görz, the number of the executions in the year 1531 already reached one thousand; in Ensisheim, six hundred. At Linz, seventy-three were killed in six weeks. Duke William, of Bavaria, surpassing all others, issued the fearful decree to behead those who recanted, to burn those who refused to recant. Throughout the greater part of upper Germany the persecutions raged like a wild chase. The blood of these poor people flowed like water; so that they cried to the Lord for help. But hundreds of them, of all ages and both sexes, suffered the pangs of torture without a murmur, despised to buy their lives by recantation, and went to the place of execution joyful and singing Psalms.[1]

Some of the recent apologists for these cruelties have said that there was at least a partial justification for such wholesale executions in the suspicion that the Anabaptists were not merely heretics, but traitors—revolutionists, advocates of sedition, as dangerous to the State as to religion. It is perhaps a sufficient answer to this plea to remark that none of the contemporary documents bring this charge against the Anabaptists. In the preambles of the various decrees issued against them, in the statement

[1] " *Geschichte des Münsterischen Aufruhrs,*" Vol. II., p. 57 *seq.*

of their offenses nothing is found but their errors in religious faith and practice. If they were suspected of being politically dangerous up to 1529, it is remarkable that no trace of such suspicion should appear in any official action taken against them. It may be properly added that up to this time neither the acts nor the teachings of the Anabaptists afforded a plausible pretext for the State to treat them as seditious.

CHAPTER XII

PERSECUTION and oppression have a tendency to develop manifestations of fanatical zeal in the oppressed and persecuted. History affords many instances of this principle, and nowhere perhaps is its working better illustrated than in Germany in the sixteenth century. The movement that we call the Reformation was a complex series of phenomena, social, political, and religious; and hardly had Luther begun his labors as a religious reformer, when another group of men began to agitate for far-reaching social reforms. These were the spokesmen of the peasants, the most miserable class of the German people.

The condition of the peasantry of Germany was rapidly changing for the worse during the sixteenth century. This was owing to the complete social revolution then in progress which we call the decay of feudalism. Many causes had been at work to disintegrate the feudal system, but none had been so powerful as the invention of gunpowder. The day when foot-soldiers of the peasant class were armed with muskets was the day of doom for feudalism. The old superiority of the armored knight was gone; battles were no longer contests of cavalry; once more infantry came to the front. As the man with the hoe, the peasant was still despised; as the man with the gun he compelled respect.

The political and social supremacy of the nobles had rested on their military power. So long as the armored knight was able to contend single-handed against a score and even a hundred ill-armed peasants in leather jerkins, so long he was powerful both to punish and to protect. The weak instinctively seek the protection of the strong, even when a high price must be paid for the favor, for it is better to give a part to one's overlord than to lose all to another. The nobility had been tolerated and even upheld because they were necessary to society. They had been permitted to usurp much power, social privilege, wealth, that in nowise belonged to them. But the tacit condition on which these usurpations were condoned was that the nobility should discharge their functions as protectors of social institutions, as preservers of peace and order.

In the sixteenth century the power of the nobility was broken. The knight ceased to be supreme in arms, and as his political and social privileges depended on his military prowess, he must now prepare himself to part with these. This fact he could not and would not see. He was no student of social science, he had no philosophy of history, but he had the usual share of human selfishness, and the disposition to hold on at all hazards to his possessions. The increase of royal power on the one hand, and on the other his own growing poverty, began to pinch him sorely. The rise of the merchant class, the increase of manufactures and commerce, had done away with the old system of barter, and introduced the use of money. Of money the knight had little, of wants he and his household had an increasing number. It was natural that he should turn to his only resource, the peasants who tilled his soil, and try to wring from them the sums that he needed. Thus began new and continually increasing exactions from the peasants, until their condition became intolerable. Discontent became everywhere rife, and frequent insurrections showed that a violent social revolution was imminent.

The rise of the Lutheran Reformation was coincident with this state of things. It was inevitable that the peasants should be encouraged to expect betterment of their condition from the religious movement thus begun, and the early teachings of Luther must have fanned this hope. The seething discontent finally broke out into a general uprising throughout Southern Germany. The peasants drew up twelve articles, in which they demanded what seem now like very moderate measures of reform, such as the right to elect their own pastors, the status of freemen, restoration of the common rights to fish and game and woodlands, just administration of the laws, and abolition of fines and undue feudal services. In a tract that he wrote on the articles, though he criticised the peasants for resorting to forcible methods of obtaining redress, Luther felt compelled to defend the substantial justice of these demands, and exhorted the nobles to yield lest ruin overtake them.

It is quite clear that we have no one upon earth to thank for all this disorder and insurrection but you yourselves, princes and lords, and you especially, blind bishops, insane priests and monks, who, even to this very day, hardened in your perversity, cease not to clamor against the holy gospel, although you know it is just and right and good, and that you cannot honestly say anything against it. At the same time, in your capacity as secular authorities, you manifest yourselves the executioners and spoilers of the poor, you sacrifice everything and everybody to your monstrous luxury, to your outrageous pride, and you have continued to do this until the people neither can nor will endure you any longer. With the sword already at your throat, your mad presumption induces you to imagine yourselves so firm in the saddle that you cannot be thrown off. If you alter not, and that speedily, this impious security will break your necks for you. . . It is you, it is your crimes that God is about to punish. If the peasants, who are now attacking you, are not the ministers of his will, others, coming after them, will be so. You may beat them, but you will be none the less vanquished; you may crush them to the earth, but God will raise up others in their place; it is his pleasure to strike you, and he will strike you.[1]

The leader of the peasants whose name has come down to us as most notable was Thomas Münzer. He was born about 1490 at Stolberg, studied at several universities, becoming a bachelor of theology at Halle, and was a man of considerable learning, unusual ability, and remarkable eloquence. With all these gifts he showed himself from the beginning of his career to be one of those hot-headed, unbalanced, fanatical men, who are born to be troublers in Israel. In 1515 he was provost of a convent at Trohsen, near Aschersleben, and in 1517 became a teacher in the gymnasium at Brunswick. In June, 1520, he became preacher of the chief church at Zwickau, the city already leaning toward Lutheranism; and it is more than suspected that he received the appointment with Luther's knowledge and sanction. In his first sermon he attacked the pope and clergy so furiously as to make a marked sensation in the town, and soon great crowds of people flocked in from the surrounding region to hear this preacher, who, according to an enemy's testimony, was " gifted with angelic eloquence."

It was by Luther's earlier writings that he had been won to the reformation cause, and he took more seriously than their author the ideas set forth in these writings. Luther's course was a curious compound of radical opinions and conservative action, but Münzer was the kind of man to insist on making action correspond to avowed opinion. He therefore attempted to carry out consistently the principle avowed by Luther in his " Babylonian Captivity," that the gospel should be the rule of political as well as of Christian life. He also dissented from Luther's forensic ideas about justification. That faith

[1] Michelet, " Life of Luther " (tr. by Hazlitt). pp. 167, 168.

alone justifies he denied, calling this a " fictitious **faith**."
In short, the disciple showed a strong tendency to outrun
his master, in unsparing application of logic and Scripture
(as he understood the latter) to everyday life.

Finding the Council and more sober citizens opposed
to his radicalism, Münzer thought to strengthen his position by attaching his fortunes to those of the " prophets," Storch, Stübner, and Thomä, and together they be·
gan to announce the speedy end of the age and the setting
up of the kingdom of Christ. These prophecies soon
produced such disorders in Zwickau that the Council was
compelled to act. The " prophets " were thrown into
prison, and Münzer was banished, going into Bohemia.

The " prophets " were released after a time, went to
Wittenberg, as already related, and then disappear from
history. Münzer, unfortunately, did not disappear.
About 1523 he in some way became pastor at Alstedt,
where he married a former nun. Here he was as conservative as previously he had been radical. He published a liturgy in German which is decidedly more Roman than Lutheran in doctrine, and contains a form of
baptism for infants. In one of his tracts published he
says that infant baptism cannot be proved from Scripture,
which is probably the reason why he has been called an
Anabaptist, but he never abandoned the practice of
baptizing infants.

By the summer of 1524 he had made the town too hot
to hold him, and for some time he wandered from place
to place, visiting Œcolampadius at Basel, possibly Hübmaier at Waldshut, and making the acquaintance of the
Swiss Anabaptists. At the beginning of 1525 he came
to Mühlhausen. Before this time, in September, 1524,
learning what his views had come to be, and what was
likely to be their outcome, Grebel, Mantz, and Blaurock
addressed a letter of warning and remonstrance to

Münzer which did not reach him, but still exists in the archives at Schaffhausen to testify to the sound views of its authors. " Is it true," Grebel asks, " as we hear, that you preached in favor of an attack on the princes? If you defend war or anything else not found in the clear word of God, I admonish you by our common salvation to abstain from these things now and hereafter." It is impossible to say what effect this fraternal reproof might have had; but not receiving it, Münzer went on his way, and by his rash attempt to mingle civil and religious reform, and enforce both by the sword, he forfeited his life.

For when he reached Mühlhausen it was the storm-center of Germany; the outbreak of the peasants had already begun and the Peasants' War was on. The peasants had a righteous cause, if ever men had one who strove for liberty with the sword, and the justice and moderation of their demands as made in their twelve articles is conceded by every modern historian. Münzer gave himself out as the prophet of God, come for the purpose of setting up the kingdom of heaven in the city, and promising destruction of princes, community of goods, and the gospel to be made the rule of life in all things.

By such means he easily made himself the head of the revolt, and thousands of the deluded peasants of Southern Germany flocked to his standard. The bubble was pricked by the lances of the allied German princes at the battle of Frankenhausen, May 15, 1525. The peasants were defeated with great slaughter; Münzer and other leaders were captured and put to death; and it is credibly recorded of the " prophet " that before his death he recanted his errors, returned to the Catholic Church, received the last sacraments, and died exhorting the people of Mühlhausen to hold fast to the true (Catholic) faith!

Though the peasants had a good cause, they had not always adopted good methods. Most of them were ig-norant, all were exasperated, and some were maddened by their wrongs. In their uprising some outrages were committed; castles had been burned and plundered and ruthless oppressors had been slain. These deeds were now made the pretext for a retaliation whose cruelty has rarely been surpassed in history. It is computed by his-torians who have no motive to exaggerate, that fully a hundred thousand were killed before the fury of the princes and the knights was appeased.

Foremost among those who urged them on was Luther. It would seem that he had become alarmed by the per-sistence of those who had sought to make him and his teachings responsible for the peasant war. His hope was in the protection and patronage of the princes, to whom the plain words he had spoken must have given deep offense. So in the midst of the uproar he sent to the press a second pamphlet, in which he turned com-pletely about, and denounced the peasants as violently as he had before rebuked the princes.

They cause uproar, outrageously rob and pillage monasteries and castles not belonging to them. For this alone, as public highwaymen and murderers, they deserve a twofold death of body and soul. It is right and lawful to slay at the first oppor-tunity a rebellious person, known as such, already under God and the emperor's ban. For of a public rebel, every man is both judge and executioner. Just as, when a fire starts, he who can extinguish it first is the best fellow. Rebellion is not a vile murder, but like a great fire that kindles and devastates a country; hence uproar carries with it a land full of murder, bloodshed, makes widows and orphans, and destroys everything, like the greatest calamity. Therefore whosoever can, should smite, strangle, and stab, secretly or publicly, and should remem-ber that there is nothing more poisonous, pernicious, and devilish than a rebellious man. Just as when one must slay a mad dog; fight him not and he will fight you, and a whole country with you.

Let the civil power press on confidently and strike as long as it can move a muscle. For here is the advantage: the peasants have bad consciences and unlawful goods, and whenever a peasant is killed therefore he has lost body and soul, and goes forever to the devil. Civil authority, however, has a clean conscience and lawful goods, and can say to God with all security of heart: "Behold, my God, thou hast appointed me prince or lord, of that I cannot doubt, and hast entrusted me with the sword against evil-doers (Rom. 13 : 4). . . Therefore I will punish and smite as long as I can move a muscle; thou wilt judge and approve." . . Such wonderful times are these that a prince can more easily win heaven by shedding blood than others with prayers.

Therefore, dear lords, redeem here, save here, help here; have mercy on these poor peasants, stab, strike, strangle, whoever can. Remainest thou therefore dead? Well for you, for a more pious death nevermore canst thou obtain. For thou diest in obedience to God's word and to duty (Rom. 13: 1), and in the service of love, to deliver thy neighbor out of hell and the devil's chains.

The charge brought against Luther was of course absurd. There would have been a revolt of the peasants had there been no Luther and no Reformation, though it is possible that Luther and his teachings hastened the outbreak and increased its violence. It is equally absurd to charge the responsibility of the revolt upon the Anabaptists, and had not Münzer been erroneously called an Anabaptist by careless writers probably no connection would have been suspected between movements that had so little in common as the religious reformation sought by the Anabaptists and the social revolution desired by the peasants. Some few Anabaptists were doubtless concerned in the revolt—it would be wonderful if such were not the case—but not the sect as a whole, or even any large proportion of them. One fact is decisive of this question: the vengeance of the princes and nobles was not directed against Anabaptists as such, on account of the peasant uprising. No contemporary charges the Anabaptists with responsibility for the disorders at Mühlhausen or elsewhere during the revolt of the peasants. That charge it was left for certain writers of the present century to advance for the first time.

It was in Northern Germany, and some years after the revolt of the peasants had been subdued, that the anarchistic and doctrinal vagaries of certain Anabaptists found their fullest development. He who has been called the leading spirit of the movement that culminated at Münster, never countenanced or taught the use of the sword in the cause of religion. Melchior Hofmann was a man of fervent piety, of evangelical spirit, of pure and devoted life; but his mind was of the dreamy, mystical type, and his lack of thorough knowledge of the Scriptures in the original tongues, and his deficiency in general mental culture made him an easy victim to speculations and vagaries. Pure in life and mild in character as he was, not a few of his teachings contained dangerous germs of evil, and their development under his successors brought great shame upon the Anabaptist cause.

Hofmann was born in Swabia, probably in the free imperial city of Hall, about 1490. He had only a slight education, and was apprenticed to a furrier. He very early embraced the Lutheran Reformation, but was by nature a radical and an enthusiast, and could be expected to remain permanently subject to no leader who halted half-way in the work of reform. A disparaging reference to him in one of Zwingli's letters, written in 1523, shows that he was then in Zurich, and later he went to Livonia, where he was in no long time thrown into prison and then banished. He was in Dorpat in the autumn of 1524, and succeeded in obtaining testimonials from a number of scholars and influential men, including Luther himself. It was about this time that he began to develop his chiliastic notions, and as a lay preacher he did not fail to advocate them.   This would bring him into no collision with the Lutherans, for Luther was himself inclined to chiliastic notions, at least during this portion of his career.   About the beginning of 1526 Hofmann went to Stockholm, where he published his first book, an interpretation of the twelfth chapter of Daniel, in which he gave free vent to his notions about the coming of Christ's kingdom, and fixed the year 1533 for the end of the age.

For the next two years he was in Denmark; being still attached to the Lutheran party, he had little difficulty in obtaining the protection of the authorities, and even got a living assigned him.   His restlessness in speculation soon made trouble for him with the Lutheran clergy, and finally his avowal of Zwinglian ideas regarding the Eucharist procured his banishment.   Thence he seems to have gone to Strassburg, arriving there at the beginning of 1529, or possibly a little before.

Up to this time there is no evidence that he had met any Anabaptists or become acquainted with their views, still less that he had any inclination toward them.   At Strassburg the Anabaptists were numerous, and the death of Denck had left them without a recognized leader. They differed from many German Anabaptists on several points; in particular, they were opposed to the use of the sword, in spite of the authority of Hübmaier and Denck. The ardor of Hofmann and the novelty of his teachings naturally fitted him to step into the vacant leadership, and in a very short time he was recognized as the head of the Anabaptists of Strassburg.   He wrote and taught indefatigably, and made numerous missionary journeys into surrounding regions.   One of these, into Holland, was fraught with momentous consequences, for in the course of it he met, converted, baptized, and indoctrinated with his notions, Jan Matthys, a baker of Haarlem, who was to be his successor, and lead the Anabaptists into a career of shame and overthrow.

After a time the magistrates of the city became alarmed at Hofmann's growing influence, and he was arrested in May, 1533, and thrown into prison. He had before this predicted that the end of the age was at hand; that Strassburg was to be the New Jerusalem, and that the magistrates would there set up the kingdom of God; that the new truth and the new baptism would prevail irresistibly throughout the earth. He had set the very year of his arrest as the time of consummation; and at first his followers were not dismayed, for this persecution, they persuaded themselves, was also foretold. But the years passed and Hofmann still languished in prison, until death released him toward the close of 1543.

In the meantime another "prophet" had arisen and his predictions were claiming the attention of the credulous. Hofmann was discredited by the failure of his prophecies, but none the less eagerly were those of Jan Matthys received. He was one of these crack-brained fanatics, half lunatic, half criminal, who never fail to gain a large following, and as certainly lead their dupes to destruction. About the time of Hofmann's imprisonment Matthys began to dream dreams and see visions; proclaimed himself to be the Elias of the new dispensation soon to begin, and sent out twelve apostles to herald the coming of the kingdom of Christ. Among other things he predicted the speedy overthrow of all tyrants and the coming of an age of gold. Converts were made to this new gospel by the thousand in Holland and Friesland.

Events just then occurring at the city of Münster attracted the attention of the Anabaptist leaders and caused that city to become the center of operations. Münster was at that time a semi-free city, ruled by its council, but situated in the territory of a prince-bishop who claimed a certain suzerainty. The citizens had been struggling to gain freedom from an ecclesiastical caste that insulted and robbed them, and a famine that occurred in this region in 1529 brought the city to the very verge of revolution.

At this juncture Bernard Rothmann began to preach the Lutheran doctrines there, and soon all the clergy of the city sided with him. A revolution, half political, half religious, ensued, and by the intervention of Philip of Hesse a treaty was made with the prince-bishop, in which Münster was recognized as a Lutheran city. But Rothmann and his colleagues had no notion of stopping here; they issued a " Confession of Two Sacraments," in which they strongly advocated believers' baptism, and defined the ordinance as " dipping or completely plunging into the water."

Just as affairs had come to this stage two of the apostles of Matthys reached the city and began preaching and baptizing. In eight days they are said to have baptized fourteen hundred people. Two weeks later Jan Matthys himself arrived, and in February the Anabaptists had so increased that they had no difficulty in electing a council from their own number, and so gained control of the government of Münster without striking a blow. From this time they had supreme power in the town, though the prince-bishop speedily laid siege to it and confined them closely within.

The Anabaptist domination was celebrated by clearing the Dom of all images, and driving from the city all who would not join them. The council then established community of goods as the law of the town, and the orgy of fanaticism and wickedness began. Daily visions and revelations came to the leaders, some of whom were evidently sincere, while others appear to have been simply devilish. Matthys was certainly one of the former, and proved it by his death. In obedience to a vision he made a sortie from the city with a few followers, and was killed while fighting desperately. John Bockhold, of Leyden, thereupon declared himself the successor, and had no difficulty in persuading the people to accept him as the prophet appointed by God. Nothing seemed too much for these credulous Münsterites to receive unquestioningly. When John of Leyden shortly afterward proclaimed that this was Mount Zion, that the kingdom of David was to be re-established, and that he was King David, nobody questioned him. The solemn farce was played out to the end. Of course King David had to have a harem, and polygamy was proclaimed as the law of the new kingdom. Perhaps the fact that six times as many women as men were now in the city had not a very remote connection with this feature of the kingdom.

The farce was about ended; it was soon to become bloody tragedy. The Münsterites, knowing that before the siege began the surrounding country held thousands who sympathized with them, were continually expecting that an armed force of Anabaptists would come to their aid. But the Anabaptists were overawed by the military force, or disgusted by the fantastic doings in the city, and no army came. The town was wasted by famine, weakened at last by dissensions, and betrayed by traitors. June 25, 1535, it fell, and Anabaptism in Germany fell with it. There was great slaughter in the town, and the captured leaders, after tortures truly diabolical in their cruelty, were hung up in cages to the tower of the church of St. Lambert, in the chief market-place, to die of starvation and exposure, and there they hung until quite recent times, when for very shame the few remaining bones were removed. The cages still hang there.

The entire responsibility for these disorders was at once thrown upon the Anabaptists. There was this excuse for so doing, that several of the ringleaders, and a considerable number of their followers, called themselves or were called by that name. Yet the principles of Rothmann, in his writings that remain, are totally opposed to his conduct at Münster. In none of the Anabaptist literature of the time is there anything but horror and detestation expressed for the Münster doings; and even before they were made the scapegoats of this uprising, their writings were full of reproofs spoken against any who would propagate religion by the sword. Münster was not more decidedly contrary to the teachings of the reformers than it was to the teachings of the Anabaptists generally. It is no more fair to hold the Anabaptists as a whole responsible for what occurred there, because Matthys and Bockhold were Anabaptists, than it is to hold the Lutherans responsible because Rothmann was a Lutheran when he began his evil career. Cornelius, the able and judicial Roman Catholic historian of the Münster uproar, says justly: " All these excesses were condemned and opposed wherever a large assembly of the brethren afforded an opportunity to give expression to the religious consciousness of the Anabaptist membership." Füsslin, a conscientious and impartial German investigator, says: " There was a great difference between Anabaptists and Anabaptists. There were those amongst them who held strange doctrines, but this cannot be said of the whole sect. If we should attribute to every sect whatever senseless doctrines two or three fanciful fellows have taught, there is no one in the world to whom we could not ascribe the most abominable errors." To which may be added the conclusion of Ulhorn: " The general character of this whole movement was peaceful, in spite of the prevailing excitement. Nobody thought of carrying out the new

ideas by force. In striking contrast to the Münzer uproar, meekness and suffering were here understood as the
most essential elements of the Christian ideal."

But though scholarly investigations, with substantial
unanimity, have now come to this conclusion regarding
the teachings and methods of German Anabaptists, this
was not the voice of contemporary opinion; that visited
the sins of the few upon the many, and pronounced all
Anabaptists alike to be enemies of society and worthy
of any punishment that could be devised. The most atrocious crimes were not avenged with a severity greater
than was visited on the members of this unfortunate sect.
The severities of former persecutions were far exceeded,
and only in the domain of the Landgrave of Hesse was
there anything like moderation or justice in the treatment
meted out to these people. This prince alone among the
Protestant rulers, while he favored the punishment of
those actually concerned in the Münster disorders, declared that merely to be an Anabaptist was not a capital
crime: " To punish with death those who have done
nothing more than err in the faith, cannot be justified on
gospel grounds."

A gathering of Protestant authorities was held August
7, 1536, at Homburg, in Hesse, to consider the policy
proper to be pursued toward the Anabaptists. Eight representatives of the nobility, seven delegates from five
cities, and ten divines were present. The divines substantially agreed with Melanchthon, whose judgment was:
" That the Anabaptists may and should be restrained
by the sword. That those who have been sent into exile, and do not abide by the conditions, are to be punished
by the sword." The representatives of the cities, particularly of Ulm and Augsburg, were of the milder opinion
that death should not be inflicted as a punishment of
heresy, though other severities might be employed. Such

of the nobles as spoke favored banishment, on pain of death in case of return. This was the penalty finally decided upon.

After the savage persecution following the downfall of Münster, one might have expected the Anabaptists to have been extirpated. Their prominent leaders, it is true, disappeared, some being put to death, some dying of hardships and excessive toils. They were not entirely without leadership, however, and their dauntless fidelity to the truth continued. In Moravia, about the middle of the sixteenth century, there were seventy communities of Anabaptists, prosperous farmers and tradesmen, acknowledged to be among the most thrifty and law-abiding element of the population. In Strassburg, in Augsburg, in Bohemia, and in Moldavia, they were also found in large numbers, and wherever found they were marked men by reason of their godly lives and good citizenship. Fifty years later, however, persecution had done its work only too well, and early in the seventeenth century we find the Anabaptists disappear from the history of Germany. They survived somewhat later in Poland, where they became quite numerous, and a large section of them adopted the Socinian theology.

The German Anabaptists committed the one sin that this world never pardons: they attempted a radical revolution, which would ultimately have transformed civil and social as well as religious institutions and—they failed. That is the real gist of their offense. Had they succeeded, the very men whom historians have loaded with execrations would have been held up as the greatest and noblest men of their age. The fame of Luther and Zwingli and Calvin would have been eclipsed by that of Grebel and Hübmaier and Denck, if the labors of the Anabaptists had been crowned with success. The true Reformation was that with which they were identified.

The Reformation that actually prevailed in the sixteenth century was a perversion of the genuine movement, resulting from the unholy alliance with the State made by those who are called "reformers." Two centuries were required before the fruits of a real Reformation could ripen for the gathering; and it was in America, not in Germany, that the genuine Reformation culminated.

CHAPTER XIII

IF the disappearance of the Anabaptists from Germany had been as complete in reality as it was in appearance, it would furnish a curious historical problem to explain so sudden a cessation of evangelical teaching and practice. But the student of history is not long in discovering that the Anabaptists did not disappear; they only took a different name. They had never chosen the name Anabaptist, and had always maintained that it was not properly applied to them. Now that the name had come to be a synonym for all that was fanatical in creed and immoral in conduct, they were only too glad to be rid of the hateful title—as hateful to them as to their oppressors. As before, so now and after, these people called themselves simply " the brethren," but in common speech a new name came to be applied to them about the middle of the sixteenth century; they were known as Mennonites.

Of Menno, surnamed Simons, we know little, save what he himself has told us. He was born in Witmarson, Friesland, in 1496 or 1497. He was educated for the priesthood, and in 1524 he undertook the duties of a priest in his father's village, called Pingjum. A year thereafter, while officiating at the altar, the thought occurred to him that the bread and wine in the mass were not the body and blood of Christ, but he put the idea from him as a temptation of the devil. He feared to study the Scriptures lest they mislead him. His life was godless and dissipated. After a time he began to study

184

the Scriptures, and received some light from them, though
his heart was still unchanged.

While in this state of mind Menno heard of the martyrdom of one Sicke Freerks or Frierichs, more commonly
known by his surname of Snyder, which designated him
as a tailor. On the 30th of March, 1531, this faithful believer was condemned, as the court record reads, " to be
executed by the sword; his body shall be laid on the
wheel, and his head set on a stake, because he has been
rebaptized and perseveres in that baptism "; all of which
was duly done at Leeuwarden. The blood of that poor
tailor produced a host of followers to the Lord, for whom
he joyfully gave all that he had, even his life; for it led
Menno Simons, after a long and hard struggle, to
decisive action.

At first he was merely surprised to hear that this man
suffered on account of what was called a second baptism.
He studied the Scriptures, but could find in them nothing
about infant baptism. He consulted in turn Luther,
Bucer, and Bullinger, but they gave him no help, for he
saw that the arguments by which they supported the
practice had no foundation in the Scriptures. Though
he now came gradually to a fuller knowledge of God's
truth, and to some outward amendment of his life, he
still held back from what he knew to be his duty. He
was ambitious, and hesitated to break with the church,
in which he hoped for a career and fame. For a time
he attempted to compromise with his conscience, and
preached the truth publicly from the pulpit. Finally, he
says, after about nine months of such preaching, the Lord
granted him his Spirit and power, and he then renounced
all his worldly honor and reputation, separated himself
from the church and its errors, and willingly submitted
to distress and poverty.

This was about the year 1536, and it seems to have

been Menno's intention to lead the quiet life of a student and writer. But about a year later, a small group of believers came to him and urged him to remember the needs of the poor, hungry souls, and make better use of the talents he had from the Lord. Accordingly, he began to preach the gospel, and continued to make known the truth with voice and pen to the end of his life.

Though not without frequent interruptions, his labors were practically continuous and very fruitful. At the beginning, the Anabaptists were greatly divided, as well as discouraged. One party still held to the views that had been practically embodied at Münster; they defended polygamy, believed in the speedy second coming of Christ, a second time incarnated to set up an earthly kingdom, which his followers were to defend and extend by the sword. The other party condemned polygamy and the sword. The strife was keen, but the weight of Menno's influence turned the scale in favor of purity and peace. From the first he repudiated the ideas of Münster. In his " Exit from Papacy " he wrote as follows: " Beloved reader, we have been falsely accused by our opponents of defending the doctrine of Münsterites, with respect to king, sword, revolution, self-defense, polygamy, and many similar abominations; but know, my good reader, that never in my life have I assented to those articles of the Münster Confession; but for more than seventeen years, according to my small gift, I have warned and opposed them in their abominable errors. I have, by the word of the Lord, brought some of them to the right way. Münster I have never seen in all my life. I have never been in their communion. I hope, by God's grace, with such never to eat or drink (as the Scriptures teach), except they confess from the heart their abominations and bring forth fruits meet for repentance and truly follow the gospel."

Menno was an apostle of the truth, preaching and founding churches across the whole of Northern Europe, from France to Russia. In spite of the severest edicts and the bloodiest persecutions, he continued faithful to his calling, and found willing hearers of the gospel wherever he went. He enforced a strict standard of morals, repressed all tendencies toward fanaticism, and gradually molded his followers into the mild, peaceful, and moral people that the Mennonites have ever since been. His last years were spent in Holstein, where he died January 13, 1561, in his sixty-sixth year. He was a voluminous writer, and during his last decade he established a printing-press and secured the wide circulation of his writings. These are mostly in the Dutch language, though some were originally written in " Oostersch " and very badly translated into Dutch. The issue of his " Fundamental Book of the True Christian Faith," in 1539, established his doctrinal teaching on solid grounds. It differed from the Reformed theology only in maintaining the spiritual idea of the church, as a communion of true saints, and the necessary consequence of this idea, the rejection of infant baptism.

Menno owed his prolonged life and labors in part to the fact that he was content to work very quietly and obscurely, in part to the protection that he received at various times from several princes and noblemen, who were favorable to evangelical teachings. He had many narrow escapes, some of which seem like special interpositions of Providence on his behalf. His daughter relates that a traitor who had agreed without fail, for a certain sum of money, to deliver him into the hands of his enemies, after several failures one day met Menno, being then in the company of an officer in search of the heretic preacher. Menno was going along the canal in a small boat. The traitor kept silence until Menno had passed them some distance, and had leaped ashore in order to escape with less peril. Then the traitor cried out, "Behold, the bird has escaped!" The officer chastised him, called him a villain, and demanded why he did not speak in time, to which the traitor replied, "I could not speak, for my tongue was bound." It is said the authorities were so displeased with the man that, according to his pledge, he had to forfeit his own head.

Certainly this servant of God was pursued with great bitterness. The governor of Friesland issued a proclamation, under date of December 7, 1542, in which it was declared that any one who gave food or lodging, or any assistance to Menno Simons, or should have any of his books, should be liable to the penalties of heresy. This was no empty threat; before this, in 1539, one Tjaert Reyndertz or Reynderson, was arraigned for the offense of lodging Menno in his house, was stretched on the wheel and finally beheaded. These local persecutions and edicts were doubtless inspired by the general edict of Charles V., executed at Brussels, June 10, 1535, which commanded that all Anabaptists or re-baptizers and their abettors should be put to death by fire; those who sincerely repented and renounced their errors should be beheaded, and the women should be buried alive. Buckle, in his "History of Civilization," estimates that by 1546, thirty thousand persons had been put to death for Anabaptism in Holland and Friesland alone. And yet it is held by many historians that this decree was never generally enforced. Had it been, one must think the country would have been nearly depopulated.

In spite of such measures, the churches established by Menno and his fellow-laborers increased in numbers rapidly. Their growth may be explained by two causes, of which one has already been mentioned. The change of name was greatly in their favor. To say "Anabaptist" produced much the same effect in those days that the cry of "mad dog" does in ours. To say "Mennonite," at most provoked a feeling of mild curiosity as to what this new sect might be—so much is there in a name, Shakespeare to the contrary notwithstanding. A second thing greatly in favor of this new development of the Anabaptists, was the fact that the Netherlands soon came to favor a much greater measure of religious liberty than was found anywhere else in Europe. In 1572 the Netherlands revolted from the authority of the Spanish crown, and in 1579 formed a federal union, with the Prince of Orange at its head. He was the most liberal-minded prince in Europe, and was strongly opposed to all persecution on religious grounds. To his influence chiefly the Mennonites owed their long immunity from active persecution, for the clergy of the Reformed Church (which became the established religion of the Netherlands) were generally opposed to toleration, and many times attempted to stir up the government against the Mennonites. After 1581 the mild, peaceable, and law-abiding character of this people gained for them a measure of toleration that other Anabaptist bodies failed to enjoy; and with the independence of the Netherlands came religious freedom, the Mennonites being formally recognized in 1672. This is probably the reason why they alone, of the Anabaptist parties of the Reformation, have survived to the present day.

One branch of Menno's followers, those especially in Lithuania, at the invitation of Empress Catherine II., emigrated to Russia, and there founded flourishing agricultural communities, especially in the Crimea. They were for a long time treated with exceptional favor. their faith not only being tolerated, but the male members being exempted from military service on account of their religious scruples against bearing arms. Their descendants abode there until, in 1871, an imperial decree deprived them of this exemption, since when many of them have emigrated to America, forming strong colonies in several of our Western States. Many others have come from Holland and elsewhere, and the majority of Mennonites are now found on American soil. In the census of 1890 twelve branches are reported, with slight differences in polity and doctrine, aggregating a membership of forty-one thousand five hundred and forty-one.

There is good reason to believe that from the first, affusion was generally practised for baptism by the Mennonites. Menno himself at times uses language that would seem to imply immersion, as when he says, " We find but one baptism in the water, pleasing to God, which is expressed and contained in his word, namely, baptism on the confession of faith. . . But of this other baptism, that is, infant baptism, we find nothing." Yet that he could have had an immersion in mind as the act of baptism is irreconcilable with his speaking of it elsewhere as " to have a handful of water applied." While he was perfectly clear about the scriptural teaching regarding the subject of baptism, he appears to have considered the act as a relatively unimportant matter. He was content to follow the prevailing practice of his time, and so were his followers.

But while the Mennonites as a whole have doubtless from the first practised affusion, there have been and are some exceptions. The congregation at Rynsburg, known as Collegiants, adopted immersion in 1619, a fact that had important relations to the Baptists of England, as we shall see. One branch in the United States, that coming from Russia, practises immersion exclusively, and another branch immerses by preference, but affuses those who prefer that form.

Neither their love of Christ nor their fear of persecution was able to keep the Anabaptists of the sixteenth century from internal dissensions; and this was especially true of the followers of Menno. Since they had no formal creeds and professed the Scriptures alone as their standard of faith and practice, it was natural that considerable differences should arise among them. They became divided into High and Low (*Obere* and *Untere*). The former held to vigorous discipline, or the " ban." The Low party would reserve the " ban " for cases of flagrant immorality. This division dates from the time of Menno himself, who was inclined towards a more strict use of the ban than many of his followers approved. A synod or assembly of the brethren held at Strassburg in 1555, felt constrained to protest against what they believed to be Menno's excessive strictness, especially in requiring a husband or wife to refuse cohabitation with an excluded partner.

Some of the disputes that arose among the brethren deserve a place in the curiosities of literature. Such is the button controversy, which arose in this wise: The traditional method of fastening the gowns of women and the coats of men had been hooks and eyes. The Mennonites held views about soberness of dress and shunning conformity to the fashions of the world similar to those afterward associated with the Friends or Quakers. Accordingly, when buttons were invented and introduced, the use of them on a garment was held to be the badge of a carnal mind, it was a conformity to the spirit of this world unworthy of a true Christian. This was the ground on which this apparently trivial controversy was fiercely fought for generations; and to this day some of the descendants of the High party, even in this country, fasten their coats with the old-fashioned hooks and eyes and are popularly known as " Hook-and-eye Dutch." In general, it may be said that the High party demanded a discipline extending far beyond Scripture precedent, and concerning itself with the minutest details of daily living. The Low party was in favor of a more rational measure of Christian liberty. In some cases the High party also insisted as an article of faith on letting the beard grow, while the Low party denied that the use of the razor was contrary to the word of God.

The Mennonite churches were not content, however, with establishing general rules; they undertook to regulate the daily lives of their members, and to interfere with all manner of private concerns. The results produced by this policy are well illustrated by the Bintgens case. Bintgens was an elder in the Franecker church, and having occasion to purchase a house for seven hundred florins, permitted the seller to insert in the deed a valuation of eight hundred florins. It was not charged that Bintgens profited by the transaction or that anybody lost; but he had been a party to a deception, and that was enough. When the matter was brought before the church, Bintgens professed sorrow for his error, and his statement was accepted. Later a party in the church demanded his deposition from the eldership. Three successive councils failed to effect a settlement, and neighboring churches became involved in the matter. For years the contest raged, some churches becoming hopelessly divided, others withdrawing fellowship from sister churches whose attitude they did not approve, and great scandal being brought upon the name of the brethren by this bitter contentiousness over so slight a matter. " Behold how great a forest is kindled by how small a fire."

Followers of Menno appeared in England in the sixteenth century, as we learn from many historical documents. They fled thither to escape the persecutions that then raged in Holland, but in this they were doomed to disappointment, for England harried the Anabaptists no less than Holland, casting them into prison and burning them at the stake. Our information regarding these people is mainly confined to royal proclamations against them, and to the records of their arrest, trial, and punishment.

In 1534, after the Act of Supremacy made Henry VIII. the supreme head of the Church of England, he issued two proclamations against heretics, in which the Anabaptists were especially named. They were first warned to leave the kingdom within ten days, and then severer measures were taken against them. In the ten articles published by royal authority in 1536, the error of the Anabaptists regarding the baptism of children is singled out for special reprobation. It is a matter of record that in this same year nineteen Dutch Anabaptists were arrested, and fourteen were burned. Ten are said to have likewise perished in the preceding year. Bishop Latimer, who was himself to suffer in like manner for the truth a few years later, says of these executions: " The Anabaptists that were burnt here in divers towns in England, as I heard of credible men, I saw them not myself, went to their death even *intrepide,* as ye will say, without any fear in the world, cheerfully; well, let them go."

In 1538 another proclamation was issued against heretics, who had in the meantime increased rapidly, and a commission of Cranmer and eight bishops was appointed to proceed against such by way of inquisition. Any who remained obdurate were to be committed, with their heretical books and manuscripts, to the flames. Four Dutch Anabaptists were burned in consequence at Paul's Cross and two at Smithfield.

That these Anabaptists were really an inoffensive folk, who were punished solely for religious offenses, is proved by still another proclamation of Henry VIII., issued in 1540, in which their alleged heresies were thus enumerated: "Infants ought not to be baptized; it is not lawful for a Christian man to bear office or rule in the commonwealth; every manner of death, with the time and hour thereof, is so certainly prescribed, appointed, and determined to every man by God, that neither any prince by his word can alter it, nor any man by his wilfulness prevent or change it."

In the sermons of Roger Hutchinson, published by the Parker Society, is a discourse preached prior to 1560, the following from which describes one tenet on which the Anabaptists of that day laid special stress:

Whether may a man sue forfeits against regrators, forestallers, and other oppressors? Or ought patience to restrain us from all suit and contention? "Aye," saith master Anabaptist; "for Christ our Master, whose example we must follow, he would not condemn an advoutress woman to be stoned to death, according to the law, but shewed pity to her, and said, 'Go and sin no more' (John 8); neither would he, being desired to be an arbiter, judge between two brethren and determine their suit (Luke 12). When the people would have made him their king he conveyed himself out of sight, and would not take on himself such office. Christ the Son of God would not have refused these functions and offices if with the profession of a Christian man it were agreeable with the temporal sword to punish offenders, to sustain any public room, and to determine controversies and suits; if it were lawful for private men to persecute such suits, and to sue just and rightful titles. He *non est dominatus sed passus;* would be no magistrate, no judge, no governor, but suffered and sustained trouble, injury, wrong, and oppression patiently. And so must we; for Paul saith, 'That those which he foreknew he also ordained before—*ut essent conformes imagini Filii sui*—that they should be alike fashioned into the shape of his Son.'"

By 1550 the growth of the Anabaptists, especially in Kent and Essex, so disquieted those in power that a new commission was issued in the name of the young king, Edward VI., with special powers to discover and punish all Anabaptists. Cranmer, Latimer, and other notable reformers were members of this body. It was by their agency that Joan Boucher, of Kent, was burned for heresy. Her error was that she held a doctrine common among the German Anabaptists, from the time of Melchior Hofmann, and given further currency by the adhesion of Menno Simons, that though Jesus was born of Mary he did not inherit her flesh; the idea being that if he had, he must have shared her sinful human nature. It was crude theology, but the harmless error of untrained minds. A wise church and one really moved by the spirit of Christ would have winked at a matter that so slightly concerned a godly life; but for this offense, and the kindred crime of being an Anabaptist, Joan of Kent suffered death at the stake.

Elizabeth was faithful to the traditions of her race, and in 1560 she warned all Anabaptists and other sectaries to depart from her realm within twenty-one days, on pain of imprisonment and forfeiture of goods. This was a peculiar hardship in the years immediately following, for persecution was raging in the Netherlands, and England was the natural refuge of the oppressed Anabaptists. Later in her reign, Elizabeth's relations with the Protestant States on the Continent led her to relax the rigors of persecution, but in the meantime fleeing from Holland to England was a leap from fire to fire. The year 1575 is memorable for a special persecution. Thirty Dutch Anabaptists were arrested in London in the very act of holding a conventicle. Most of them were finally released, after a long detention in prison, but Jan Pieters and Hendrik Terwoort were burned for rejecting infant baptism and the bearing of arms. A Confession of Faith that Terwoort penned while in prison contains the first declaration in favor of complete religious liberty made on English soil:

Observe well the command of God: " Thou shalt love the stranger as thyself." Should he then who is in misery, and dwelling in a strange land, be driven thence with his companions, to their great damage? Of this Christ speaks, " Whatsoever ye would that men should do to you, do ye even so to them: for this is the law and the prophets." Oh, that they would deal with us according to natural reasonableness and evangelical truth, of which our persecutors so highly boast! For Christ and his disciples persecuted no one; on the contrary, Jesus hath thus taught, " Love your enemies, bless them that curse you," etc. This doctrine Christ left behind with his apostles, as they testify. Thus Paul, " Unto this present hour we both hunger, and thirst, and are naked, and are buffeted, and have no certain dwelling place; and labor, working with our own hands; being reviled, we bless; being persecuted, we suffer it." From all this it is clear, that those who have the one true gospel doctrine and faith will persecute no one, but will themselves be persecuted.

The writings of this period and the published sermons of English divines (such as Latimer, Cranmer, Hutchinson, Whitgift, and Coverdale) are full of references to the Anabaptists and their heresies. Occasionally some light is thrown upon the question of their teachings. Thus, in 1589, Doctor Some wrote " A Godly Treatise," in which he charged the Anabaptists with holding the following deadly errors:

That the ministers of the gospel ought to be maintained by the voluntary contributions of the people;

That the civil power has no right to make and impose ecclesiastical laws;

That people ought to have the right of choosing their own ministers;

That the high commiccion court was an anti-Christian usurpation;

That those who are qualified to preach ought not to be hindered by the civil power, etc.

Traces of the presence in England of Anabaptists of foreign origin continue during the reign of Elizabeth, but with the decline of persecution on the Continent their numbers dwindled, and they at length disappeared. They may have converted to their views a few Englishmen here and there, but they do not seem to have made any permanent impression on the English people, nor is the historical connection clear between them and the later bodies of Englishmen bearing the same name.

The last person burned at the stake in England, during the reign of James I., Edward Wightman, was an Anabaptist. Almost nothing is known of him previous to his arrest, except that he was a resident and probably a native of Leicestershire. Whether he was a member of an Anabaptist church, and if so, where the church met, is not known. He was arrested in March, 1611, and the proceedings against him occupied a whole year. In his examination fourteen specific questions were propounded, with the object of making clear his heresies. In reply to these questions he declared that he did not believe in the Trinity, that Christ is not of the same substance as the Father, but only a man; he denied that Christ took human flesh of the substance of the Virgin Mary;[1] he affirmed that the soul sleeps in the sleep of the first death as well as the body; he declared the baptism of infants to be an abominable custom; he affirmed that there ought not to be in the church the use of the sacraments of the Lord's Supper to be celebrated in the elements of bread and wine, and of baptism to be celebrated in the element of water, as they are now practised in the Church of England; but only the sacrament of baptism, to be administered in water to converts of sufficient age of understanding, converted from infidelity to the faith.

From this it is evident that Wightman's views were derived from the Continental Anabaptists, and apparently

[1] The Hofmann heresy, for which Joan Boucher also suffered. This clearly marks the connection of Wightman with the Continental Anabaptists.

from those who had come from Poland, or in some way imbibed the teachings of Socinus. He may also have derived from that source his idea about immersion, if his language implies that, which is not quite certain. For " baptism to be celebrated *in* the element of water " must be read in connection with " Lord's Supper to be celebrated *in* the elements of bread and wine." And it seems entirely probable that in the one case " in " has the force of " with " as in the other, and has no reference to the act—a conclusion made still more probable by the added phrase " as they are now practised in the Church of England." The practice of the Church of England then was to celebrate baptism in the element of water by pouring it upon the head of a babe. Wightman objected to the babe; he does not make it clear that he objected to the pouring. His death occurred April 11, 1612, and so profound was the sensation caused that no further executions for heresy occurred.

PART II

A HISTORY OF BAPTIST CHURCHES

CHAPTER XIV

THE EARLY DAYS

WITH the first decade of the seventeenth century we reach solid ground in Baptist history. Before that we must proceed by conjecture from one isolated fact to another, and many of our conclusions are open to doubt; but after 1610 we have an unbroken succession of Baptist churches, established by indubitable documentary evidence. The most that we can say of the various Anabaptist groups of the Continent, is that on the whole certain of them seem to have held those views of Scripture teaching that are fundamental in the Baptist faith of to-day. But from about the year 1641, at latest, Baptist doctrine and practice have been the same in all essential features that they are to-day. Subsequent changes have not affected the substance of faith or the chief matters of practice in the denomination as a whole.

The history of English Baptists does not begin on English soil, but in Holland. The leader in the new movement was the Rev. John Smyth. Much obscurity hangs over his early life, and he has by many writers been identified with several other men, bearing a name then as now very common. He was a pupil and friend at Cambridge University of Francis Johnson, later one of the Separatist leaders. As Johnson did not matriculate until 1579, it follows that this cannot have been the John Smyth who matriculated as sizar in 1571. John Smyth took his Master's degree in 1593, whence we may conclude that he was born not later than 1570, and possibly several years earlier. He is said to have been ordained by Bishop Wickham, of Lincoln, but he was never, as has been frequently stated, vicar of Gainsborough, as the records of that parish show. He was, however, appointed lecturer or preacher in the city of Lincoln, September 27, 1600; and though deposed as "a facetious man" by vote of the Corporation, October 13, 1602, appears to have held the office until 1605.

He tells us himself that he passed through nine months of doubt and study before deciding to leave the Church of England, but by 1606 he had reached a decision and joined himself to a company of Separatists in Gainsborough, of whom he became the recognized "teacher" —for they disliked "ministers" and all similar terms. Thomas Helwys and John Murton were the leading members of this group. A few miles distant, in the manor of Scrooby, there was another group of Separatists, in close fellowship with the Gainsborough group. Prominent among the Scrooby group were William Bradford, William Brewster, and John Robinson, the last being the "teacher." Scattered throughout the surrounding region were a score or more of adherents, who were rapidly increasing in numbers.

This was the time when James I. was vigorously making good his threat regarding sectaries in England: "I will make them conform, or I will harry them out of the land." Persecution became so violent that these Separatists despaired of maintaining themselves in England, and Thomas Helwys, whose wife had been imprisoned for her schism, induced the Gainsborough group to emigrate to Holland. They established themselves at Amsterdam, where they became the second English church, and their teacher supported himself by practising medicine.

The first English church was composed of Separatists, mostly from London, who had come to Amsterdam at various times from 1593 onward, and had as their pastor Francis Johnson, who had been a tutor of Smyth at Cambridge. Not long after the Gainsborough exodus, the church of Scrooby fled to Holland, going first to Amsterdam and thence to Leyden. Their pastor was John Robinson. It was this congregation, with certain additions, that afterward became the Pilgrims of the Mayflower.

Our concern is, however, with the second church at Amsterdam. Pastor Smyth here became acquainted, possibly for the first time, with the theology of Arminius, and here, it is also reasonable to suppose, he learned the Mennonite theory of the nature of the church. If he had had doubts before concerning infant baptism they were now confirmed into conviction that it is not warranted by the Scriptures, and that a scriptural church should consist of the regenerate only, who have been baptized on a personal confession of faith. He gave utterance to these views in a tract called " The Character of the Beast " (1609). Before this (1608) differences had arisen over a question of comparatively slight importance between the two English churches, and the result had been an interruption of their communion. Now a still more important step was taken: Smyth, Thomas Helwys, and thirty-six others formed the first church composed of Englishmen that is known to have stood for the baptism of believers only.

Smyth is generally called the " Se-Baptist," which means that he baptized himself. There can be no doubt that such was the case, since an acknowledgment of the fact still exists in his own handwriting. In this respect he resembled Roger Williams. He held that the real apostolic succession is a succession not of outward ordinances and visible organizations, but of true faith and practice. He therefore believed that the ancient, true apostolic succession had been lost, and that the only way to recover it was to begin a church anew on the apostolic model. Accordingly, having first baptized himself, he baptized Helwys and the rest, and so constituted the church. They soon after issued a Confession of Faith, Arminian in its theology, but distinct in its claims that a church should be composed only of baptized believers, and that only such should " taste of the Lord's Supper."

It is also certain that the baptism of Smyth and his followers was an affusion, for in a few months he became dissatisfied with what he had done, confessed that his Anabaptism was an error, and applied with some others for admission into a Mennonite church. A committee of Mennonite ministers was appointed to examine into the doctrine and practice of the applicants, and in their report they said: " We . . . also inquired for the foundation and form[1] of their baptism, and we have not found that there was any difference at all, neither in the one nor the other thing." Several Confessions—at least four in all—were issued by Smyth and this church, in which baptism is defined as " the external sign of the remission of sins, of dying and being made alive," as " washing with water," as " to be ministered only upon penitent and faithful persons," and the like; but nothing is said in any of them of immersion as the form of baptism.

Smyth died in 1612, but before that the church he had been instrumental in founding, now reduced to some ten members, had disappeared from Holland. Persecution seems to have been less severe in England, and Thomas

[1] Some have been inclined (so Newman, "History of Anti-pedobaptism," p. 387) to understand "form of their baptism" not to refer "to the mode of applying the water," but "rather to the words spoken in connection with the administration of the ordinance." But this is directly contravened by the authority of John Smyth himself. In his "Character of the Beast" (p. 54) he clearly makes the distinction between the *matter* of baptism, a believing subject, and the *form* of baptism, a washing with water.

Helwys, John Murton, and others returned to London, probably some time in 1611, and founded the first Anabaptist church composed of Englishmen known to have existed on English soil. This church was also Arminian in theology, and churches of this type came later to be called General Baptists, because they held to a general atonement for all men, while orthodox Calvinists then held to a "particular" atonement, for the elect only. By the year 1626 there were five such churches in England, though all were small, and in the aggregate contained about one hundred and fifty members. In 1644 they had increased to forty-seven churches, according to their opponents; possibly there were more. Once they had a fair opportunity to preach New Testament truth among their countrymen, these churches throve rapidly in England.

The fact must not be overlooked, however, that ten Baptist churches in England claim an earlier origin than this whose story has thus been told. Hill Cliff (1522), Eythorne, Coggeshall, Braintree (1550), Farringdon Road (1576), Crowle, Epworth (1599), Bridgewater, Oxford, Wedmore (1600). To substantiate these claims there is little evidence but tradition, of no great antiquity. Thomas Crosby, the earliest of our Baptist historians, who sought with praiseworthy diligence for all accessible facts, and was personally familiar with some of these localities, had either never heard such traditions or did not consider them even worthy of mention. In no case is there the smallest scrap of documentary evidence for such antiquity as is claimed. No title-deeds or records extend back much over two hundred years, few extend so far back. There is some archæological evidence, in one or two cases, to prove that a certain site was used for religious services or as a burial-place, long before the beginning of the seventeenth century. The gap between these slender premises of fact and the conclusion sought to be drawn from them is so wide that only the most robust faith could span it. One who is capable of believing in the great antiquity of English Baptist churches on evidence so slender is quite capable of believing on no evidence at all—which is the quickest and safest way. Let us return, then, to the history.

The Calvinistic or Particular Baptists had a quite different origin. The account of that origin given by Baptist historians generally, including the former editions of this work, rests on the authority of Thomas Crosby, the earliest historian of the Baptists. The documents on which Crosby depended have been made accessible, and show that he did not accurately follow his sources. Assuming the credibility of the documents—the question cannot be discussed here—the essential facts are as follows:

A congregation of Separatists, or Dissenters from the Church of England, was gathered by the Rev. Henry Jacob in London, in 1616. After some years Jacob went to Virginia and John Lathrop became the pastor. Many were added to them, and discussions rose whether the parish churches could be regarded as true churches. In 1633 there was a peaceable division on this issue, and a new church of seventeen persons was formed. This new church was evidently what we should now call a church of mixed membership; some of its members were certainly of Anabaptist views, for the record adds: " Mr. Eaton, with some others [but not all], receiving a further baptism." Mr. John Spilsbury soon became pastor of this flock, which in 1638 received another secession of six members from the Jacob church, this composed wholly of Anabaptists. Not long after, this church seems to have wholly adopted Baptist principles and practices, and is therefore entitled to be called the first Particular Baptist church in England.

Returning now to the original church of Jacob and Lathrop, we find that Mr. Lathrop also emigrated to New England, leaving the flock again without a shepherd. The records of the church then go on to say:

1640. 3rd Mo: The Church became two by mutuall consent just half being with Mr. P. Barebone, & ye other halfe with Mr. H. Jessey. Mr. Richd Blunt wth him being convinced of Baptism yt also it ought to be by dipping in ye Body into ye Water, resembling Burial and riseing again Col. 2. 12, Rom. 6, 4 had sober Conferance about in ye Church, & then wth some of the forenamed who also were so convinced; and after Prayer & Conferance about their so enjoying it, none having then so practiced it in England to professed Believers, & hearing that some in and ye Nether Lands had so practiced, they agreed and sent over Mr. ich'd Blunt (who understood Dutch) with Letters of Commendation, and who was kindly accepted there, and Returned wth Letters from them Jo: Batten a teacher there, and from that Church to such as sent him.

1641. They proceed on therein, viz Those Persons yt ware perswaded Baptism should be by dipping ye Body had mett in two Companies, and did intend so to meet after this, all those Agreed to proceed alike togeather: and then manifesting (not by any formal Words) a Covenant (wch Word was Scrupled by some of them) but by mutuall desires and agreement each Testified: Those two Companyes did set apart one to Baptize the rest: so it was Solemnly performed by them.

Mr. Blunt baptized Mr. Blacklock yt was a Teacher amongst them, and Mr. Blunt being baptized, he and Mr. Blacklock Baptized ye rest of their friends yt ware so minded, and many being added to them they increased much.

Another method of reviving immersion was taken by the Baptists of this period, as their writings bear witness. Thomas Crosby has stated it very accurately in these words:

But the greatest number of the English Baptists, and the more judicious, looked upon all this [Blunt's mission to Holland] as needless trouble, and what proceeded from the old popish

doctrine of right to administer the sacraments by an uninterrupted succession, which neither the Church of Rome nor the
Church of England, much less the modern dissenters, could prove
to be with them. They affirmed, therefore, and practised accordingly, that after a general corruption of baptism, an unbaptized person might warrantably baptize, and so begin a
reformation (1 : 103).

This was apparently the method adopted by the Spilsbury church, for its pastor strongly argued against the
theory of succession, and upheld the right of a church
of Christ by its own act to recover lost ordinances.
" Where there is a beginning," he pithily says, " some
must be first."

In these two ways the practice of immei ing believers
in Christ was introduced among those churches that a
few years later came to be known as Particular Baptists.
We have no such definite account of the introduction of
immersion among the Arminian churches, but we have
no sufficient grounds for supposing that they anticipated
their Calvinistic brethren. The only thing that points in
that direction is a passage in " Religion's Peace," a book
written by Leonard Busher in 1614. Busher may have
been at one time connected with the Helwys congregation at Amsterdam, and his book bears internal evidence
of having been written and published there, but we cannot connect him more closely than this with the Baptists
in England. In his book he says: " And such as shall
willingly and gladly receive it [the gospel] he hath commanded to be baptized in the water; that is, dipped for
dead in the water." It is not a perfectly safe inference,
however, from this teaching that there was a corresponding practice. That sort of logic would prove that both
Luther and Calvin were immersionists, and lead us into
all sorts of absurdities if it were consistently applied
throughout the history of the church. Nothing is

A Group of Radical Leaders

MUNSTER—THE CHURCH OF ST. LAMBERT

Menno Simons

WILLIAM OF ORANGE

WILLIAM KIFFEN

The true and Lively Effigies of Mr.
HAN: KNOLLIS Minister of ye̅ Gospell
Aged 67. Yeares.

Oliver Cromwell

JOHN BUNYAN

commoner than to find lack of correspondence between teaching and practice.

The churches afterwards known as General Baptists had from the first maintained close relations with the Mennonite churches of Holland. Their members, on going to Holland, were received without question into the Mennonite churches. Certain of their church disputes were referred to the Mennonite churches for arbitration. These facts indicate that they were agreed on the practice of baptism, which we know to have been aspersion among the Mennonites. But from the middle of the seventeenth century, or a little before, all traces of this union cease. The only reasonable explanation of the facts is that given by Mennonite writers, namely, the adoption of immersion by the English churches, which thus practically pronounced their Mennonite brethren unbaptized.

For many years we find that the question of baptism was still debated among these English churches. Some, who agreed with their brethren in all other things, had not yet adopted the practice of immersion and were called the Old Men, or Aspersi; while the others were called the New Men, or Immersi, " because they were overwhelmed in their rebaptization." [1] So late as 1653 we find the same difference of opinion still persisting. A Baptist writer of that date complains of what he calls a " mere demi-reformation that is made on this point on a party of men in Lincolnshire and elsewhere (of whom I suppose there are several congregations), who having long since discovered the true way of baptism as to the subjects, namely: That professing believers only, and not any infants, are to be baptized, but remaining ignorant of the true way and form of administering the ordinance, are fallen into the

[1] B. Rynes, "*Mercurius Rusticus.*" London, 1646, p. 21.

frivolous way of sprinkling believers; which to do is as much no baptism at all, as to dip infants is no baptism of Christ's ordaining. Which people, for whose sakes, as well as for others, I write this, will be persuaded, I hope, in time, to be as to the outward form, not almost only, but altogether Christians, and rest no longer in that mere midway, mongrel reformation." [1] This is the last known case of the kind, and from about this time it is certain that all the Anabaptist churches of England adopted immersion, and are thenceforth properly called Baptists.

A great mass of pamphlets and books relating to baptism began to pour from the presses of England from 1640 onward. This revival of the practice of immersion by the Baptist churches is the only and also the sufficient explanation of this phenomenon. The controversy thus precipitated also accounts for the importance thenceforth assumed by the question of baptism in Baptist Confessions and in polemical writings by the Baptists of this period. Others had before this practised immersion, being convinced that it is taught by the Scriptures, without teaching that immersion is essential to valid baptism. The opposition of the other English sects to the novel practice of immersion developed the Baptist doctrine rapidly. The other Separatists of the period with one accord attacked immersion as new-fangled, unnecessary, immodest, dangerous to life, and the like. Baptists retorted by asserting that nothing else than immersion could be accepted as baptism. When the Continental Anabaptists practised immersion, no special opposition was made to their practice, and they were therefore never impelled to lay any special emphasis upon its necessity. In this one difference of circumstance is the full explanation of the difference of doctrine obtaining between the immersing Anabaptists and the modern Baptists.

[1] " Baby Baptism mere Babyism," by S. Fisher. London, 1653, p. 464.

By the year 1644 the number of Particular Baptist churches had increased to seven. In that year these seven churches united in issuing a Confession of Faith, composed of fifty articles, which is one of the chief landmarks of Baptist history.

The Confession, besides giving a brief exposition of gospel truth according to the Calvinistic theology, pronounces baptism " an ordinance of the New Testament given by Christ, to be dispensed upon persons professing faith, or that are made disciples; who, upon profession of faith, ought to be baptized, and afterward to partake of the Lord's Supper." It then specifies:

That the way and manner of the dispensing this ordinance is dipping or plunging the body under water; it being a sign, must answer the thing signified, which is, that interest the saints have in the death, burial, and resurrection of Christ: and that as certainly as the body is buried under water and risen again, so certainly shall the bodies of the saints be raised by the power of Christ in the day of the resurrection, to reign with Christ.

And a note to this section adds: " The word *baptizo* signifies to dip or plunge (yet so as convenient garments be upon both the administrator and subject, with all modesty)." English Baptists were accused by their opponents of baptizing converts in a state of nakedness, and doing other scandalous things, hence the statement in parentheses was necessary, and the 1651 edition of the Confession adds these words: " Which is also our practice, as many eye-witnesses can testify."

The Confessions issued before this time are not so explicit in defining baptism as immersion, but they are equally plain in placing baptism before participation in the Lord's Supper. One of the fourfold Confessions issued by the Smyth-Helwys church in Holland says: " The Holy Supper, according to the institution of Christ, is to be administered to the baptized." Indeed, in the whole history of Baptists not a Confession can be produced that advocates the invitation or admission to the Lord's table of the unbaptized. Nevertheless, some English Baptist churches, being formed of Separatist elements, did from the first claim and exercise liberty in respect to this ordinance.

The Confession of 1644 is outspoken also in the advocacy of religious liberty as the right, and of good citizenship as the duty, of every Christian man. The following article is worth quoting in full, as the first publication of the doctrine of freedom of conscience, in an official document representing a body of associated churches:

XLVIII. A civil magistracy is an ordinance of God, set up by him for the punishment of evil-doers, and for the praise of them that do well; and that in all lawful things, commanded by them, subjection ought to be given by us in the Lord, not only for the wrath, but for conscience' sake; and that we are to make supplications and prayers for kings, and all that are in authority, that under them we may live a quiet and peaceable life in all godliness and honesty.

The supreme magistracy of this kingdom we acknowledge to be King and Parliament. . . And concerning the worship of God, there is but one lawgiver. . . which is Jesus Christ. . . So it is the magistrate's duty to tender the liberty of men's consciences (Eccl. 8: 8), (which is the tenderest thing unto all conscientious men, and most dear unto them, and without which all other liberties will not be worth the naming, much less the enjoying), and to protect all under them from all wrong, injury, oppression, and molestation. . . And as we cannot do anything contrary to our understandings and consciences, so neither can we forbear the doing of that which our understandings and consciences bind us to do. And if the magistrates should require us to do otherwise, we are to yield our persons in a passive way to their power, as the saints of old have done (James 5: 4).

This is a great landmark, not only of Baptists, but of the progress of enlightened Christianity. Those who published to the world this teaching, then deemed revolutionary and dangerous, held, in all but a few points of small importance, precisely those views of Christian truth that are held by Baptists to-day. For substance of doctrine, any of us might subscribe to it without a moment's hesitation. On the strength of this one fact, Baptists might fairly claim that, whatever might have been said by isolated individuals before, they were the pioneer body among modern Christian denominations to advocate the right of all men to worship God, each according to the dictates of his own conscience, without let or hindrance from any earthly power.

Among the names signed to this Confession are two of special significance in this early period of Baptist progress in England—William Kiffen and Hanserd Knollys. Kiffen was born in London, in 1616. His family was of Welsh extraction. He lost his parents by the plague that scourged London in 1625, and was taken care of by relatives, whom he charged with misappropriating his patrimony. They apprenticed him to "a very mean calling" (brewer), and in his fifteenth year he ran away from his master. While wandering aimlessly about town, he saw people going into church and went in with them. The sermon on the fifth commandment, and the duties of servants to masters, caused him to return to his master, and also provoked in him a desire to hear other Puritan ministers. Soon he was convicted of sin, and after an experience not unlike that which Bunyan relates in his "Grace Abounding," he found peace in believing. He joined himself to an independent congregation (probably that church of Henry Jacob, of which so much has already been said), and some time afterwards left this to join the Baptist church of which John Spilsbury had become pastor. Not long thereafter he became pastor of a newly constituted Baptist church in London. This was certainly prior to 1644, but how long we do not know.

About the same time that he became a Baptist preacher, Kiffen also became a merchant. His first venture was in a trading voyage to Holland, in 1643, and two years later he engaged in business in that country with a young man of his congregation, and he adds: " It pleased God so to bless our endeavors, as from scores of pounds to bring it to many hundreds and thousands of pounds." This is his modest way of saying that he became one of the wealthiest and most influential merchants of London. He himself valued his success mainly because it enabled him to preach the gospel with less hindrance, and he used his large means generously to propagate the truth as he understood it. To his shrewd liberality the Baptists of England owed much of their progress during the seventeenth century.

Kiffen's wealth exposed him to many persecutions, but also, it is likely, obtained for him many favors from those in power. He was the friend of kings and high officials, and though he doubtless valued such favor, he not infrequently found it costly. It is related that on one occasion Charles II. requested of this rich subject a " loan " of forty thousand pounds. Kiffen's ready wit did not fail him in this emergency. He answered, with all respect, that he could not possibly *lend* so large a sum, but he hoped his Majesty would honor him by accepting a *gift* of ten thousand pounds. His Majesty was ever ready to bestow that particular form of honor on anybody, and graciously accepted the offer. Kiffen used to relate the story with glee in after years, and declared that by his timely liberality he had saved thirty thousand pounds. Full of years and labors and honors, Kiffen died in 1701.

Hanserd Knollys, one of the most godly, learned, and

laborious among the English Baptists of this time, was born at Chalkwell, Lincolnshire. His parents were religious people, as well as possessed of some wealth. He was prepared by a private tutor and then sent to the University of Cambridge, where he took his degree in due course. Having had a religious training from boyhood, he was in a condition of mind and heart to be impressed by sermons that he heard while a student, and he was converted. His piety while at the university was marked, and in his after years this early promise was quite fulfilled.

After graduation, he was master of a school at Gainsborough for a while; but in June, 1629, he was ordained by the bishop of Peterborough, first deacon, then presbyter, of the Church of England. Not long after, the bishop of Lincoln presented him to the living of Humberstone, where he engaged most zealously in the work of a parish minister. He ordinarily preached four times on Sunday, and besides preached on every holiday. Both his training and natural inclinations inclined him toward the Puritan party in the church, and after some three years of service, his conscientious scruples regarding the wearing of the surplice, the sign of the cross in baptism, admitting to the Lord's Supper persons of notoriously wicked lives, and the like, made his position untenable. He had only to stifle his convictions, to compound with his conscience, to retain his place of honor and comfort in the church, with fair prospects of promotion. Bu, he could not do this, and he manfully resigned his living to his bishop, frankly stating his reasons; and so much was he respected for his honesty, that the bishop connived at his continuing to preach in the diocese, without wearing the surplice or reading the service, though such procedure was strictly forbidden by law.

This was a position impossible to maintain long; a

man who did this was neither one thing nor another. Accordingly, about 1636, Knollys joined himself to the Separatists, as those Puritans were called who had been compelled by conscience to come out of the Church of England. This exposed him to active persecution, and he determined to emigrate to New England, where he understood that the Separatists had liberty. He landed in Boston, in 1638, after a voyage of much hardship. It is related of him, as showing how low his fortunes had ebbed, that by the time he had embarked on shipboard he had but six brass farthings left; but his wife produced five pounds that she had saved in happier days, and they were enabled to reach the new land.

Soon after his arrival he had an opportunity to go to the new settlement of Piscataway (afterward called Dover), in New Hampshire, which needed a pastor. We have testimony to show that while here he opposed the baptism of infants, and probably for this reason Cotton Mather classes him among the Anabaptists. Mather, however, bears testimony to the excellent character of Knollys.

In 1641, Knollys was summoned home to England by his aged father, and he was so little of a Baptist as yet that he became a member of the Separatist congregation, of which at that time Henry Jessey was pastor. The records of that church inform us that in 1643 Knollys was unwilling to have his infant child baptized, which led to conferences on the subject and finally to a division, sixteen members withdrawing and forming a Baptist church. Whether it was this church or another that he gathered is uncertain, but in 1645 he was formally ordained pastor of a Baptist church in London, and from that time was known as one of the efficient leaders of this people.

The Episcopal hierarchy had been abolished, and " liberty of prophesying " was now supposed to be enjoyed by all godly ministers. But the Presbyterians were determined on the ruins of the Church of England to erect an establishment of their own, and to silence all who did not agree with them. For a time Knollys preached in the parish churches, but was summoned to give account of himself before a committee of divines at Westminster. They forbade him to preach, but he only ceased to preach in the parish churches, gathering a congregation in a house of his own at Great St. Helen's, London. This was a sample of the " liberty " experienced by our Baptist forefathers under the dominion of the Presbyterians and the Long Parliament.

After the Restoration, Knollys suffered long-continued hardships for the sake of the gospel. His popularity as a preacher was so great, and his influence so generally acknowledged by Nonconformists, that to silence him was a special object of the upholders of the Church of England and the Act of Uniformity. He was imprisoned many times; even in his eighty-fourth year he was in jail for six months, an act of revenge on the part of James II. because Knollys refused to use his influence with Baptists and other Dissenters to gain their approval for the illegal dispensations issued by that monarch. To escape these persecutions, Knollys and his family were obliged to change their residence often, and once he left England and spent some time in Holland and Germany.

After a short illness, Knollys died in his ninety-third year, having given an example of constancy to his convictions that is worthy of all admiration. A Puritan to the core, somewhat narrow and stern according to our notions to-day, he was yet a very lovable man, and compelled the respect of even those who most widely differed from him in matters of faith and practice.

Both William Kiffen and Hanserd Knollys are known

to have been buried in Bunhill Fields, London, where also the mortal remains of John Bunyan rest. Bunyan's tomb is still pointed out to the curious visitor, but all trace of the others has disappeared. A stone once marked the grave of Kiffen, and its inscription has been preserved by a diligent local historian, and that is now his sole memorial.

CHAPTER XV

THE contest between Charles I. and his people had come to an acute crisis before the Confession of 1644 was printed. He had showed, under the tutelage of Laud in the Church, the same imperious temper and the same persecuting spirit that he showed under Strafford's counsel in the State. It was all one to him whether Hampden refused to pay ship-money, or the obstinate Scots refused to accept his liturgy. Baptists fared hard during the earlier years of his reign, but from the meeting of the Long Parliament, in November, 1640, they had peace, and increased rapidly in numbers. Almost to a man they were supporters of the Parliamentary cause, which was the cause of liberty, religious as well as civil. Large numbers of Baptists took service in the armies of Parliament, some of whom rose to a high rank, and were much trusted by the Lord Protector, Cromwell.

The period of the civil war was thus one of comparative immunity for those who had been persecuted, yet the toleration practically enjoyed by the Baptists was not a legal status; they still had no civil rights that their stronger neighbors were bound to respect; and it was only the dire necessity of uniting all forces against the king that led the Presbyterian Parliament to refrain from active measures of repression. The leading Westminster divines rebuked Parliament in sermons and pamphlets for suffering the Baptists to increase, but political considerations were for a time paramount. A single incident illustrates the Presbyterian idea of liberty of conscience at this time. In 1646, one Morgan, a Roman Catholic, unable to obtain priests' orders in England, went to Rome for them, and on his return, was hanged, drawn, and quartered, for this heinous offense. The unspeakable papist could not be tolerated on any terms by the Presbyterian party.

Against a general toleration the Presbyterians protested vigorously. Thomas Edwards declared that " Could the devil effect a toleration, he would think he had gained well by the Reformation, and made a good exchange of the hierarchy to have a toleration for it." Even the saintly Baxter said: " I abhor unlimited liberty and toleration of all, and think myself easily able to prove the wickedness of it." Well might Milton, incensed by such teachings and by attempts in Parliament to give them effect, break forth in his memorable protest, moved by a righteous indignation that could not find expression in honeyed words or courteous phrases:

> Dare ye for this adjure the civil sword
> To force our consciences, that Christ set free,
> And ride us with a classic hierarchy?

And with bitter truth he added:

> New Presbyter is but old Priest writ large.

Not in vain was his subsequent appeal to Cromwell for protection from these wolves in sheep's clothing, who had broken down one tyranny only to erect on its base another more odious:

> Peace hath her victories
> No less renowned than war; new foes arise,
> Threat'ning to bind our souls with secular chains;
> Help us to save free conscience from the paw
> Of hireling wolves, whose gospel is their maw.

Nothing but the overthrow of the Long Parliament, and with it the Presbyterian domination, prevented a more tyrannous and implacable persecution than any that disgraces the fair page of England's annals. One of the last acts of the Presbyterian party was to pass a law (1648) making death the penalty for eight errors in doctrine, including the denial of the Trinity, and prescribing indefinite imprisonment for sixteen other errors, one of which was the denial of infant baptism.

Fortunately for the Baptists, the furious extremists among the Presbyterians were never able to do more than occasionally annoy those whom they so cordially detested. It is related of William Kiffen that on July 12, 1655, he was brought before the Lord Mayor, charged with violation of the statute against blasphemies and heresies, in that he had preached "that the baptism of infants was unlawful." The accused merchant-preacher was treated with great consideration by the mayor, who, on the plea of being very busy, deferred further consideration of the case. There is nothing to indicate that Mr. Kiffen ever heard more about the matter. Others, less powerful, were by no means so fortunate.

But the excesses of the Presbyterian party hastened its downfall. The real power in the State was the army, composed mainly of Independents, but containing many Baptists. As the revolution proceeded, it inevitably became a military despotism, the head of the army exercising the civil authority more or less under forms of law.

During the Protectorate a fair measure of religious liberty prevailed. Cromwell himself came nearer than any public man of his time to adopting the Baptist doctrine of equal liberty of conscience for all men. He came, at least, to hold that a toleration of all religious views—such as existed among Protestants, that is to say—was both right and expedient; though he seems to have had no insuperable objections to a Presbyterian or Independent Church, established by law and maintained by the State. He was compelled to maintain a State religion, but he maintained it in the interest of no one sect. He admitted all whom we now call evangelical Christians to an equal footing in religious privileges, appointing a committee of Triers, of different sects, to examine the qualifications of incumbents and candidates. The only standard these Triers were permitted to set up was godliness and ability to edify; no minister was to be either appointed or excluded for his views of doctrine or polity. Several Baptists served as Triers, and many others received benefices during this time—a very inconsistent course for Baptists to take, and one that it is not easy to pardon, for they sinned against light.

From time to time Baptists were accused of sedition, and various pretexts were found to justify their persecution; but Cromwell could never be induced to move against them. It has been reserved for writers of our own day to press these stale slanders against a loyal and upright people. By such it has been urged, with insistence and bitterness, that the Baptists were not sincere in their professions of zealous devotion to the principle of liberty of conscience for all; or, at least, that the declarations already quoted from their Confessions and from their published writings did not represent the Baptists as a whole—that there were Baptists as intolerant and as desirous of persecuting their opponents as the most zealous Presbyterian of them all.

The events of 1653 are said to furnish full confirmation of this view of the case. In that year the "Rump" Parliament was dissolved, and Cromwell was proclaimed Lord Protector, according to the provisions of an Instrument of Government framed by a convention he had called for the purpose of devising a scheme to regulate the affairs of the nation. It would seem that some of the Baptists were ardent republicans, and in these proceedings of Cromwell they saw only the workings of his ambition to be king. We know that four years later certain Baptists protested against the proposition to confer this title upon him, and that their protest had weight. Some of them protested now; and the Rev. Vavasor Powell denounced Cromwell from the pulpit at a meeting in Blackfriars of certain Fifth Monarchy men. There were fears also for a time of trouble in Ireland from the Baptists, who were reported to be extremely disaffected with the new government. On these facts a charge is based that a part of the Baptists, at least, were disposed toward a religious movement that must have resulted in persecution.

The simple fact is that the Baptists, as a body, were loyal to the Commonwealth and its head as the *de facto* government of England; and the few who were disaffected opposed Cromwell on civil grounds. Among these was Gen. Thomas Harrison (who, however, did not become a Baptist until 1657). This party was republican and suspected Cromwell of kingly ambitions, and hence opposed him. Certain of these men, notably Harrison, also believed that the time was drawing near for the Fifth Monarchy. These were enthusiasts, misled by the study of prophecy—as had happened in the former ages of the church, among the medieval Anabaptists and the earlier Montanists, for example—into a notion that the last times were at hand, and that Christ was about to set up an earthly kingdom and reign with his saints a thousand years. Men's laws and traditions were to be altogether swept away, and the world was to be ruled by the law of Christ. This would, of itself, exclude the idea of persecution when once this kingdom should have been established; and before its establishment persecution would not have been possible. It is not true that the Fifth Monarchy men, as a body, believed in setting up this kingdom by the sword, as their public declarations clearly show. To prove that a Baptist was concerned in these Fifth Monarchy demonstrations does not show that he cherished any idea of punishing dissent by any form of persecution; still less does it show that his brethren sympathized with any persecuting notions.

But we have abundant testimony that the great body of the Baptists had no sympathy with the chiliastic ideas that lay at the basis of the Fifth Monarchy movement; that they utterly condemned all conspiracies against the *de facto* government; and that they exhorted all their brethren to follow their example in rendering loyal obedience to the powers that be. An extant letter from William Kiffen and others to the Baptists in Ireland gives interesting evidence as to the feeling of the English Baptists. The writers express sorrow that " there is raised up in many amongst you (the Baptists in Ireland) a spirit of great dissatisfaction and opposition against this present authority," and exhort them to think better of their determination to protest publicly against Cromwell. They say :

And this we are clearly satisfied, in that the principles held forth by those meeting in Blackfriars, under pretense of the Fifth Monarchy, or setting up the kingdom of Christ, to which many of those lately in power adhered, had it been prosecuted, would have brought as great dishonor to the name of God, and shame and contempt to the whole nation, as we think could have been imagined.

The letter closes with a solemn appeal in these words:

We do therefore beseech you for the Lord's sake and for the truth's sake, that it be not evil spoken of men, seriously weigh these things; for surely if the Lord gives us hearts we have a large advantage put into our hands to give a public testimony in the face of the world. That our principles are not such as they have been generally judged by most men to be; which is, that we deny authority and would pull down all magistracy. And if any trouble should arise, either with you or us, in the nation, which might proceed to the shedding of blood, would not it all be imputed and charged upon the baptized churches? And what grief and sorrow would be administered to us, your brethren, to hear the name of God blasphemed by ungodly men through your means? This we can say, that we have not had any occasion of sorrow from any of the churches in this nation with whom we have communion; they, with one heart, desiring to bless God for their liberty, and with all willingness to be subject to the present authority. And we trust to hear the same of you, having lately received an epistle written to us by all the churches amongst you, pressing us to a strict walking with God, and warning of us to take heed of formality, the love of this world; that we slight not our mercy in the present liberties we enjoy.

Whether to this appeal or to the sober second thought is to be attributed the subsequent quiet of the Irish Baptists is not quite certain, but a letter in Thurloe's " State Papers " informs us that there was no further trouble:

As to your grand affairs in Ireland, especially as to the Anabaptist party, I am confident they are much misconceived in England. Upon the change of affairs here was discontent enough, but very little animosity. For certainly never yet any faction, so well fortified by all the offices, military and civil, almost in the whole nation, did quit their interest with more silence.

The Baptists were conscious that toleration was not likely to continue long unless the principle were incorporated in the law of the land. They continued in their writings and Confessions, therefore, to urge the duty of all Christians to tolerate those who differed from them in religious belief. With this they uniformly coupled a disclaimer of any such doctrine of liberty as implied license, and enforced the duty of the Christian to render obedience to the civil magistrate in all secular affairs.

In the year 1660 Charles Stuart was brought back with great rejoicing to the throne of his fathers. The Baptists must have seen in this event the death blow to their hopes of religious liberty, yet it does not appear that they raised voice or hand against the new king, though they were far from trusting his smooth words and promises of toleration. He was hardly seated on his throne when one Thomas Venner and a band of Fifth Monarchists and other irreconcilables made an insurrection, whose object was the dethronement of the new monarch and the setting up of the kingdom of Christ on earth. The slanders of the time accuse the Baptists of complicity in this disturbance. Beyond the repetition of these stale slanders there is not a particle of evidence producible that any Baptists took part in the insurrection. Conclusive evidence that they did not we have in their protest made at the time, and in the verdict of every candid Pedobaptist historian who has carefully gone over the facts. Venner himself was a Pedobaptist, and it is not known that a single Baptist was among his followers. Nevertheless, persecution on account of alleged disloyalty and heresies was active and bitter.

The death of Thomas Harrison cannot, however, be called a case of persecution. His case stands by itself. The difference between a patriot and a rebel has been defined somewhat as follows: " The man who succeeds is a patriot; the man who fails is a rebel." If George Washington had failed, he would have been hanged like Robert Emmet, and schoolboys would now be reading books in which his treason would be appropriately condemned. Thomas Harrison failed at last, after a period of complete success, and he went to his grave so loaded down with ignominy that few have had courage since to plead his cause. He deserves a rehearing in the court of the world's justice.

He was born in Cheshire, and his father was a butcher; hence, as Mrs. Hutchinson sneeringly remarked in her " Memoirs," he was " a mean man's son." Nor does Mistress Lucy fail to record several ancedotes, illustrating his love of display and fine clothes, as a foil to the perfections of Colonel Hutchinson. Nevertheless, when the pinch came, Harrison, the " mean man's son," played the Christian hero, while the well-born colonel played the coward and meanly truckled to save his life—and succeeded, but lost his honor forever.

Little is known of Harrison's early life. He must have had a fair education, and became clerk to a solicitor. Early in the struggle between Charles I. and his Parliament he enlisted in the parliamentary army, beginning as cornet, the equivalent of a second lieutenant of cavalry. By bravery and fidelity he was advanced to the rank of captain, and having attracted the notice of Cromwell, was made a colonel of cavalry after the remodeling of the army. It was the policy thereafter to promote officers who, besides military capacity, were men of piety and intelligence, and Harrison rose fast, until he became major-general and ranked next to Cromwell himself in the respect of the army. By various means, in none of which do his enemies charge him with any dishonor, he acquired a considerable estate, and lived in a manner becoming the second man in England. It is this rapid promotion and access of power that doubtless roused the jealousy of the Hutchinsons and that explain the references to Harrison in pious Mrs. Lucy's " Memoirs."

When the war was over and Charles I. was a prisoner, the question rose what to do with him. The army was tired of fighting, and demanded summary measures. This demand was resisted until it was discovered that Charles was plotting for further uprisings on his behalf, and then his fate was sealed. By vote of Parliament, a high court of justice was appointed to try the king. Harrison was one of the most prominent members of the court, and his name was signed in bold characters to the death warrant of Charles I. The verdict of history is that while Charles Stuart richly deserved his fate, it was a political blunder thus to make of him a martyr; but that Harrison could not be expected to see at the time. His act was that of patriot who did what he believed to be best for his country. It is difficult to read with patience what has been written by many historians concerning the death of a king who plunged his country into civil war because he neither could nor would keep his word, and who deserved forty deaths by his perfidy and cruelty.

But Harrison had no mind to have King Noll substituted for King Charles; he had had enough of kings, and was for a republic. So was the army. Cromwell's doings were regarded with great suspicion; his title of Lord Protector was looked upon as a preliminary to assuming a higher title; his government was more arbitrary and despotic than that of the Stuarts. Harrison and the army were uneasy and became estranged from their former leader. So near to an open breach did they come that twice, as a matter of precaution, Cromwell imprisoned Harrison for a time, without any warrant but his sword, with no accusation, and finally released him without trial. At length Cromwell was compelled to give a definite refusal to the request, doubtless made with his own connivance and at his desire, that he would assume the title and state of king. The refusal was made with many sighs, but the army was hopelessly opposed, and Harrison in this matter represented the army. It was due to his firmness that the house of Cromwell did not succeed the house of Stuart on the throne of England.

General Harrison and his wife were baptized in 1657, in the dead of winter, when it was so cold that the ice had to be broken for the immersion. This was but three years before his death, and he was never so identified with Baptists as has been commonly supposed, though he had rather inclined toward that despised body of Christians for years before he joined them.

After the restoration, Harrison well knew that he could expect no mercy. The regicides, as the judges of Charles I. were called, were expressly excepted from all proclamations of amnesty. Nevertheless, he refused either to fly or to truckle, but remained quietly at home, calmly awaiting the worst. He had not long to wait. He was arrested, sent to the Tower, and soon after tried. He was permitted to make no defense, and an executioner stood at his side in the dock with a halter in his hand. His condemnation was inevitable, but English courts of justice were never so disgraced, even in the days of the brutal Jeffreys, as by the means taken to secure it.

The sentence of death was carried out with equal barbarity. We have accounts of it from two eye-witnesses, Samuel Pepys and General Ludlow. Both agree that Harrison bore himself with calmness and fortitude. He was first hanged, then cut down while still living, his bowels cut out and thrown into the fire before his eyes; then his head was cut off, his body divided into quarters, and these gory members displayed in public places. And this in Christian England, in the year 1660! No wonder that, as Ludlow says, Harrison's bearing throughout his trial and execution was such " that even his enemies were astonished and confounded." They alleged nothing discreditable in his life, and his death was as honorable to him as it was disgraceful to the people of England.

Nor was the case of John James one of persecution in form, though there is every reason to believe it was such in fact. He was arrested while preaching to his flock, a Seventh-day Baptist church in London, and brought to trial on the charge of treason. The evidence against him seems to be rank perjury, attributing to him such sayings as that " the king was a bloody tyrant, a bloodsucker, a bloodthirsty man," that " he much feared they had not improved their opportunity when they had the power in their hands; that it would not be long before they had power again, and then they would improve it better." Every effort was made to induce some of the congregation to confirm these charges, but they unanimously maintained that they never heard such words. But there was no great difficulty in suborning wretches to swear away the life of a Dissenting preacher, and he was speedily found guilty. On the 26th of November he was hanged, drawn, and quartered at Tyburn, and his head was placed on a pole near his meeting-house in Whitechapel.

It is probably unjust to hold Charles II. responsible for the persecutions that disgraced his reign. There is no good reason to suppose him insincere in his Breda declaration of " a liberty to tender consciences, and that no man shall be disquieted or called in question for differences of opinion in matters of religion, which do not disturb the peace of the kingdom." The good faith of his promise, in the same declaration, to approve any measure of toleration that his Parliament might pass cannot be questioned, for he was anxious that such a measure might be enacted, so that the Roman Catholics of England might enjoy toleration.

But the first Parliament of Charles was composed largely of young men, not old enough to remember the misrule of the first Charles and his ministers, but distinctly remembering the harshness and insolence of the Puritan rule. Vindictive legislation was certain to be enacted by such a body, and neither the king nor his advisers could do much to restrain these anti-Puritan legislators. A new Act of Uniformity reënacted the prayer-book of Elizabeth, with a few modifications, and required that every minister who had not received Episcopal ordination should procure such orders before August 24, 1662. On that day, the anniversary of the massacre of St. Bartholomew, two thousand of the most learned and godly ministers in England were driven from their pulpits—a loss from which the Church of England has never recovered to this day.

A series of laws was now passed against those who refused conformity to the Established Church and its rites. In 1663 the Conventicle Act forbade all religious meetings in private houses of more than five persons not belonging to the family. In 1665 the Five Mile Act prohibited any Dissenting minister from going within five miles of any borough or corporate town. In 1673 the Test Act excluded from all public offices every one who could not produce a certificate from a clergyman that he had within a year partaken of the communion according to the rites of the Church of England. By these laws, those who refused, for conscience' sake, to conform to the church established by law were deprived of all their religious and a great part of their civil rights.

Doubtless Charles II. had promised more than any mortal could have performed; doubtless, also, he might have performed more had he cared to do it. These were not laws after his heart—they bore too hard on Romanists for that—but as he was powerless to protect them, he cared little that all other Dissenters from the Church of England were harshly treated. Baptists did not fare harder than many others. If they kept perfectly quiet they were not molested; but if they assembled for religious meetings they became violators of law, and the man who preached to them was reasonably certain of a long incarceration, if he did not receive stripes and the stocks as well. Yet in spite of this persecution, Baptists increased in numbers rapidly. Britons are a sturdy folk, and rather disposed to sympathize with one who is hit hard; so the more Baptists were forbidden to meet, the more people flocked to their meetings.

The typical Baptist preacher of the time was John Bunyan, a man of the common people, a tinker by trade, one who knew little literature but his English Bible, but who knew that from lid to lid as few know it in these days. We learn of his early life only from his own account: that he was wild, irreligious, fonder of sports than of the church, is plain; but his self-accusations of desperate wickedness we may discount heavily. When a man calls himself the vilest of sinners he always uses the words in a strict theological sense, and would quickly resent being charged with actual vileness, as Bunyan did, when he hotly denied the charge that he had been unchaste. After a long conflict of soul, in which he more than once gave himself up as eternally lost, Bunyan was at length soundly converted. He was never a very orthodox Baptist; he seems to have had his children christened in the Established Church, and it is uncertain whether he was himself ever baptized on profession of faith; he repudiated the name Anabaptist or Baptist as the badge of a sect, and desired to be called merely a Christian; he vigorously promulgated and defended the practice of communing with the unbaptized; yet in spite of these vagaries his fundamental notions were those of a Baptist. As a preacher he had great influence in his day, but his chief work was done with the pen. It is one of the marvels of literature that a man of such antecedents and training should have written books that from the day of publication took an undisputed rank among the classics of our language. The "Pilgrim's Progress," the hardly less popular "Holy War," and "Grace Abounding," are a trio not to be matched in the history of Christianity.

This achievement of Bunyan's we probably owe to the fact that his active evangelical work was interrupted by a long imprisonment, amounting with several short intervals to about thirteen years. His crime was the preaching of the gospel, nothing more; but he would have been released much sooner had he been willing to pledge himself not to offend again. This the sturdy preacher would not do; if he had the opportunity again he must preach, and so he avowed; consequently in prison he stayed until the administration of the law was greatly relaxed, and he was set free with a multitude of others in like case.

It is to his third and last imprisonment that we owe his immortal allegory—a book rendered into more languages than any other save the Bible itself; a book which, next to the Bible, has been the most effective teacher of peasant and prince; which has been the never-failing delight of childhood, has comforted our weary hours in manhood, and will be our treasure in old age. As our experience broadens and deepens we shall see new beauties in it, for it is a book of which it may be truly said that it "was not of an age, but for all time."

How many of us have taken the journey with Christian, not in imagination merely, but in sober fact. We have borne the same intolerable burden, have entered, like him, the little wicket-gate at Evangelist's bidding— falling perchance, by the way, into the Slough of Despond, or misled by Mr. Worldly Wiseman's bad advice—and have, like him, lost our heavy load at the foot of the cross. We have had to climb the Hill Difficulty, and not a few of us have been seduced into By-path

Meadows, only to fall into the clutches of Giant Despair, and to be cast into Doubting Castle. We have been tempted by the gay shows of Vanity Fair, and have passed through the dangers of the Enchanted Ground. We have been cheered on our way by Hopeful and Faithful, instructed by Interpreter, and entertained at the House Beautiful. On one day we have caught glimpses of the Delectable Mountains, only on the next to enter the Valley of Humiliation, and fight for our lives with Apollyon. We have seen one and another of our companions pass through the dark river, whose waters our feet must soon enter, and happy are we to whom a vision has been granted of the Shining Ones, conducting them into the gates of the City which, when we have seen, we have wisht ourselves among them.

The events of the reign of James II. were favorable to the development of a spirit of toleration among Protestants, who were driven into a closer political and religious alliance by the fear of Roman Catholic supremacy. The king in some cases exercised his pretended power of dispensation to protect Baptists from the execution of their laws; but while they accepted the immunity thus offered, they gave no approval to the high-handed proceedings of the monarch. In pursuance of his policy of securing Nonconformist support, the king appointed William Kiffen alderman of the ward of Cheap. Mr. Kiffen was much disturbed, but as counsel advised him that refusal might entail a fine of thirty thousand pounds, he reluctantly qualified for the office. He succeeded in obtaining his discharge, however, nine months later. The project was a failure. Neither Baptists nor any other Nonconformists were to be hoodwinked, nor could they be flattered or bribed into approval of the overriding of the laws of England by royal prerogative, even though those laws might press hard on themselves.

The king's persistence could not overcome the opposition of the people, but it could and did lose him his crown.

The revolution that overthrew James placed on the throne the Prince of Orange, the descendant of that heroic leader of the Netherlands in their long struggle to throw off the yoke of Roman Catholic Spain, the first ruler in modern history who was statesman enough and Christian enough to incorporate the principle of religious liberty into his country's laws. Thanks to William III., the Act of Toleration was passed in 1689, which, though a mass of absurdities and inconsistencies when carefully analyzed, was yet a measure of practical justice to the majority, and of great relief to all. The penal laws against dissenters from the Church of England were not repealed, but Baptists and most other Protestant Dissenters were exempted from their operation. Roman Catholics and Jews were left still subject to the penal laws, and men so enlightened and liberal-minded as Tillotson and Locke protested against granting toleration to them. From that day the grosser forms of persecution ceased forever, as regarded all Protestant bodies, though the principle of complete religious liberty has never yet found general acceptance in England.

The Baptists of the seventeenth century had many curious customs, some of which were borrowed from them by the Friends, and survive among the latter body to this day. The quaint garb of the Quaker is that of the seventeenth century Baptist. In public worship men and women sat on opposite sides of the house, both participating in the exhorting and "prophesying," as the "Spirit moved." Whether singing was an allowable part of worship was fiercely disputed, and a salaried or "hireling" ministry was in great disfavor. The imposition of hands was practised, in the ordination not only of pastors, but of deacons, and in many churches hands were laid on all who had been baptized, an act that has given place among American Baptists, at least, to the " hand of fellowship." Fasting was a common observance, feet-washing was practised by many churches, though its obligation was earnestly questioned, and the anointing of the sick was so common as to be almost the rule. Pastors and deacons were often elected by the casting of lots, and love feasts before the Lord's Supper were a common practice.

The supervision of members' lives was strict. Marrying out of meeting, as among the Friends, was followed by excommunication, and the amusements that might be indulged in were carefully limited. Disputes between husbands and wives, between masters and servants, were made subjects of church discipline and adjudication, and such offenses as covetousness, slander, and idleness were severely dealt with. To the Baptists of to-day this kind of discipline seems a meddlesome interference with personal rights and private affairs, and it has fallen into disuse in all but a few localities.

CHAPTER XVI

THE SECOND REFORMATION AND ITS CONSEQUENCES

FEW people have borne the ordeal of persecution better than the English Baptists; but for a century after the passage of the Act of Toleration it seemed that they were unable to bear freedom. In the history of Christianity it has often happened that the people of God have grown marvelously in spite of opposition and persecution, but have languished in times of comparative prosperity—that a sect that fire and sword could not suppress has degenerated and disintegrated or finally disappeared when every external hindrance to prosperity had been removed. The English Baptists were to furnish another instance of this kind. After 1689 they were given a measure of toleration such as they had never known in England—since it was toleration secured and clearly defined by law, not given by the arbitrary will of one man. There was no external obstacle to their making rapid, continuous, and solid growth. Every indication pointed toward a career of uninterrupted progress and prosperity. Yet fifty years after the passage of the Act of Toleration, the Baptists of England were scarcely more numerous than they were at the accession of William III., while as to spiritual power they had dwindled to a painful state of deadness and inefficiency.

At first, indeed, they appeared likely to grow with unusual rapidity. The Confessions issued by them at about this time show how quickly they felt the impulse of hope, and how rapid, for a season, was their development. In 1677, the Particular churches published a modified form of the Westminster Confession, which they reissued in 1688. This still forms the basis of the English Confessions, and, under the name of the Philadelphia Confession, is the system of doctrine approved by a large number of Baptist churches of our Southern and Southwestern States. The General Baptist brethren issued their Confession in 1678, and it is noticeable that its Arminianism is of a type that can hardly be distinguished from the milder forms of Calvinism. But while the immediate effect of toleration was stimulating, its later result was unfavorable to sound growth. Centralizing tendencies manifested themselves, false doctrine crept in, and there was a marked decline of spirituality.

The centralizing tendencies were strongest among the General Baptists. By 1671, a General Assembly had been organized. This body from the first undertook to exercise powers incompatible with the independence of the churches. Not content with such legitimate activities as proposing plans of usefulness, recommending cases requiring pecuniary support, and devising means for the spread of the gospel, it undertook the reformation of inconsistent or immoral conduct in ministers and private Christians, the suppression of heresy, the reconciling of differences between individuals and churches, and giving advice in difficult cases to individuals and churches. Some Baptists of our own day, who lament the lack of a " strong government," will find this something closely approaching their ideal.

But mark the sequel. One Matthew Caffyn, a Sussex pastor of undoubted piety and alleged (but doubtful) learning, was charged with unsound views concerning the nature of Christ. There is little doubt that his theology, if sound at first, came to be Arian. He denied the Deity of Christ, though calling him " divine "—a fine-spun distinction that some modern Unitarians also make. Two parties sprang up in the Assembly, and the body was finally divided in 1689, when Caffyn's views were pronounced heretical. A new Assembly was formed, and by 1750 the major part of the General Baptists had become Unitarian in their beliefs. This was followed by worldliness, lax discipline, the superficial preaching of mere morality, and the members fell away in large numbers. In a petition that he presented to Charles II., Thomas Grantham declared that there were twenty thousand General Baptists in England; in the days of George II. there were probably not half that number; and of these a large part had the form of godliness without the power. The "strong government" had miserably failed to repress heresy or to prevent schism.

The Particular Baptists organized the first Associations; the Somerset, in 1653, which became extinct about 1657; and the Midland, formed in 1655 and reconstructed in 1690, which still exists. Their General Assembly was organized in 1689, by the agency of the London churches, and this body also still lives. At its fourth meeting, in 1692, the Association had in its fellowship one hundred and seven churches. Warned by the experience of their General brethren, they "disclaimed all manner of superiority or superintendency over the churches." They were willing to give advice in regard to queries, but had no notion of becoming a court of appeals to settle church quarrels and try heretics. This was not for lack of heretics to try, for the Particular churches had their difficulties at this time with certain troublers in Israel, who professed Antinomian doctrines and complete sanctification, the results of which teachings were disputes and divisions that caused a great decline.

Hyper-Calvinism was developed in one section of the Particular churches, and everywhere proved a blighting doctrine. The London Association, formed in 1704 by delegates from thirteen churches, deemed it necessary to condemn the Antinomian perversion of Calvinism—regarding its action, however, not a judicial decision, but the deliberate opinion of a representative body of Baptists. The ablest and most learned of the Baptists of this time, John Gill, cannot be absolved from responsibility for much of this false doctrine. He was the son of a Dissenting minister and a native of Northamptonshire (born at Kettering, 1697). As a Dissenter he could not be matriculated at either of the Universities, but, pursuing his education under private tutors, he became a great scholar—in the classics, in biblical studies, and in rabbinical lore he was the equal of any. His vigorous mind was not weighed down by his erudition. Though not eloquent as a preacher, he was an industrious writer of books highly esteemed in their day and very influential. His " Commentary " on the Bible is more learned than perspicuous, and Robert Hall once characterized it as " a continent of mud, sir." If this be regarded as a hasty and unjust criticism, the praise of Toplady must be acknowledged to go to the other extreme: " If any man can be supposed to have trod the whole circle of human learning, it was Doctor Gill. . . It would perhaps try the constitutions of half the *literati* in England, only to read with care and attention the whole of what he said. As deeply as human sagacity, enlightened by grace, could penetrate, he went to the bottom of everything he engaged in."

Doctor Gill's " Body of Divinity," published in 1769, was a great treatise of the rigid supralapsarian type of Calvinism, and long held its place as a theological textbook. This type of Calvinism can with difficulty be distinguished from fatalism and antinomianism. If Gill did not hold, as his opponents charged, that the elect live in a constant state of sanctification (because of the imputed righteousness of Christ), even while they commit much sin, he did hold that because of God's election Christians must not presume to interfere with his purposes by inviting sinners to the Saviour, for he will have mercy on whom he will have mercy, and on no others. This is practically to nullify the Great Commission; and, in consequence of this belief, Calvinistic Baptist preachers largely ceased to warn, exhort, and invite sinners; holding that, as God will have mercy on whom he will have mercy, when he willed he would effectually call an elect person, and that for anybody else to invite people to believe was useless, if not an impertinent interference with the prerogatives of God. What wonder that a spiritual dry-rot spread among the English churches where such doctrines obtained! Could any other result be reasonably expected as the fruits of such a theology?

It must, however, in justice be said that this was a time of general decline in religion among Englishmen, which began with the Restoration, and became marked from the beginning of the Hanoverian period. Many causes combined to bring religion to this low estate. In the desire to avoid Romanism on the one hand and Puritanism on the other, the Established Church had fallen into a colorless, passionless, powerless style of teaching. The clergy were estranged from the House of Hanover, and the whole church system was disorganized. By successive withdrawals of its best men, the Church had been seriously weakened, while the Dissenting bodies had not been correspondingly strengthened. Deism had made great strides among people and clergy, and Christianity was but half believed and less than half practised.

Here, indeed, was the great secret of the religious collapse that had overtaken England. There was a serious deterioration in the moral fiber of the people, the cause of which is not far to seek. This deterioration plainly had its source in that general and widespread corruption of the highest orders of society that began with the reign of Charles II. and had continued ever since. During the reign of the Stuarts the body of the poeple continued, as to moral character and religious ideas, substantially what they had been. After a generation or two, however, the example of the higher classes was not without its effect. When king and courtiers made a scoff of religion, when they lived in open lewdness and ostentatious impiety, the ideals of the people could not fail to be greatly affected though the change might be slow. The corruptions sown during the Stuart period were bearing abundant fruit in church and society long after the Stuarts had lost the throne of England forever. Phillimore, a historian of English jurisprudence, sums up the matter in saying: " The upper classes were without refinement; the middle, gross without humor; and the lower, brutal without honesty."

But it was through the clergy that the effects of the Restoration chiefly made themselves felt on the religious life of the nation. In the Established Church the manners and morals of the clergy, as depicted in contemporary literature, were frightful. The drunken, lecherous, swearing, gaming parson is a familiar character in the plays and romances of the period, and survives even to the beginning of the present century. Preferment in Church depended upon subserviency to those who were masters in State, and the clergy took their tone from the court. Not only was personal piety a bar to advancement rather than a recommendation, but virtual infidelity in the State bred rationalism in theology. The clergy became timid, apologetic, latitudinarian in their teaching, and the people became like unto them. Religion never sank to so low an ebb in England as during the first half of the eighteenth century.

Lest this should be thought too black a picture, painted by an unfriendly hand, let an English churchman be heard. Bishop Ryle says: " From the year 1700 till about the era of the French Revolution, England seemed barren of all good. . . There was darkness in high places and darkness in low places; darkness in the court, the camp, the Parliament, and the bar; darkness in the country and darkness in town; darkness among rich, and darkness among poor—a gross, thick, religious and moral darkness; a darkness that might be felt."

But a man had been raised up for just this emergency, and by a long and peculiar experience he had been prepared to cope with the powers of darkness. John Wesley was the son of an English clergyman, educated at Oxford, in his youth an ardent believer in High Church principles and full of self-righteousness. Going on a mission to the new colony of Georgia, he fell into company with some Moravians, and received his first instruction in the true meaning of the gospel. On his return to England, he sought out others of this people; and it was in the year 1738, at the meeting of a Moravian Society in London, that John Wesley felt, as he tells us, for the first time: " I did trust in Christ, Christ alone, for salvation; and an assurance was given me that he had taken away my sins, even mine, and saved me from the law of sin and death." Soon England was shaken by the preaching of the new birth and immediate justification by faith, and the second Reformation had begun. Driven from the pulpits of the Established Church—of which he was, and remained to the day of his death, a presbyter in full standing—Wesley began, though with fear and trembling, to preach in the fields. In this he had been preceded by George Whitefield, a fellow-student at Oxford, and a member also of a small religious club that had been nicknamed " Methodists."

Whitefield was the greater preacher, Wesley the greater organizer and leader. Together, and powerfully aided by other helpers only less eloquent and less able, they accomplished the greatest religious revolution of modern times.

Not only did they call into being societies all over the kingdom, which, at John Wesley's death numbered one hundred thousand members; but, as has been well said, the Methodists themselves were the least result of the revival. A great wave of religious zeal swept over the entire English nation, and left permanent results upon the national character, institutions, laws. Upon the Church of England itself the effect was most marked, possibly because here reformation was most needed. The clergy were roused from their lethargy; the whole spirit of the church was transformed and permanently altered for the better. Skepticism was checked, and religion became once more respectable among the titled and the rich. An " Evangelical " party arose, which ruled the Church of England for the next fifty years, and included among its members some of the most godly ministers and laymen that church has ever possessed. A new moral enthusiasm was roused in the nation, as was manifest in the changed attitude of the people toward all policies in which ethical issues were involved. The abolition of the slave trade may be directly traced to the revival, as well as the new philanthropy that from this time forward became a national trait. In short, in the throes of this movement, England was born again, and the new life on which she then entered has endured to the present hour.

It is superfluous to say that the Baptists of England participated in the benefits of this second Reformation. With it begins a new era in their history, an era of growth, of zeal. of missionary activity, which gave them a leading place among the Nonconformists of England. While this is true regarding all the Baptist churches, perhaps the most immediate and striking results of the Wesleyan movement may be traced in the growth of the General Baptists.

Among the early converts of the Wesleyan revival was a youthful Yorkshireman, the son of a miner, himself a worker in the mines from his fifth year. Dan Taylor was of sturdy frame and great native intelligence, though his education was naturally of the slightest. Soon after his conversion, he began to visit the sick and lead prayer-meetings with the zeal not unusual in new converts, but with an ability so unusual that his brethren encouraged him to attempt preaching. His first sermon was preached in a dwelling-house near Halifax, in September, 1761. The leading Methodists of Yorkshire encouraged his efforts and urged him to visit Mr. Wesley and be enrolled in the ranks of the regular Wesleyan preachers; but there were things in the discipline and doctrine of the societies that he did not approve, and about midsummer, 1762, he withdrew finally from all connection with the Methodists.

At this time there were a few Christians in the village of Heptonstall, not far from Halifax, who had done the same. They invited Taylor to preach to them. For some months he preached to them in the open air, under a tree. The prospect was discouraging, the country wild, and the people rough and unpolished, yet he determined to remain and preach the gospel to them. On the approach of winter, they obtained a house to meet in, taking up part of the chamber floor and converting the rest into a gallery. The house was duly registered under the Act of Toleration, and during the week Taylor taught a school in it, to eke out his support. These people had left both the Church of England and the Methodists.

but had joined no other body. They began to study the New Testament, with a view to determining some plan of church order and some principles of doctrine. Taylor diligently used such books as he could obtain, and the result of his investigations was to convince him that believers' baptism is the only thing warranted by the Scriptures. There were Particular Baptists about Halifax, but they were bitterly hostile to all who held the Arminian theology; and since Taylor persisted in holding that Jesus Christ had tasted death for every man and made propitiation for the sins of the whole world, they would not help him to obey Christ—though several expressed their firm persuasion that he was a genuine Christian, and were even well satisfied of his call to the ministry. He learned at length that in Lincolnshire there were Baptists of sentiments like his own, and with a friend he set out to travel a distance of one hundred and twenty miles on foot. They found, however, a congregation of General Baptists at Gamston, Nottinghamshire; and though they were received rather coolly at first, after a conference of three days they were baptized in the river near-by, February 16, 1763.

Returning, Taylor and his people organized a General Baptist church, the only one at that time in Yorkshire, and in the autumn he was ordained to the ministry, at Birchcliff. At first they connected themselves with the Lincolnshire churches of like faith, but speedily became aware of the great degeneracy that had occurred. Many of the General Baptists had come to deny the atonement, justification by faith alone, and regeneration by the Holy Spirit. As Taylor made the acquaintance of General Baptists in the midland counties, he found them more evangelical. A preliminary conference was held at Lincoln about Michaelmas, 1769, and a formal organization was effected in London, June 7, 1770, of " The Assembly of the Free Grace General Baptists," commonly known as the " New Connexion." Two Associations, a Northern and a Southern, were also formed at once. The Northern consisted in 1772 of seven churches and one thousand two hundred and twenty-one members, which by 1800 had increased to twenty-two churches and two thousand six hundred members. The Southern Association never showed much vitality. In Yorkshire, as we have seen, there was but one church at the beginning, but at the end of fifteen years there were four.

The progress of the New Connection was due almost wholly to Dan Taylor. He was the life and soul of the movement. Everything that he set his hand to prospered; when he took his hand away things languished. His mind was naturally vigorous, and he found means to cultivate its powers and make of himself a fairly educated man. His body seemed incapable of fatigue and his labors were herculean. If anything demanded doing, he was ready to do it. Did an Association wish a circular letter to the churches, he wrote it; was a minister in demand for a sermon, a charge, or any other service, from Berwick-on-Tweed to Land's End, Dan Taylor was on hand. He led in the establishment of the fund for the education of ministers, in 1796, and was principal of the academy—or, as we should say nowadays, theological seminary—established for the purpose in 1798. He edited the " General Baptist Magazine "; he traveled up and down England, traversing, it is said, twenty-five thousand miles, mostly on foot. And he preached constantly; a sermon every night and three on Sunday was his ordinary allowance, and on special occasions he preached several times a day. Even the labors of John Wesley are equaled, if not surpassed, by this record.

One story has been preserved that well illustrates a trait of his character, his indomitable energy. At one time in his life he had some difficulty with his eyes and feared he might lose his sight. He was at first appalled by the prospect, as anybody would naturally be; then he determined that he would learn the whole Bible "by heart," so that when his eyesight was gone he might still be able to preach the gospel. He began his task, and had actually accomplished a good part of it when his trouble left him, and he desisted. No wonder that such a man was a successful evangelist; such determination and pluck will make a man successful in any calling; and qualities of this kind, as well as the anointing of the Holy Spirit, are needed, if one is to be a great evangelist. God makes no mistakes; he never selects for a great work the lazy, half-hearted, weak-willed man, but one who has energy and grit and perseverance, as well as piety. It is impossible to bore through granite with a boiled carrot; it requires a steel drill.

Dan Taylor fell asleep in his seventy-eighth year, and the phrase almost literally describes his end, for suddenly, without a groan or sigh, he expired while sitting in his chair. His work was well done, and English Baptists still feel the result of his manly piety and zealous labors.

The change that gradually came over the Particular Baptists is not, to so great an extent, identified with the character and labors of a single man. It is still true, however, that to the influence of Andrew Fuller such change is largely due, especially the modification of the Baptist theology, that was an indispensable prerequisite to effective preaching of the gospel. Fuller was born in Cambridgeshire in 1754, and at the age of fourteen became deeply convicted of sin. It was long before the way of life became clear to him, but at length he reached a faith in Christ from which he never wavered. The witnessing of a baptismal service in March, 1770—until then he had never seen an immersion—wrought immediate conviction in his mind that this was the only form of obedience to the command of Christ, and a month later he was himself baptized. In the spring of 1775 he was ordained to the ministry, and in 1782 became pastor of the church at Kettering, which he served until his death, in 1815. He was a sound and edifying preacher, but not a great orator; nevertheless, few pulpit orators have had so wide a hearing, or so deeply influenced their generation.

Fuller was, first of all, mighty with his pen. He was mainly self-educated, and never became a real scholar, but he had a robust mind capable of profound thought, and he learned to express himself in clear, vigorous English. The result was to make him one of the most widely read and influential theological writers of England or America. Large editions of his writings were sold in both countries, and they bid fair to be still " in print " when much-vaunted works of a later day are forgotten. Fuller boldly accepted and advocated a doctrine of the atonement that, until his day, had always been stigmatized as rank Arminianism, viz., that the atonement of Christ, as to its worth and dignity, was sufficient for the sins of the whole world, and was not an offering for the elect alone, as Calvinists of all grades had hitherto maintained. Along with this naturally went a sublapsarian interpretation of the " doctrines of grace," and this modified Calvinism gradually made its way among Baptists until it has become well-nigh the only doctrine known among them.

But Fuller was also great as an organizer and man of affairs. He became secretary of the missionary society of the Baptists, and in pursuance of his duties traveled from one end of England to another many times; five times he traversed Scotland for the same object, and once he made a like tour of Ireland. He was a man of splendid physique, tall and strongly built, and eyes deep-set under bushy brows lighted up a massive face that was a good index of his character. To his sturdy mind, enlightened zeal, and indefatigable labors, the Baptist cause in England, and in America as well, owes a debt that can hardly be acknowledged in words too emphatic.

But the most important of those results that may be directly or indirectly traced to the Wesleyan revival, remains to be described. The man destined to do more than any other toward the regeneration of English Baptists, and to be an inspiration to all other Christians, was some years younger than Andrew Fuller. This was William Carey. He was born in 1761, not of Baptist parentage; on the contrary, his father was an old-school Churchman, and bred his son in holy horror of all " Dissenters." But Carey heard the gospel preached, he was convicted of sin, and converted, and like most young converts, took to reading his Bible with new zest. The New Testament speaks for itself to any one who will honestly read it to learn what it teaches, and Carey soon learned what a Christian church ought to be and what a converted man ought to do. He not only saw his duty, but did it, though it required him to join himself to certain of the despised Dissenters. He was baptized on profession of faith, in the river Neu, on October 5, 1783, by Dr. John Ryland. Little did Doctor Ryland know that he was performing the most important act of his life, and as little did he guess that this humble youth was to become a great man. " This day baptized a poor journeyman shoemaker " is the curt entry in the good doctor's diary.

It was evident, however, from the beginning that Carey was a young man of promise. He became a member of the Baptist church at Olney, of which Rev. John Sutcliffe

was pastor. He showed gifts in exhortation that warranted his pastor and friends in urging him to preach,
and he was not long in making his fitness for the ministry evident. In 1787 he was called to the pastorate of
a little Baptist church at Moulton, and ordained. He
already had a wife and two children, and the Moulton
church was so poor that he could be paid only seventy-
five dollars a year. He was obliged, therefore, during
the week to work as a cobbler for the support of his
family. At the same time he had a thirst for learning,
and as he worked his custom was to keep by him a book
for study. In this way he is said in seven years to have
learned to read five languages, including Greek and Hebrew. If young men and women whose educational advantages have been limited would but take a tithe of the
pains to utilize their odd minutes that Carey took, they
might do anything they chose. It is true Carey had a
remarkable gift for acquiring languages, but even more
remarkable than this was his determination to learn, in
spite of difficulties. It is that determination which is
lacking in most, more than ability to learn.

Carey not only studied text-books, but read all good
books that he could borrow, and among these was a copy
of Captain Cook's voyages. He also kept a school after
a time, and of course had to teach the children geog-
raphy. In these ways his mind was turned toward the
destitute condition of the heathen and their need of the
gospel. But when he began to talk to others about it,
he met with little encouragement, and it is said that once
when he began in a Baptist gathering to speak of a mission
to the heathen, Doctor Ryland exclaimed: " Sit down,
young man; when the Lord gets ready to convert the
heathen he will do it without your help or mine! " It
is not recorded whether Carey sat down or not, but he
certainly did not give up advocating missions to the

heathen. Apart from the hyper-Calvinism disclosed by Doctor Ryland's remark, it is not wonderful that Carey received so little encouragement at first. English Baptists were poor, and so great an enterprise might well have seemed to them beset with unsurmountable difficulties. But Carey wisely declined to consider the matter of possibilities; he looked only at the question of duty. The Duke of Wellington replied to a young clergyman who asked if it were not useless to preach the gospel to the Hindus: " With that you have nothing to do. Look to your marching orders, ' Go, preach the gospel to every creature.' " The soldier was right and the preacher stood justly rebuked.

With difficulty Carey got together money to print and circulate a tract called " An Enquiry into the Obligations of Christians to Use Means for the Conversion of the Heathens." Not long after this came from the press his great opportunity arrived—he was appointed to preach the sermon at the meeting of his Association at Nottingham, May 30, 1792. He chose as his text Isaiah 44 : 2, 3, and announced as the " heads " of his discourse: " Expect great things from God; attempt great things for God." It was one of the days on which the fate of denominations and even of nations turns. It roused those who listened to a new idea of their responsibility for the fulfilment of Christ's commission. Even then, nothing might have come of it but for an impassioned personal appeal of Carey's to Andrew Fuller, not to let the meeting break up without doing something. A resolution was passed, through Fuller's influence, that a plan be prepared for establishing a missionary society, to be presented at the next ministers' meeting.

That meeting was held in Andrew Fuller's study, at Kettering, October 2, and then and there " The English Baptist Missionary Society " was organized. Its constituent members were twelve, and out of their poverty they contributed to its treasury the sum of thirteen pounds two shillings and six pence. What a sum with which to begin the evangelization of the world! The history of this society is an instructive commentary on the Scripture, " For who hath despised the day of small things." The London churches, the richer churches among Baptists, stood aloof from this movement. It was the poorer country churches that finally raised enough money to send out in June, 1793, Carey and a Baptist surgeon named Thomas, who had previously been in India and, as he had opportunity, had preached the gospel as a layman and a physician.

The British East India Company was bitterly opposed to the preaching of the gospel in India, fearing that the natives might be provoked to rise against the government. It is not exaggerating to say that Christianity has done more than any other thing, more than strong battalions, to maintain England's rule in India. But the directors could not foresee this. One said he would see a band of devils let loose in India rather than a band of missionaries. Englishmen who survived the Sepoy rebellion were rather less anxious to see devils let loose in India, and much more favorably disposed toward missionaries. For a time Carey, and the next missionaries sent—Marshman and Ward—established themselves at Serampore, a Danish settlement not far from Calcutta. Here a missionary press was set up, and Doctor Carey did the great work of his life in translating and printing the Scriptures in the various Indian languages. He had, as we have seen, a special aptitude for the acquisition of languages. He had shown this before leaving England, but he lemonstrated it more clearly after he reached India. The rapidity and ease with which he acquired the various languages spoken there have never been surpassed, and he became in a short time one of the world's greatest Oriental scholars.

To every man his gifts. Others could preach the gospel to the heathen as well as Carey, or better, for he never seems to have developed special power as a preacher. But no one could equal him as scholar, translator, writer. He wisely spent his time and strength in translating the Scriptures and other Christian literature into the Indian languages and dialects, in making grammars, and the like. Thus he not only did a great work for his own generation, but one that will last for all time, or so long as these languages shall be spoken. Before his death, there had been issued under his supervision, he himself doing a large part of the work, versions of the Scriptures in forty different languages or dialects, spoken by a third of the people on the globe; and of these Scriptures two hundred and twelve thousand copies had been issued.

In his later years, men like Sydney Smith ceased to sneer at the " consecrated cobbler," and Carey was honored as a man of his learning, piety, and exalted character deserved. In 1801 he was made professor of Bengali in Lord Wellesley's new College of Fort William, at Calcutta; and titles and honors were showered upon him toward the close of his life. The learned societies of Europe recognized him as one of the greatest scholars of his age. But he was to the last a humble missionary of the religion of Christ. He is justly regarded as the father of modern missions, for though Baptists were not the first in modern times to engage in this work, it was Carey and his work that drew the attention of all Christians to it, that quickened the Christian conscience, and that gave the missionary cause a great forward impulse which it has never since lost.

From the first the mission thus established prospered,

in spite of the obstacles thrown in its way by British officials and the fire of ridicule kept up in the rear by men who ought to have been in better business. The first secretary of this body was Andrew Fuller, to whose indefatigable labors was due much of its growth in financial strength and missionary zeal. The society has several times extended its operations, and in addition various enterprises have been conducted by churches and individuals in Africa and Italy. In this work, and in many other forms of service, the General and Particular Baptists united, prior to their formal union.

CHAPTER XVII

THE NINETEENTH CENTURY

OF the English Baptist churches now in existence, but one hundred and twenty-three were established before the Act of Toleration, and during the next half-century only sixty-eight more were added to the number. From 1750 onward, as the effects of the Wesleyan movement began to be felt, the growth was more rapid, and in the second half of the eighteenth century one hundred and sixty-five Baptist churches were constituted, of which more than one hundred belong to the last two decades. From this time, seven decades of the nineteenth century show a rapid and ever-increasing rate of progress. The first half of the century saw an addition of seven hundred churches; the second half exceeds even this growth, showing a total number of nine hundred and sixty-one churches established. The last two decades are less remarkable for increase in the number of churches, but on the other hand, they show a gratifying advance in the strength and efficiency of the churches already founded.

It does not seem fanciful to trace a close connection between this growth of the churches and the development of organization that followed the Carey movement. The first step was taken by the formation of the Baptist Home Mission Society in 1779, followed by the Baptist Union in 1832. Both societies did much to unite the churches in evangelistic efforts, but the older society was more distinctively missionary in its aims and methods. In 1865 the society was united with the Irish Missionary

Society (formed in 1814) to form the British and Irish Baptist Home Mission, and now for some years this has been merged in the Baptist Union for Great Britain and Ireland, which became an incorporated body in 1890. The General Baptists had established a missionary society in 1816, and other societies of various kinds at other times; but in 1891, the General Baptists united with the Particular Baptists, and now all the various missionary and benevolent societies of both bodies are administered as departments of the Baptist Union. The distinctions of doctrine anciently maintained by these two wings of the denomination long since practically disappeared, and it was proper that distinctions in administration should no longer be maintained.

The missionary movement begun by Carey and his coadjutors had a stimulating effect by no means confined to his own denomination. Missionary societies were speedily formed by other bodies of Christians, and even the Church of England was stirred to do something for the evangelizing of heathen lands. And this new activity was not limited to strictly missionary effort. The great work of Carey, as we have seen, was the translation of the Scriptures into the Eastern tongues, and a multitude of others followed in his footsteps. In 1804 a large number of evangelical Christians, of some ten or more different denominations, formed the British and Foreign Bible Society, for the circulation of the Scriptures in all lands, without note or comment. It was due to the activity of Rev. Joseph Hughes, a Baptist minister of Battersea, that this society was formed, and he was its first secretary. Baptists generally were active in the support of the society, and for a generation grants were freely made from its treasury to aid the printing of Carey's translations. This was done with full knowledge of the fact that Carey and others translated all

words, including *baptizo* and its cognates—official correspondence left no question possible regarding this point.
In 1835 Messrs. Yates & Pearce had ready for publication a revised copy of Carey's Bengali Bible, and applied to the British and Foreign Bible Society for aid
in printing it. This application was refused, unless they
would guarantee that "the Greek terms relating to Baptism be rendered, either according to the principle
adopted by the translators of the authorized English
version, by a word derived from the original, or by such
terms as may be considered unobjectionable by other denominations composing the Bible Society." The demand
was, in plain English, either that the Baptist missionaries
should not translate *baptizo* and its cognates at all, or that
they should make a wrong translation!

More than six hundred Baptist ministers presented to
the society, in 1837, a protest against its unjust, un-
catholic, and inconsistent action; and in January, 1840,
a final remonstrance was addressed to the society by the
Baptist Union. Nothing, of course, came of these protests, and therefore on March 24, 1840, the Baptists of
England formed the Bible Translation Society, in order
to "encourage the production and circulation of complete translations of the holy Scriptures, competently au-
thenticated for fidelity, it being always understood that
the words relating to the ordinance of baptism shall be
translated by terms signifying immersion." This society
is still in existence, and enjoys the distinction of having
printed and distributed over six million copies of the
Scriptures, at a cost of one million five hundred thousand
dollars.

Two of the greatest preachers of the nineteenth century came from the ranks of the English Baptists. The
first, Robert Hall, belongs in part to the preceding

century. He was born near Leicester, in 1764, the young-
est child of a family of fourteen, weak in body, and pre-
cocious in mind. He was an accomplished theologian at
the tender age of nine, having then mastered (among
other works) " Edwards on the Will " and Butler's
" Analogy." Notwithstanding such precocity, he did not
prove to be a fool, but was one of the few " remarkable
children " who turn out really remarkable men. In his
fifteenth year he began his series of studies for the ministry at Bristol College, where his progress in learning
was rapid; but as a preacher he seemed likely to be a
failure. On his first public trial he repeatedly broke
down, through an excessive sensibility that made public
speech an agony to him, almost an impossibility. He
mastered this weakness, however, and thenceforth steadily increased in power as an orator. Four years spent at
King's College, Aberdeen, where he was first in all his
classes, brought him to his majority. His pastorates
were at Cambridge, Leicester, and Bristol, and in each
city his ministry was greatly successful. Many of his
sermons were printed and had a wide circulation. No
preacher of his time was more highly esteemed by the
leaders of thought in Great Britain. Hall was master
of an ornate and stately kind of eloquence long extinct
in the pulpit, much esteemed in its day and perhaps too
little esteemed now. To the present generation his sentences seem cumbrous, his style is pronounced affected
and stilted, his tropes frigid. Indeed, the reader of to-
day is at a loss to understand how his sermons could
ever have won such encomiums as they received. Yet
at his death, in 1831, it was universally agreed that one
of the greatest lights of the pulpit had been extinguished.

The other preacher, Charles Haddon Spurgeon, was
a man of quite different mold. His father and grand-
father had been Congregationalist preachers, and from

his birth, in 1834, he was predestined to the same career. This did not become clear to him, however, until his conversion in his seventeenth year. He felt it his duty to unite with a Baptist church, and soon after his baptism began to preach. He had received a fair education, about equal to that given by a good American academy, and was already a teacher in a private school. His success as a preacher led him to forego any further training, and from his eighteenth year until his death, in 1892, he was constantly engaged in what was to him the most delightful and the most honorable of all callings. It was a dangerous experiment; only one man of a thousand could have escaped disaster, but Spurgeon was that man. In the autumn of 1853 he was called to the Southwark Baptist Church, where his predecessors had been such men as Keach, Gill, and Rippon, and there he spent the rest of his life.

The success of the young preacher was immediate and wonderful. During the rest of his life Spurgeon had continuously the largest congregations of any preacher in the world, and soon his sermons were printed and scattered broadcast, until through the press he spoke weekly to more than half a million people. But he was more than a voice crying in the wilderness; he bears the supreme test of greatness that can be applied to a preacher—he not only gained a great reputation for eloquence, but proved himself a builder. His church grew to more than five thousand members—the largest Baptist church in the world. He founded the Pastors' College for the education of ministers, and hundreds of graduates attest by godly living and fruitful ministry the worth of what he thus did. He established the Stockwell Orphanage, in which more than five hundred children have been maintained and educated annually for nearly thirty years. A Colportage Association, a Book Fund, and a successful religious magazine were among his other practical achievements. And when he was called to his reward, all these institutions went on, with little impairment of their efficiency; what he had built was so solidly built that the shock of his death could do it no serious harm.

During the latter part of Spurgeon's life there was, as he believed, a great declension in theology among the English Baptists. By diligent study through life he had become, if not exactly a great theologian, a well-read, well-trained minister, especially versed in the Scriptures and the writings of the great Puritan divines. From first to last he was the unfaltering advocate of the pure gospel of Christ. A moderate Calvinist as to theology, he preached an atonement for the whole world and salvation through Christ's blood to every one who will believe. He stood like a rock against the advancing tide of lax teaching and lax practice, and at least retarded, if he did not check, the movement that he described as " the down grade." This led him to sharp controversy with many of his brethren, and finally induced him to withdraw from the Baptist Union.

Besides Hall and Spurgeon, the Baptist pulpit of England produced other great preachers during the last century, two of whom at least are still living—Alexander McLaren, the eloquent Manchester divine (born at Glasgow, 1825), and John Clifford (born 1836), everywhere known as one of the most scholarly, able, and polished preachers of his time. Nor have there been lacking laymen of equal eminence—to mention three examples only—Major-General Havelock, the hero of the Indian Mutiny (1795-1857); Thomas Spencer Baynes, LL. D. (1823-1887), long professor of logic and metaphysics at the University of St. Andrews, and a writer of world-wide repute; and Sir Robert Lush (1807-1881), one of the foremost men at the bar, and Lord-Justice of the High Court of Appeals. It would be easy, but also unprofitable, to make a long catalogue of distinguished names, only less worthy of mentioning than these. Enough has been said, however, to show that Baptists have been by no means an obscure and feeble folk in England for the last hundred years or more.

The English Baptists began the century just closing not differing greatly in numbers from their brethren in America; but their rate of increase has been much smaller. Why so marked a difference of growth? American Baptists are accustomed to answer, To the difference in the effective maintenance of Baptist principles. The Baptists of America have been consistent and united, while their English brethren have been divided and inconsistent. The answer may be far from satisfactory, it may ignore many important elements of the problem, and yet it may be at least a partial explanation of the unquestionable fact.

As we have already seen, from the beginning there were so-called Baptist churches of mixed membership— that is to say, not exclusively Baptist, but composed in part of Pedobaptists. This is due to the circumstances of their origin. In nearly every case which is matter of record, the early Baptist churches of the seventeenth century were formed from previously existing Separatist churches of the Congregational order. The separations between those who had come to hold to believers' baptism only and those who still held to Pedobaptism were generally peaceful, frequently friendly. In some cases there was no formal separation, the majority holding to believers' baptism and tolerating Pedobaptism in the minority. In other cases a church was organized on the principle of permitting full liberty in the matter of baptism, both as to subjects and form. That churches so composed should remain in full fellowship with Pedobaptist churches is nothing surprising; why should they not commune with Pedobaptist churches, since they admitted Pedobaptists to membership in their own churches, which, of course, carried with it the privilege of communion? To admit some Pedobaptists to the Lord's table and exclude others would have been inconsistency too ridiculous.

From the first, therefore, there was a division of sentiment and practice. Baptists like William Kiffen, John Spilsbury, and Hanserd Knollys, stood for the consistent Baptist position that the church should be composed of baptized believers only, and that only such are warranted or invited by New Testament precept and example in coming to the table of the Lord. On the other hand, Baptists like Henry Jessey, John Tombes, and John Bunyan, favored the laxer practice of communing with all Christians, while Jessey and Bunyan at least were pastors of churches of mixed membership. There was hot debate over this question of open communion, as any one may see who will take the trouble to examine a copy of Bunyan's " Complete Works," of which there are many editions. Words decidedly warm passed between Bunyan and Kiffen, and of course neither party was convinced by the arguments of the other. Mixed churches and open communion remained the practice of a considerable part of the English Baptists, and had the advocacy of some of the ablest men in the denomination.

The natural result, one that might have been predicted from well-known principles of human nature, was that the growth of English Baptists was relatively slow, even in times when their piety and zeal were high. Baptist growth has always been in proportion to the stanchness with which Baptist principles have been upheld and prac-

tised. So it ever has been with all religious bodies.
Nothing is gained by smoothing off the edges of truth
and toning down its colors, so that its contrast with error
may be as slight as possible. On the contrary, let the
edges remain a bit rough, let the colors be heightened,
so that the world cannot possibly mistake the one for
the other, and the prospect of the truth gaining acceptance, is greatly increased. The history of every religious denomination teaches the same lesson : progress
depends on loyalty to truth. Compromise always means
decay.

The present century has witnessed the most rapid
change among the Baptists of England with regard to
the communion. The most powerful factor in producing
this twofold defection was Robert Hall. Starting from
premises that Socinus would have heartily approved, he
reached the conclusion that the neglect of baptism is to
be tolerated by the churches as an exercise of Christian
liberty (a Christian at liberty to disobey Christ!), and that
sincerity rather than outward obedience is the test that
the " genius of Christianity " proposes. Under the influence of such teachings, large numbers of Baptist
churches became " open." This change has been followed
by its logical result—a result inevitable wherever " open "
communion is adopted and given full opportunity to work
itself out—the formation of churches of mixed membership. In many of these, the trust-deeds distinctly specify
that Baptists and Pedobaptists shall have equal rights,
and it is not uncommon for such a church to have a
Pedobaptist pastor. In many other so-called Baptist
churches of England the ordinance of baptism is seldom
or never administered; Pedobaptists are received to
membership on equal terms with the baptized; they are
chosen to office, and even to the pastorate. In short, so
effectually is the church disguised as frequently to be

reckoned by both Baptists and Independents in their statistics.[1]

Spurgeon's attitude towards these questions has very often been misunderstood. He did not absolutely agree with the practice of the American Baptists regarding the communion, but he did very nearly, and it is an abuse of terms to call him an "open communionist." He did not advocate or practise the promiscuous invitation of all Christians to the table of the Lord. The communion service was held on Sunday afternoon in the Tabernacle, and admission was by ticket only. Members of the church, of course, were furnished with tickets. Any person not a member, desiring to attend and partake of the Supper, must satisfy the pastor or deacons that he was a member in good standing of an evangelical church, when he would receive a ticket. At the end of three months he would be quietly told that he had had an opportunity to become acquainted with the church, and they would be glad to have him present himself as a candidate for membership; otherwise he would do well to go elsewhere, where he could conscientiously unite. This is a more restricted communion than is practised by most Baptist churches in America, for in large numbers of our churches Pedobaptists occasionally partake of the communion without any such careful safeguards. Spurgeon did not believe in mixed membership; he abhorred it. No one could be a member of the Metropolitan Tabernacle church unless he was a baptized believer— credibly a believer, and certainly baptized. From our point of view, it was very unfortunate that he gave the approval of his example to even occasional communion with those whom he believed unbaptized. His practice

[1] Thirty-four such churches are set down among the Baptist churches of England in the "Baptist Handbook," and of these six had Congregational pastors in 1901.

was to this extent illogical and inconsistent, and somewhat weakened the general healthfulness of his influence. He frankly admitted this in private conversations, on many occasions, and explicitly said that were he a pastor in America he should conform to the practice of American Baptists. Compared, however, with the " open communion " Baptists of England, he was strongly orthodox and rigidly conservative.

Among the ministers who established the first Baptist churches in England was a large proportion of men who had been educated at Oxford and Cambridge for the Church of England, but there were also from the first men whose early education had been very slight. Among these latter, such preachers as Kiffen and Bunyan were certainly not a whit inferior to the better-trained men. Nevertheless, it was not long before the Baptist churches felt the importance of establishing schools for the education of their ministry. These are always called " colleges " in England, but differ from the colleges of America in being not schools of arts, but schools of theology. The oldest of these schools now surviving is Bristol College, founded in 1770 by the Northern Baptist Education Society. There are usually twenty-five students in attendance. They have opportunity to pursue studies in arts in Bristol University College, and some of the students take their degrees at London University. Another college was instituted in 1797 in London, and has had numerous habitations since then, but is now located at Midland, Nottingham. Thirteen students is a good attendance for this institution. Rawdon College, near Leeds, in Yorkshire, was founded by the Northern Baptist Education Society, in 1804, and has been in its present home since 1859. The best known of these colleges is perhaps that established in 1810 at Stepney, but removed in 1856 and since then known as the Regents' Park College. Dr. Joseph Angus was for many years its honored head. The two last-named schools have an annual attendance of from twenty-five to thirty, and from Regents' Park some five hundred ministers in all have gone forth. The Pastors' College, founded by Mr. Spurgeon, in 1856, has about sixty students. The strict-communion churches established a college, now located at Manchester, in 1866, which has an attendance rarely or never exceeding twenty students.

The other parts of the United Kingdom are not without similar provision. The Welsh Baptists at present have two theological schools: Cardiff College, founded in 1897, and formerly located at Pontypool; and Bangor College, instituted at Llangollen, in 1862. An annual attendance of about twenty students is reported from both colleges. A single theological college is maintained by Baptists at Glasgow. It furnishes strictly theological education to students who have taken the arts course in a Scottish University, leading to the degree of M. A. A college at Dublin, with six students, is also reported by the Baptists of Ireland.

Besides the General and Particular Baptists, there have been and still are several organizations in England, holding Baptist principles in general, but adding to them some distinguishing peculiarity of faith or practice.

The Six-principle Baptists were so called from the stress they laid on the " six principles " enumerated in Heb. 6 : 1, 2: Repentance, faith, baptism, laying on of hands, the resurrection of the dead, and eternal life. Of these, the fourth is the only one really peculiar to this body—the laying of hands on all after baptism, as a token of a special impartation of the Spirit. In March, 1690, the churches holding these views formed an Association.

This continued with varying fortunes for some years; at its strongest, numbering but eleven churches in England, though there were others in Wales when the Calvinistic Baptists withdrew, and the rest of the churches were gradually absorbed into the General body.

The Seventh-day Baptists (so called from their observance of the seventh day of the week for rest and worship, instead of the first) were founded in 1676 by the Rev. Francis Bampfield, a graduate of Oxford, and at one time prebend of Exeter Cathedral. This has always been a small body, and at the present time but one church survives, the Mill Yard, in Whitechapel, London. This church was, a few years ago, reduced to a membership of about half a dozen, and could secure no pastor of its own faith in England. The property being very valuable, special efforts were made in behalf of the church, a pastor was sent to them from America, and they became more prosperous than for many years before.

CHAPTER XVIII

THERE are traditions among the Welsh Baptists of an ancient origin, and some of their historians have not hesitated to claim for them an antiquity reaching back to the days of the apostles. When such claims are submitted to the ordinary tests of historic criticism, however, they vanish into thin air. Baptist history in Wales, as distinguished from tradition, begins with the period of the Commonwealth. The most moderate and judicious of the Welsh Baptist writers, Rev. Joshua Thomas, says that the oldest church in the principality is one formed at or near Swansea, in Glammorganshire, in 1649.[1] But one church now in existence, the Wrexham, in Denbighshire, claims an earlier date, 1630; and as a few years ago it was content with the year 1635 as the true date of its origin, it is probable that neither is matter of record.

The honor of organizing this first Baptist church in Wales belongs to John Myles. He was born about 1621, and matriculated at Brasenose College, Oxford, in 1636. Whether he ever took orders in the Church of England is not positively known, but it is probable that he did. At any rate, he began to preach the gospel about 1645, and by 1649 was so highly esteemed as to be named one of the Triers for Wales during the Protectorate. In that year, a few baptized believers were gathered, and they continued to increase until the Restoration, when Myles

---

[1] There is a tradition of an earlier church of Welsh Baptists at Olchon, in Herefordshire (1633), but no record survives to prove that such a church ever existed

and most of the church emigrated to the colony of Massachusetts.

The man to whom the Baptist cause in Wales owes most in its early years is Vavasor Powell. He was born in 1617, and was descended from a Radnorshire family of great antiquity and distinction. It is not known where he received his education, but it is certain that he became a scholar of notable attainments and that he early obtained preferment in the Established Church. He was led to entertain Puritan sentiments by intercourse with some of that persuasion, and by the reading of their literature, and in 1642 came to London and joined the Parliamentary party. He was for a time settled at Dartmouth, in Kent, where his ministry was very fruitful, but calls from his native Wales led him to return thither, which he did in 1646, bearing with him the highest testimonials as to his piety and gifts, signed by Charles Herte, prolocutor, and seventeen other divines of the Westminster Assembly.

Precisely when Powell became a Baptist is not known, but it must have been before 1655, for in that year Thurloe speaks of him as "lately rebaptized." [1] It is probable that most or all of the churches he established were of mixed membership. He favored the practice of open communion also. From these lax practices the Welsh Baptists were soon emancipated, and became what they still are, notable for the consistency and zeal with which they advocate and maintain the distinctive principles of their denomination. The zeal and eloquence of Powell exceeded his consistency; he was a most laborious and successful evangelist throughout the principality, and by the Restoration he had established some twenty churches, of which some had from two hundred to five hundred members. He died in 1670. He has been

[1] " State Papers," IV., 373.

called the Whitefield of Wales, and his abundant and fruitful labors seem well to merit such a title.

But eight of the existing churches of Wales were founded in the seventeenth century, and before the Act of Toleration only thirty-one were added to the number. From the passage of that Act, however, the growth of Baptists in the principality has been rapid, especially since 1810. The formation of Associations began in 1799, and the Baptist Union of Wales was organized in 1867.

More potent than the influence of organization in the promotion of this growth has been a succession of godly and eloquent Baptist preachers. One of the most celebrated of these was Christmas Evans, so named because he was born on the 25th of December, 1766. In spite of poverty and many difficulties, he obtained a good elementary education, and shortly after his conver-sion and baptism was ordained to the ministry at the age of twenty-two. We may judge of the state of affairs in Wales at the time, when we are told that after he had been nearly ten years in the ministry and was highly esteemed, he was paid by two churches that he served, the salary of seventeen pounds a year! Nevertheless, he continued to labor, not only as pastor of churches, but as evangelist in general to Wales, until he rested from his labors in 1838. In a ministry of half a century he had preached all over his native country, with great power, and with equal eloquence and originality.

Through the efforts of such men, the Baptist cause has made rapid progress in Wales throughout the nine-teenth century, which saw at its close eight hundred and thirty-five churches and a membership of one hundred and six thousand five hundred and sixty-six (including Monmouthshire). Though for a time Arminian doctrines threatened to make serious inroads, the Welsh Baptists have as a whole remained ardent Calvinists down to the present time. Of their churches two hundred and fiftynine maintain services in the English language, and of these quite a proportion—some say nearly half—have adopted the open communion practices of their neighbors in England. This is especially true of churches in the large towns. The churches that adhere to their native language also adhere to the well-established principles and practices of the faith.

The Baptist churches of Scotland do not pretend to any great antiquity. The oldest church now existing was founded in Keiss, in Caithnesshire, in 1750. It was formed upon the estate of Sir William Sinclair, who was immersed in England, and became a preacher of the truth on his return. The next oldest churches are in Edinburgh. The Bristo-place church was constituted in 1765, by Rev. Robert Carmichael, originally of the Church of Scotland, then a Glasite and later an Independent preacher, who finally rejected the doctrine and practice of infant baptism, and going to London for the purpose, was baptized by Doctor Gill. The other church owes its origin to Archibald McLean, who also began his career in the Scotch church and then became a Glasite, having been at one time a member of Mr. Carmichael's church. Not long after his former pastor, he also became a convert to Baptist views, and sought baptism on personal profession of faith. Besides these churches, one in Glasgow claims the date of 1768 for its foundation, and two in Paisley are said to have been organized in 1795. There are no other Baptist churches in Scotland formed earlier than 1803.

Archibald McLean almost deserves to be called the founder of the Scotch Baptist churches. He was born in 1733, received the rudiments of a classical education, from which he afterwards advanced by his own exertions to considerable learning, and became a printer at Glasgow. He had in early life been much influenced by the preaching of Whitefield, and was finally constrained himself to become a preacher. He was even more influential by pen than by voice, and his collected writings in six volumes are still a monument to his industry and solidity of mind. His membership for a time in a Glasite or Sandemanian church had important consequences. It was the special endeavor of that peculiar sect to return as far as possible to apostolic simplicity, and to make the churches of to-day an exact reproduction of those of the New Testament. From many of his Sandemanian notions McLean never freed himself, and the Baptist churches of Scotland have perpetuated not a few of these notions, such as insisting on having a plurality of elders in every church, on the weekly celebration of the Lord's Supper, and the like. Later investigations of the New Testament period have disclosed the fact, apparently not suspected by McLean and men of his time, that no single form of organization was common to all the churches of that period, and that it is unsafe to assert a practice found in a single church to be necessarily the norm for all other churches through all time.

Next to McLean, possibly the Baptists of Scotland owe most to the brothers Haldane, Robert (1764-1842) and James Alexander (1768-1851). Both were educated for the navy and served for some years with distinction. Robert inherited a large fortune and retired to his estate at Airthrey, where he became much interested in religion, and finally sold his estate, that he might have means to carry out his projects. James likewise became interested in religion, and retired from service to become a preacher. In 1799 he was ordained pastor of an Independent church in Edinburgh, for which his brother built him in 1801 a fine edifice, known as the Tabernacle. Other congregations were established in Glasgow, Dundee, and other cities.

The Haldanes had been bred in the Church of Scotland, but these churches were Independent or Congregational, and this movement was watched with great interest by the English Independents. There was much dissatisfaction at this time with the State church system in Scotland, and the prospects of Congregationalism seemed bright. In 1808, however, both brothers became convinced that infant baptism is not scriptural, and resolved to teach and maintain believers' baptism. This was the signal for the temporary disruption of their movement, but James continued his work in Edinburgh and evangelistic tours throughout the kingdom, while his brother's purse [1] was at his service always. For fifty years this eloquent preacher held his own with the great pulpit lights of Edinburgh, and during his time of service thirty-eight Baptist churches were founded—about one-third of the total number in Scotland at the present time. The formation of the Baptist Home Mission Society for Scotland in 1816 must be credited with a part of this growth, no doubt, though its work has been chiefly in the highlands and among the islands. In 1856 the Scottish churches united in the Baptist Association of Scotland, which was dissolved in 1869, when the Baptist Union of Scotland took its place.

There were, at the beginning of this century, one hundred and twenty-two Baptist churches in Scotland, having sixteen thousand eight hundred and ninety-nine members.

We can fix the beginning of Baptist churches in Ireland within a few years. The oldest church there was

---

[1] Within fifteen years he is known to have given away $350,000; and it is said that during his life he educated 349 ministers, at a cost of $100,000.

formed in Dublin by Thomas Patience, assistant pastor to Kiffen in London. It claims the date of 1640 for its birth, but this is obviously absurd, since Kiffen became pastor of the newly formed church in Devonshire Square, London, in that year. There is no reason to suppose that the church antedates the conquest of Ireland by Cromwell in 1649, and in fact our earliest knowledge of such a church is 1653. There are but two other churches now existing which date back to the seventeenth century, and but one other that is so old as the closing decade of the eighteenth—for one hundred and forty-three years not a single church seems to have been formed, at least not one that is now in existence. Comment is almost needless.

Baptist churches have ever found Ireland an uncongenial soil; and after more than two centuries of struggle there are little more than two dozen churches of the faith in the island. To have produced the illustrious scholar, Alexander Carson, is the chief contribution to Baptist progress of our Irish brethren, and one of which a larger body might be proud. He was born in County Tyrone, in 1776. Early in life he became a believer in Christ, and later was graduated with the first honor at the University of Glasgow. He became pastor of a Presbyterian church at Tubbermore, Ireland, and while in that service came to see from his study of the original Scriptures that the churches of the New Testament were congregational, not presbyterial, in polity; and that they were composed of baptized believers only. There were few Baptist churches in Ireland, there was no society to which he could appeal for support; of his salary of one hundred and forty pounds he received one hundred pounds from the royal treasury. If he became a Baptist he must not only sever all connection with old friends, but risk starvation. He did what he felt to be clearly his duty, was baptized, and began to preach to such as would listen. He soon gathered a church, and lived to see it grow to five hundred members, many of whom walked from seven to ten miles in order to attend its services.

Doctor Carson was an industrious student, and became a great scholar; but for his inability to sign the Confession of Faith he might have been professor of Greek in the University of Glasgow. His work on baptism was a complete reply to all the objections that had been raised by the ignorant and prejudiced against the teaching and practice of Baptists regarding this ordinance of Christ. Every contention of his has since been amply sustained by the scholarship of the world—not by Baptist scholarship alone, but by Pedobaptist.

There were in Ireland at the close of the nineteenth century thirty-one Baptist churches, with two thousand six hundred and ninety-six members.

The capture of Quebec, in 1759, marks the beginning of Protestant conquest in Canada. Baptists were among the first to profit by the new order of things under the Baptist rule. In the following year Shubael Dimock emigrated from Connecticut and settled in Nova Scotia. He had separated from the churches of the Standing Order, and for holding unauthorized religious meetings had suffered both corporal punishment and imprisonment. His son Daniel had gone even further and denied the scripturalness of infant baptism. These new settlers were accompanied by a Baptist minister, the Rev. John Sutton, who remained in the province about a year, baptizing Daniel Dimock and some others. Daniel Dimock baptized his father about 1775, but so far as is known no Baptist church was organized. A visit to the province in 1761 by the Rev. Ebenezer Moulton, of Massachusetts, is said to have been followed by conversions and baptisms at Yarmouth and Horton, a church being formed at the latter place about 1763, of both Baptists and Congregationalists. This minister was the ancestor of Mrs McMaster, the founder of Moulton College.

It was in 1763 that the first real foothold was gained in Canada by the Baptists. Members of the Second Church in Swansea, Mass., and of two or three neighboring churches, to the number of thirteen, constituted a Baptist church, chose the Rev. Nathan Mason as their pastor, and emigrated in a body to Sackville, then in Nova Scotia, but since 1784 in the province of New Brunswick. They remained for eight years, during which time their numbers had increased to sixty; then, for some reason, the original immigrants returned to Massachusetts, and the church became scattered and finally ceased to exist. A new organization was, however, formed in the same place in 1799.

Up to the year 1775, therefore, the net progress of the Baptists had been small; there was a handful of believers, scattered here and there, but not a single church had been able to maintain an existence. In that year Henry Alline was converted and became an evangelist of the Whitefield type, traveling up and down Nova Scotia and preaching the gospel with great power. He was a Congregationalist, and many of his converts formed churches of that order, but in a number of instances Baptist churches trace their origin to this revival of religion.

The first of these was constituted of ten members, October 29, 1778, at Horton, and remains to this day not only the oldest but one of the strongest churches in the province. The Rev. Nicholson Pearson was chosen pastor, and in the two following years fifty-two were added to the church. This growth in numbers, however, was in part accomplished by the adoption of open communion and mixed membership. Congregationalists being admitted to full fellowship on equal terms with baptized believers. It was not until 1809 that the Horton church became what we understand by the phrase, a Baptist church. The practice of mixed membership, or at any rate of open communion, was general among the Baptist churches of this province until the early years of the last century, they having gradually felt their way toward their present position. The Horton church is notable for having had but three pastors in the first century of its existence: Rev. Nicholas Pearson, from 1778 to 1791; Rev. Theodore Seth Harding, from 1795 to 1855, when he was succeeded by Rev. Stephen W. De Blois, who was still pastor at the celebration of the centenary. Churches were organized rapidly between 1780 and 1800, including those of Lower Granville, Halifax (1795), Newport (1799), Sackville (1799), as well as Annapolis and Upper Granville, Chester, Cornwallis, Yarmouth, and Digby, the dates of whose organizations are unknown. Of these churches the First Halifax seems to have been the only one that admitted to membership only baptized believers; and it is doubtful whether even that church practised restricted communion during this period. In this respect the early history of the Baptists of Canada differs widely from that of the first Baptist churches in the United States.

The first Baptists of Lower Canada seem to have arisen among a settlement of American Tories, not far from the Vermont line. Elders John Hebbard and Ariel Kendrick, missionaries of the Woodstock Association, of Vermont, visited them in 1794, and their preaching was followed by an extensive revival. A few years later, Rev. Elisha Andrews, of Fairfax, Vt., visited these people at their request, baptized about thirty converts, and organized the Eaton church. A number of other churches

were soon afterward formed in this region, several of which were for a time affiliated with the Richmond Association, of Vermont. The Domestic Missionary Society of Massachusetts, and other like New England organizations, paid much attention to this field, frequently sending missionaries thither.

The beginnings in Upper Canada seem to have been practically simultaneous, but quite without concert, with those in the lower province. In 1794 Reuben Crandall, at that time a licentiate, settled on the northern shore of Lake Ontario, in what is now Prince Edward County, and the following year he had gained converts enough to organize the Hallowell church. Of this body there now remains no authentic record, but another church formed at Haldimund in 1798 proved more permanent, and is now in its second century of vigorous life. Other ministers from "the States" followed, and other churches were gathered in like manner. About the year 1800, Titus Fitch, another licentiate, located in Charlotteville township, where his labors resulted in the formation of a church of thirty members in 1804. It appears to have been the fashion in those days when a young licentiate was not called by a church, for him to go out in the region beyond and call a church—a fashion that may be commended to the rising ministry of our day for their imitation.

It will therefore be seen that the first Baptist churches of Canada, in all its provinces alike, for the most part owe their origin either to colonies from the United States or to the labors of missionaries from this country. The most marked exception is found in the group of churches that compose the Ottawa Association that, together with their pastors, were largely composed of Scotch immigrants, and trace their line of descent as Baptists to the labors in Edinburgh of the brothers Haldane. Baptist growth was slow up to 1830, and has never been rapid in Quebec, whose population is so largely French and Catholic. It was likewise retarded unduly by various internal disagreements, chief of which was the question of close or open communion. The great majority of Canadian Baptists have, for a generation, belonged to the Regular or strict-communion wing of the denomination.

Alexander Crawford, a Scotchman, and one of the Haldane missionaries, was the first (1814) to preach and baptize according to the New Testament order in Prince Edward's Island, and the first churches adhered rigidly to the practice of the Scotch Baptists. In 1826 the first church was formed at Bedeque that was from the beginning associated with the churches of the Maritime Provinces, though most of the others fell into line eventually. The differences between the churches of Scotch origin and the other Baptists of the provinces were numerous; the former insisted strenuously on a plural eldership, on the weekly celebration of the Lord's Supper, and especially that members of the church should not marry those who belonged to other denominations. A domestic and foreign missionary society was formed in 1845, and the Island Baptist Association in 1868. The latter organization was especially useful in promoting denominational advance. From thirteen churches and six hundred members it has grown to twenty-five churches and over two thousand members.

The first union of these Baptist churches was formed in 1800, at Granville, by ten churches, under the title of the Nova Scotia and New Brunswick Baptist Association. In one respect it differed from other bodies of this kind, though in the main it pretended to "no other powers than those of an advisory council"; for more than a quarter of a century it assumed the function of examining and ordaining candidates for the ministry—

the sole instance of the kind, it is believed, in the
history of Baptists. In 1809 the practice of open communion was discontinued by the associated churches. Four
churches withdrew from fellowship with the others for
a time, but afterwards returned. By 1821 the growth
of this body led to its division, for greater convenience,
into two Associations, one for each province. The Nova
Scotia Association, in turn, was divided, in 1850, into the
Eastern, Central, and Western Associations. The New
Brunswick Association, in 1847, divided into Eastern
and Western Associations; a Southern Association was
organized in 1850; and in 1868 the Prince Edward's
Island Association assumed an independent existence.
These successive developments of organization are landmarks of denominational growth, indicating, better than
statistics, the progress of the churches in numbers and
spiritual efficiency. At present these Associations represent three hundred and ninety-nine churches, with forty-
four thousand eight hundred and forty-one members.

In Ontario and Quebec the growth has been equally
marked. The first organization of the churches of Upper
Canada was the Thurlow Association (afterward the
Haldimand), formed in 1803; the Eastern and Grand
River Associations followed, in 1819; and others at frequent intervals thereafter. In Quebec the progress was
slower; the earliest churches, as we have seen, remained
affiliated with Vermont Associations. It was not until
1830 that a Baptist church was established in Montreal,
and not till 1835 that the Ottawa Association was formed.
In 1845, the Montreal was formed from the Ottawa.
The Baptist churches of these provinces now number
four hundred and thirty, with forty thousand two hundred and seventy members, and report three thousand
five hundred and eight baptisms for 1900. In the
last decade these churches have increased in membership

twenty-eight per cent., while those of the Maritime Provinces in the same period have gained less than ten per cent. If these rates are maintained another decade, the churches of Ontario and Quebec will be considerably stronger, numerically, at least, than their elder sisters.

Early in their history the Baptists of the Maritime Provinces acknowledged the obligations of the Great Commission, and to the best of their power fulfilled them. A missionary society was formed as early as 1815 in Nova Scotia, and a similar organization followed in New Brunswick in 1820. Both of these societies vigorously prosecuted work at home and abroad for many years. In 1846 these societies were consolidated into one, known as " The Baptist Convention of the Maritime Provinces." Each Association in Nova Scotia, New Brunswick, and Prince Edward's Island is entitled to send two delegates to each meeting of this body, and each contributing church may send one member. Two Boards for Home and Foreign Missions direct the Convention's aggressive work, in addition to which there are Boards for Ministerial Education and Ministerial Relief; while close relations are maintained with Acadia College by nominating every three years six new members of its Board of governors.

The Canada Baptist Missionary Society was organized in June, 1837, through the agency of the Ottawa Association, and its headquarters were in Montreal. After some years of checkered existence, it finally succumbed to the stress of the communion controversies. In spite of its disclaimers, it was suspected of being too friendly to open communion, and lost the support of the strict communionists. The latter finally formed the organizations in which they could have more confidence: the Western Canada Baptist Home Mission Society, in 1854, and the Foreign Mission Society of Ontario and Quebec, in 1866. The latter was for the first seven years of its life an auxiliary of the American Baptist Missionary Union, but since 1873 has been independent, and maintains a flourishing mission among the Telugus. Home mission work among the Indians has been a special feature of the Canadian Baptist missionary enterprises. The Grand Ligne Mission among the French Catholics, founded in 1835, was for a time undenominational and independent, but for more than fifty years has been carried on under Baptist auspices, though Pedobaptists have also, to some extent, promoted the work. It is said that more than five thousand have been brought to the knowledge of the truth through this mission, many of whom are unofficial missionaries among their own people in Canada and New England.

In 1888 a bill was passed by the Dominion Parliament consolidating all the previously existing societies (except the Grand Ligne Mission), including some not named above, into " The Baptist Convention of Ontario and Quebec." Five Boards—Home Mission, Foreign Mission, Ministerial Superannuation and Widows' and Orphans', Publication, Church Edifice—conduct the work formerly done by these various societies, and the churches thus have direct relations with a single delegated body, which is their agent in all general denominational work. This seems to be almost an ideal method of organization, and must be a powerful promotive of denominational unity and efficiency. Since 1881 Manitoba and the Northwest has had a separate Convention.

In 1828, when the Baptists of Nova Scotia had but twenty-nine churches and one thousand seven hundred and seventy-two members, they established an academy at Horton; in 1838 they established Acadia College; and in 1861 a seminary for young women. The three institutions are still prosperous, and have together about three hundred and thirty students. The institutions are governed by a Board of trustees appointed by the Convention of the Maritime Provinces. The New Brunswick Baptists established an academy at Frederickton, which ceased to exist some years ago; it had a successor at St. Martins, with better prospects of permanence for a time, but that has also succumbed. The Baptists of Quebec were unfortunate in their sole educational venture, that of establishing a college at Montreal. It was founded in 1838, and after a few years erected a fine stone building, which proved too costly an enterprise. After struggling vainly with debts for some years, in 1849 it was found necessary to sell the property, liquidate the debts, and let the college perish. Many causes contributed to its downfall, its location being perhaps the chief.

The Baptists of Ontario have been more fortunate, in part perhaps by reason of greater prudence. They established a college at Woodstock about 1860, with both an arts and a theological department. Many of the most useful ministers of the Dominion, and some in the United States, received their training there. In 1880, the liberality of the late William McMaster founded the Toronto Baptist College, a theological seminary at first, to which the theological department of Woodstock was transferred. The new institution was enlarged later into McMaster University, an arts department being established in connection with the theological, and Woodstock being voluntarily reduced to the grade of an academy and feeder of the university. A college for women, known as Moulton College, has since been established by Mrs. McMaster (*nee* Moulton), and is affiliated with the university. The result of these new enterprises has been a great stimulus of interest in education among Canadian Baptists. The new century opened with an enrollment of over four hundred students in the three institutions. The

gross assets amount to about nine hundred thousand
dollars, making available for the three schools an income
of about forty thousand dollars.

But little material is accessible for the history of the
Baptists of Australasia. Rev. John Saunders, a Baptist
minister, who had established two churches in London,
became very desirous of preaching to the convicts and
planting a Christian church at Botany Bay. He formed
the Bathurst Street Church, Sidney, in 1834. His ardu-
ous labors finally broke his health, but a worthy successor
was found in Rev. James Voller, by whose effort an Association was formed, that in 1891 reports twenty-six
churches and one thousand four hundred and sixty-one
members. The Baptist church in Melbourne, Victoria,
was organized in 1845 by Rev. William Ham, and the
cause has prospered continuously. There are now forty-
four churches and four thousand five hundred and fifty-
eight members. In South Australia the first Baptist
church to be established was the Hinders Street Chapel
of Adelaide, which dates from 1861. Progress here has
been hindered by an excess of the spirit of independency
and too little co-operation, but there are fifty-two churches
and three thousand six hundred and sixty-five members.
The Wharf Street Chapel in Moreton Bay, Queensland,
was built in 1856, after Rev. B. G. Wilson had preached
there for several years, and from this the Baptists of the
colony have increased to twenty-seven churches and two
thousand one hundred and seventy members. During
the past few years there has been a slight loss here.

From New Zealand are reported twenty-eight churches
and two thousand seven hundred and seventy-eight members; and besides the work among the white people a
mission is maintained among the Maoris, of whom there
are still about fifty thousand. The Baptist cause here

owes its present prosperity largely to the labors of Rev. D. Dolomore, who went thither in 1851. The first church was organized in 1854, and from that time growth was steady, especially in the southern section. A Baptist Union was formed about 1880, which has been a great help to the churches, especially in uniting them in missionary efforts. Work was begun by the Baptists in Tasmania in 1834, but there have been meager results here, in spite of many years of hard labor, there being at present but nine churches and five hundred and seventy-four members.

CHAPTER XIX

THE history of American Baptists naturally divides into three periods or movements. The first coincides nearly with the colonial period of our secular national history. It is marked by faithful witness to the truth on the one hand, and by bitter persecution on the other. The second period also corresponds with an era of secular history, the time of territorial expansion, and is marked by unexampled growth and missionary activity (1776-1845). The third period, extending from about the time of the Mexican War to our own day, may be called the period of evangelism and education. These divisions are largely arbitrary, of course, and there are no well-marked lines of division, the periods designated overlapping each other. The division has, however, a certain mnemonic value; and as we proceed the characteristics attributed to each period will be seen to be justified by the facts.

The historians of Puritan New England assert that among the early immigrants to their colony were some tainted with Anabaptism. One of those suspected of this offense was Hanserd Knollys. Of the details of his stay in America little is known save that it was barely three years. He arrived at Boston in 1638, and very soon after became pastor of a church at Piscataway (now Dover), N. H. There is no evidence that Knollys held Baptist views at this time; as we have already seen (p. 216), he was ordained pastor of a Baptist church in London (England) in 1645, and all the circumstances of his life up to that time compel the conclusion that he had only recently become a Baptist. While he was pastor at Piscataway his church was rent by a dispute regarding infant baptism (this we know from an Episcopalian visitor to the colony in April, 1641), which warrants the conclusion that though there were people of Baptist sentiments in the church it was not a Baptist church. To escape persecution the church in large part removed in 1641 to Long Island, and thence to New Jersey, where they formed a Baptist church (probably in 1689) and gave to it the same name the New Hampshire colony had borne. This is the story of the origin of the oldest Baptist church but one (Middletown, formed in 1688) in New Jersey. If we conclude that Knollys and his church were not Baptist, then the first Baptist church organized in America was that of Providence. But before speaking of that we must consider the previous history of its founder.

Much obscurity hangs over the early life of Roger Williams, but he was probably the son of a merchant tailor of London, James Williams, and his wife Alice. He was born about 1607, and Sir Edward Coke, the great English lawyer, attracted by his promise, secured for him entrance to Sutton's Hospital. Here he completed his preparatory studies and then entered the University of Cambridge, where he took his bachelor's degree in 1627. He was offered several livings in the Church of England, but it does not appear that he was ever actually beneficed. He was apparently ordained, since he is described on his arrival at Boston as " a godly minister." He embraced Puritan principles, and it is even probable that he was a Separatist in principle before leaving England. He determined to leave England, and in 1631 landed in Boston, where he hoped to find greater religious freedom. He found the Puritans fully as intolerant as

Laud, and was by no means satisfied with the half-way reformation that they were disposed to make. He saw the inconsistency of the New England theocracy, in which the functions of the Church and State were so inter-blended that the identity of each was in danger of being lost. He had grasped the principle that the Church and the State should be entirely separate and independent each of the other. It is not at all probable that Williams had imbibed these notions from the English Baptists, or that he even knew of their holding such doctrines. At this time he was not, at any rate, an Anabaptist. He found no fault with the Congregational doctrine or dis-cipline, but denounced the principle of a State Church, and upheld the right of soul liberty on natural and scriptural grounds alike.

In spite of his heterodoxy, Williams was called to be minister to the church at Salem, where he was highly esteemed for his zeal and eloquence. The Salem church had acted against the will of the Massachusetts authori-ties, and to prevent trouble Williams went for a time to Plymouth. He returned to Salem as pastor again, but was soon summoned before the court in Boston and condemned to banishment. The first (and no doubt the chief) charge against him was, " That the magistrate ought not to punish the breach of the first table, other-wise than in such case as did disturb the civil peace." This was also stated in the decree of banishment as the chief cause: " Whereas, Mr. Roger Williams, one of the elders of the church of Salem, hath broached and di-vulged new and dangerous opinions against the author-ity of magistrates." Nothing can be clearer, as a matter of historical record, than that the chief cause of the banishment of Roger Williams was his teaching with regard to religious liberty, that the magistrate has no right to punish breaches of the first table of the law—

T

those commandments, namely, that relate to the worship of God.

After his banishment, Williams made his way, in the dead of winter, to Narragansett Bay. While at Plymouth he had learned something of the Indian dialects, and he was kindly received. At what is now Providence he founded a settlement, many of his former Salem charge removing to this place. The original settlers in 1638 entered into a compact reading thus: " We whose names are hereunder written, being desirous to inhabit in the town of Providence, do promise to submit ourselves in active and passive obedience to all such orders or agencies as shall be made for the public good of the body in an orderly way, by the major consent of the present inhabitants, masters of families, incorporated together into a township, and such others whom they shall admit into the same, only in civil things." A similar agreement was signed in 1640; the principle was embodied in the code of laws adopted by the colony in 1647, and was finally incorporated in the royal charter given by Charles II. in 1663: " Our royal will and pleasure is, that no person within the said colony, at any time hereafter, shall be in any wise molested, punished, disquieted, or called in question, for any differences of opinion in matters of religion, and do not actually disturb the civil peace of the said colony." Thus was founded the first government in the world, whose corner-stone was absolute religious liberty.

It is true that a few other countries had before this, and for periods more or less brief, tolerated what they regarded as heresy; but this was the first government organized on the principle of absolute liberty to all, in such matters of belief and practice as did not conflict with the peace and order of society, or with ordinary good morals. And though this government was insignificant in point of numbers and power, it was the pioneer in a great revolution, its principle having become the fundamental law of every American State, and influenced strongly even the most conservative European States. Though he did not originate the idea of soul liberty, it was given to Roger Williams, in the providence of God, to be its standard-bearer in a new world, where it should have full opportunity to work itself out, and afford by its fruits a demonstration that it is of God and not of man.

Up to this time Williams was not a Baptist; but his continued studies of the Scriptures led him to the belief that the sprinkling of water on an unconscious babe does not constitute obedience to the command of our Lord, " Be baptized." Having arrived at this conviction, he wished to be baptized; but in this little colony, separated from other civilized countries by an ocean or a wilderness, where was a qualified administrator to be found? In the meantime, other converts to the truth had been made, whether by his agency or by independent study of the word. They resolved to follow the precept and example of Christ in the only way possible to them. Some time about March, 1639, therefore, Williams was baptized by Ezekiel Holliman, who had been a member of his church at Salem; and thereupon Williams baptized ten others, and the first Baptist church on American soil was formed. It is highly probable, though not conclusively established, that this baptism was an immersion. No other baptism is known to have been practised, in a single instance, by American Baptists. There are a number of other instances in the history of American Baptists of the formation of a church after this manner—the constituent members either being ignorant that there were other Christians who agreed with them, or being so far distant from any other Baptists that the procurement of an administrator was out of the question.

Williams was, however, one of the most erratic and unstable men of his time; and a few months later he came to the conclusion that this baptism by one who had not himself been baptized in an orderly manner was not valid baptism. He withdrew himself from the church, and for the rest of his life was unconnected with any religious body, calling himself a "seeker." He seems to have been misled by an idea that, if logically carried out, would unchurch every church, by making all administration of ordinances invalid.

Whether the present First Baptist Church of Providence is the lineal successor of this church founded by Roger Williams is a difficult historical question, about which a positive opinion should be expressed with diffidence. Tradition maintains that the line of succession has been unbroken; but the records to prove this are lacking. The facts appear to be that after the departure of Williams, one of those whom he had baptized, Thomas Olney, became the head of the church, to which was added soon after a number of new-comers, chief among which were William Wickendon, Chad Brown, and Gregory Dexter. The original members were of Puritan antecedents and Calvinists; the new-comers appear to have been Arminians, and inclined to make the laying on of hands after baptism an article of faith. It has been conjectured that the three men named were associated with Olney in a plural eldership, but all these matters are doubtful since the earliest records of the Providence church begin with the year 1775,[1] and back of that we have only tradition and conjecture. All that is certain is that controversy began and continued until it reached the acute stage in 1652, when the church was divided. A part, the smaller, apparently, adhered to the original faith of the church, and remained under the pastoral

[1] Callendar, " R. I. Hist. Coll.," Vol. IV., p. 117.

care of Thomas Olney. This wing of the church became extinct somewhere about 1720. The larger part of the members adhered to Wickendon, Brown, and Dexter, and became a Six-principle church, remaining such until a comparatively late time. In 1771, through the influence of President James Manning, the majority adopted a Calvinistic creed, whereupon the Six-principle minority seceded. Both these branches still survive, the former now bearing the title of the First Baptist Church of Providence.

There is another church that disputes with this the honor of being the oldest Baptist church in America. Its founder, Dr. John Clarke, is one of the most interesting characters of his time, but his early history is much involved in dispute and obscurity; the true date of his birth even is unknown. According to one authority, perhaps the best, he was born in Suffolk, England, October 8, 1609. We know that he was a scholar in his manhood, with a knowledge of Greek and Hebrew such as men seldom gained in England outside of the universities; but which university he attended, and what degree he took, are facts not as yet discovered by investigation. An extant legal document bearing date of March 12, 1656, is almost the only relic of his life in England; in that he describes himself as a physician of London. There seems no room for doubt that he was of the Puritan party, and that he left England to escape persecution and enjoy the greater freedom of the new world.

When he reached Boston, in November, 1637, it must have seemed to him that he had truly jumped from the frying-pan into the fire. There had been trouble among the Puritans there, and Sir Henry Vane and others had been deprived of their arms and ordered to leave the colony. Clarke became the leader of certain of these in establishing a colony elsewhere. A constitution was

drawn up and signed in March, 1638, which made the
law of Christ the law of this new community.   An experiment was made in New Hampshire, but the climate
was thought too cold, and a location was sought farther
south.   This led to the purchase from the Indians of the
island of Aquidneck, which was renamed Rhode Island.
Two settlements were formed, the northern one called
Portsmouth and the southern Newport.   The original
code of laws has not been preserved, but in 1641 it was
" Ordered that none be accounted a delinquent for doctrine, provided that it be not directly repugnant to the
government or laws established."   The Providence compact limiting the authority of the magistrate to civil things
was made in 1639, and is the older instrument, but
Newport divides with Providence the honor of first
establishing this principle in civil government.

In the same year in which the colony was founded, a
church was organized in Newport, and Mr. Clarke became
its teaching elder, apparently from the first.   What sort
of a church this was we do not positively know.[1]   There
is no evidence at present known to exist by which the
religious opinions and practices of Clarke up to this time
may be determined.   He may have been imbued with
Baptist doctrine before coming to America, but there is
nothing in his conduct inconsistent with the theory that
he came here simply a Puritan Separatist, like Roger
Williams.   Our first definite knowledge of this church
comes from the report made in March, 1640, by the
commissioners from the church in Boston.   Of the faults
they allege, Anabaptism is not one, whence it seems a
safe conclusion that at this time this was not a Baptist
church.   When and how it became such we do not know.
The date 1644 is purely traditional, and the first positive

[1] A majority had been members of Cotton's church in Boston.   Winthrop's
Journal shows that from September, 1638, Clarke was their preacher.

knowledge we have is October, 1648, when we know [1] that a Baptist church existed in Newport, having fifteen members. In 1654 or 1656 a controversy arose in this church, as in that in Providence, and with a like result— a Six-principle church was constituted, under the leadership of William Vaughn, who had previously received the rite of laying on of hands from Wickendon and Dexter at Providence.

Doctor Clarke retained his connection with the church he founded until his death, though much of his time was absorbed by public duties. In the autumn of 1651 he was sent by the colonists to England, to obtain a new and better charter. He remained there twelve years, finding it impossible to gain his end during the Protectorate. Shortly after his arrival he printed his " Ill News from New England," which shares with Roger Williams' " Bloody Tenet of Persecution," the praise of advocating liberty of conscience at a time when that doctrine was decried even by those who called themselves friends of liberty. Finally, what he could not procure from the Cromwells he succeeded in obtaining from Charles II., who on July 9, 1663, set his hand to a charter that secured civil and religious liberty to the colony of Rhode Island—a charter under which the State was governed until the year 1843.

Returning to Newport in 1664, Clarke became one of the chief citizens of the colony. He was deputy governor in 1669, and again in 1671, having declined the office in 1670. Soon after he retired to private life, and died suddenly April 20, 1676. His services to his State, and to the cause of liberty, were quite as great as those of the better known Williams. But for him the charter of 1663 would never have been obtained; and there is good reason to infer, from internal evidence, that a good

[1] Callendar, " R. I. Hist. Coll.," IV., 117.

part of that instrument was drawn by him. He was the most eminent Baptist of his time in New England, and his name deserves to be held in the highest honor.

The formation of Baptist churches in Massachusetts was greatly impeded by the resolute opposition of the colonial authorities. A theocratic government had been established, in which all rights of citizenship were denied to those who were not members of the churches of the Standing Order.[1] From the first there were individuals who came into collision with this government, by reason of their Anabaptist convictions. These the magistrates proceeded to deal with sharply. In 1644 [2] one Thomas Painter, of Hingham, refused to have his child baptized, and stoutly protested against such a ceremony as " an anti-Christian ordinance," whereupon he was tied up and whipped. In the same year, and for several years following, there are records of several presentments to the Salem court of men who withheld their children from baptism or argued against infant baptism. These men were proceeded against on general principles, without authority of law, but in November, 1644, the General Court enacted a statute that whoever " shall either openly condemn or oppose the baptizing of infants, or go about secretly to seduce others from the approbation or use thereof, or shall purposely depart the congregation at the ministration of the ordinances, or shall deny the ordinance of magistracy, or their lawful right and authority to make war, or to punish the outward breaches of the first table, and shall appear to the court wilfully and obstinately to continue therein after due time and means of conviction, every such person or persons shall be sentenced to banishment."

[1] Order of the General Court, quoted by Wood, "History of the First Baptist Church of Boston," p. 6.

[2] Backus (Vol. I., p. 93) shows there was an attempt to organize a church at Weymouth in 1639.

The most prominent among the violators of this law was Henry Dunster. A native of Lancashire (born about 1612), he was educated at Magdalen College, Cambridge, where he took his bachelor's degree in 1630 and the master's in 1634. He probably took orders in the Church of England, but his advancement was made impossible by his adoption of Separatist ideas, and he decided to seek a career in the new world. He arrived at Boston toward the end of the summer of 1640, and in the following year he was chosen, almost by acclamation, to be the president of the new college established by the Massachusetts colony. For this post his learning, his piety, and his skill in affairs combined to make him an ideal occupant, and for twelve years he discharged the duties connected with his important office with universal satisfaction and applause.

In the year 1653 the birth of a fourth child brought to an issue doubts that he appears to have entertained for some time regarding infant baptism. He now definitely made known his conviction that only believers should be baptized, and set forth his reasons in several sermons. Great excitement was at once provoked by this procedure of Dunster's, and no wonder. The denial of infant baptism was a blow at the very foundations of the Puritan theory of Church and State, and Dunster had become a dangerous enemy of the Commonwealth. Either he must be suppressed or the whole social fabric of Massachusetts must be remodeled. We need not be surprised that the former alternative was chosen. Dunster was virtually compelled to resign the presidency of the college, but it is possible that no further proceedings would have been taken against him save for his own indiscretion. He insisted on being heard during a service of the Cambridge church, and set forth his views at length. For the offense of thus disturbing worship, he was indicted, tried, and condemned to receive an admonition from the General Court. He was also presented for refusal to have his child baptized, and required to give surety for his further appearance in court at Boston, in September, 1657. No record of further proceedings against him remains, and his death in 1659 removed him from the jurisdiction of the General Court of Massachusetts.

What he thus escaped may perhaps be inferred from the treatment of John Clarke, the founder of the Newport church, and Obadiah Holmes, who was destined to be Clarke's successor. While they were spending the Lord's Day with a brother who lived near Lynn, it was concluded to have religious services in the house. Two constables broke in while Mr. Clarke was preaching from Rev. 3 : 10, and the men were haled before the court. For this offense they were sentenced to pay, Clarke a fine of twenty pounds, and Holmes one of thirty pounds, in default of which they were to be " well whipped." A friend paid Clarke's fine, and he was set at liberty whether he would or no; but on September 6, 1651, Holmes was " whipped unmercifully " (the phrase is Bancroft's) in the streets of Boston, for the atrocious crime of preaching the gospel and of adding thereto the denial of infant baptism.

These repressive measures were quite unavailing; Anabaptist sentiments continued to increase among the Puritans, and in addition, immigrants began to come who had been Baptists in the old country. John Myles, who, as we have seen, was the founder of the first Baptist church in Wales, was one of the victims of the Act of Uniformity, and soon after it went into effect he and a number of the members of the Ilston church came to the new world and at first settled at Rehoboth. Here, in 1663, they organized a Baptist church, which was, in

1667, removed to a new settlement, named Swansea, in memory of the city near which they had dwelt in Wales. This church, the first formed in the Massachusetts colony, has had an uninterrupted existence to this day. As became its origin, it was a strongly Calvinistic body, but a second Swansea church was formed in 1685 that was as strongly Arminian.

The time was now ripe for an organized protest against the errors of the Puritan churches, by the formation of a Baptist church in Boston itself. The leader of this enterprise was Thomas Goold, or Gould, a friend of President Dunster, a resident of Charlestown. Influenced, no doubt, by his friend's teaching and example, Goold refused, in 1655, to present an infant child for baptism, and was duly admonished therefor by the Charlestown elders. A course of warning, expostulation, and discipline continuing for ten years so far failed to convince Thomas Goold of his error, that on May 28, 1665, a Baptist church was organized in his house, where meetings of Baptists had been held more or less regularly for several years. A storm of persecution at once broke upon this little band of nine, of whom two were women. The Swansea church, being situated on the borders of Rhode Island, was comparatively undisturbed; not so the church in Boston. At the time of its organization the Puritan churches were torn by the dissensions that finally resulted in the adoption of the Half-way Covenant; but, as in all family quarrels, both parties to the contest were ready to pounce upon any intruder. Such they considered this new Baptist church to be, and a determined effort was made to suppress it. Shortly after its organization the members were summoned before the court and ordered to " desist from such theire meeting, & irreligious practises, as they would Answer the contrary at theire peril."

They were not the desisting kind, however, and per
sisted in teaching their " damnable errors," and holding
meetings, whereupon nearly all of them were at one time
or another, and several more than once, imprisoned or
fined, or both. Thomas Goold, who had become the first
pastor of the church, was the severest sufferer, though
he had several companions; and his health was so broken
by his frequent and long imprisonments that he died in
October, 1675. In 1670 he removed to Noddle's Island,
and the church met in his house there, coming from
Boston, Woburn, and other places for the purpose.

In the latter part of the year 1678 the church began
to build a meeting-house in Boston, on what is now Salem
Street, a modest frame building, on ground owned by
two of the members. This was indeed flying in the face
of the Puritan State, and by order of the General Court
the marshal nailed up the doors and posted the following
notice upon them:

All Psons are to take notice yt by orde of ye Court ye dores
of this howse are shutt up & yt they are Inhibitted to hold
any meeting therein or to open ye dores thereof, without lishence
from Authority, till ye gennerall Court take further order as they
will answer ye Contrary att theire p'ill, dated in boston 8th
march 1680, by orde of ye Councell

EDWARD RAWSON *Secretary.*

This was, however, the last serious persecution of the
church. The court did not venture to enforce its order
beyond a single Sunday; on the following Lord's Day the
doors were found open, and there was no further interference with the worship of the church. Before 1671,
while the persecution was at its height, twenty-two
(including eight women) had united with the church.
After persecution ceased the growth was naturally still
more rapid. Much indignation had been caused, both in

the colony itself and in England, by the Puritan persecutions of Baptists and Quakers—the latter suffering even more than Baptists, some even to death—and there was great danger that the charter would be lost. This, in fact, befell a few years later. The Puritan theory had broken down—a theocracy had been proved an impossible form of government in New England. In 1691 a new charter was given by William and Mary; Plymouth and Massachusetts Bay were consolidated into the one colony of Massachusetts, and the charter assured " liberty of conscience to all Christians, except Papists." Baptists were henceforth exempt from persecution, but not from taxation to support a State church.

For a long time the growth of Baptists in New England continued to be slow. The next church to be established was that at Kittery, Me., the Province of Maine then being part of the Massachusetts colony. Two settlers at that place, William Screven and Humphrey Churchwood, came to hold Baptist views, made their way to Boston, and were baptized into the fellowship of the church on June 21, 1681. Mr. Screven was licensed to preach, and on his return to Kittery, organized a church. He was imprisoned and fined ten pounds by the provincial authorities for pronouncing infant baptism " no ordinance of God, but an invention of men." Finding that there was no prospect of their being permitted to serve God in peace, the little church of seventeen made preparations for removal. They settled near the site of the present city of Charleston, S. C., and reorganizing in 1684, established the First Baptist Church of that town. Not for more than fourscore years was another attempt made to plant a Baptist church in Maine.

Aside from a church formed among the Indians at Chilmark, in Martha's Vineyard (1693), these were the only Calvinistic Baptist churches formed in New England during the seventeenth century.[1]   There were, however, two churches of the Arminian or Six-principle order in Rhode Island—the North Kingston (1665), and the Tiverton (1685).   There was also a Seventh-day church in Newport that had been founded in 1671.   In all, therefore, there were ten small churches, with probably not more than three hundred members, in the year 1700.

The only direction in which any considerable progress was made for about half a century was in Connecticut. There some Baptists, probably removed from Rhode Island, were found early in the eighteenth century, and a church was organized in 1705, at Groton, of which Valentine Wightman became the pastor.   This was a Six-principle church.   But the churches formed at New London (1710), Wallingford (1731), Southington (1738), and North Stonington (1743) were either Calvinistic churches from the beginning or soon became such.[2]

This slow progress is by no means surprising.   The atmosphere of New England was not favorable to spiritual vigor in the first half of the eighteenth century, and the policy pursued toward Baptists there had prevented immigrants of that faith from turning their faces in that direction.

In the Middle States the conditions of growth were, on the whole, more favorable.   The only persecution experienced was in the colony of New York, and that was for a brief time under the governorship of Peter Stuyvesant.   Misled by the liberal promises of the Dutch West India Company a number of Baptists had settled on

[1] There were but eight, all told, in Massachusetts at the beginning of the Great Awakening (1740).

[2] How Connecticut felt toward Baptists may be seen from this early statute: "Nor shall any persons neglect the public worship of God in some lawful Congregation, and form themselves into separate companies in private Houses, on Penalty of Ten Shillings for every such Offense each person shall be guilty of." ("Colony Law Book," p. 139.)

Long Island, in what are now Gravesend and Flushing. One of the most prominent was John Bowne, who had come to this country from England in 1635, first settling at Salem, Mass. He may not have been a Baptist at this time, but he was a dissenter both from the Church of England and the Established Church of Massachusetts. He offended the Dutch authorities by his tenderness towards the "abominable people called Quakers," who were then being punished in New Amsterdam with little less severity than was shown in New England. Bowne was arrested and fined for giving aid and shelter to these people, and on his refusal to pay his fine, he was banished and sent by ship to Holland.

He at once appealed to the directors of the company, and they promptly condemned their agent. The Dutch were too hearty lovers of religious liberty, and had experienced too much of the horrors of the Inquisition, to play for any length of time the rôle of persecutors. The choleric and tyrannical Peter soon received orders from Holland: "Let every man remain free, so long as he is modest, moderate, his political conduct irreproachable, and so long as he does not offend others or oppose the government." But before the policy could be thus changed, Baptists had suffered considerably, and later under the English rule the same difficulty was experienced. The first Baptist minister to labor in New York City, so far as is known, was Rev. William Wickendon, of Providence, in 1656; and for these labors he was heavily fined, but after an imprisonment of some months, being too poor to pay the fine, he was released and banished from the colony. Whether he had succeeded in gathering a church is uncertain, but if he did, it was soon scattered by persecution, for an ordinance of 1662 imposed a severe fine on anybody who should even be present at an illegal conventicle.

The next trace of Baptists in this colony is at Oyster Bay, L. I., where one William Rhodes, a Baptist minister from Rhode Island, began to preach and baptize converts about 1700. By 1724 a church had been organized, and Robert Feeks was ordained pastor. Before this, however, a Baptist church had been organized in New York, where Rev. Valentine Wightman began to preach about 1711. One of his converts was Nicholas Eyres, a wealthy brewer, in whose house the meetings were held. He was baptized in 1714, a church was formed, and Eyres soon became its pastor, at the same time continuing in business. In spite of some persecutions and many discouragements, they continued to flourish until internal dissensions wrecked them, and not long after 1730 the church became extinct.

The most important and influential of the early Baptist centers was the group of churches in the vicinity of Philadelphia. In 1684 Thomas Dungan gathered a church at Cold Spring, Pa., but it became extinct about 1702. In 1688 the church at Pennepeck (Lower Dublin) was organized. This church, of twelve members at the beginning, had as its first pastor Elias Keach, son of the well-known Baptist minister of London, Benjamin Keach. The First Church of Philadelphia was founded in the following year, but its members were connected with the Lower Dublin Church until 1746, when they were formally constituted a separate and independent church. The Welsh Tract Church was constituted in 1701.

The liberal offers of complete religious liberty in New Jersey drew Baptists to that colony as early as 1660. The first church organized was that at Middletown in 1688, composed mainly of those who had fled from persecution in New York and other colonies. Piscataway (1689), Cohansey (1690), Cape May (1712), and Hopewell (1715), were the next to follow. Congregations

ANDREW FULLER

The Kettering House Where the English Baptist Missionary Society Was Organized in 1792

CHARLES HADDON SPURGEON

The Myles Memorial

JOHN MYLES
1621 — 1683
FOUNDER OF
THE FIRST BAPTIST CHURCH
IN MASSACHUSETTS

The First Baptist Meetinghouse in Boston

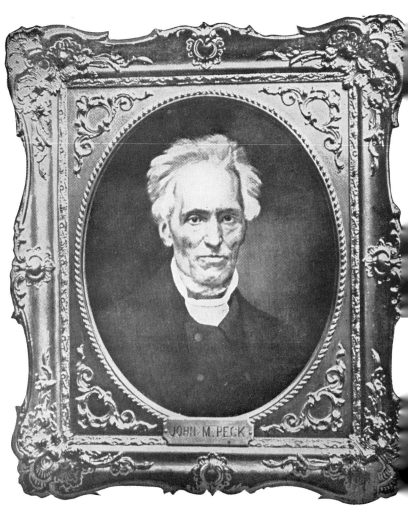

JOHN M. PECK

Adoniram Judson

THE HAYSTACK MONUMENT

were also gathered at Salem, Burlington, Scotch Plains, and other places, that in later years were constituted separate churches.

The nucleus of each of these churches, so far as their history is known, appears to have been a few men and women who had been Baptists before coming to this country. Others had held Baptist beliefs for some years, but had never before connected themselves with a Baptist church, possibly for lack of opportunity in their old homes. The major part of these people were English; in and about Philadelphia there were many Welsh Baptists; a few came from Ireland. The affiliations of American Baptists are thus directly with our brethren of Great Britain. It is the fashion in some quarters to call the church founded by Roger Williams "the venerable mother of American Baptist churches." She is then that anomaly in the world, a mother who never bore children, for no church now existing can be shown to have been established by her labors prior to 1800, if thereafter. The part played by Roger Williams and his church in the history of American Baptists is ludicrously small, when the facts are compared to the ink that has been shed on the subject.

All these churches last described were in intimate fellowship, the Philadelphia group being by common consent the center of interest. For their mutual convenience and edification, almost from their origin, a custom grew up of holding "general meetings" from time to time for the ministry of the word and the gospel ordinances. From being held once a year, these meetings came to be semi-annual, in the months of May and September. These were for many years what their name implied—general meetings—being attended by as many as could make it convenient, and were wholly devotional and evangelistic. In 1707 the meeting was for the first time a delegated body, five churches appointing delegates, and this is the beginning of the Philadelphia Association. From the first the New Jersey churches were members, and as the body increased in age and strength it attracted to itself all the Baptist churches within traveling distance of it, having as members churches in southern New York and Virginia. Its adoption of a strongly Calvinistic Confession in 1742 (or possibly earlier) was a turning-point in the history of American Baptists, as it ensured the prevalence of that type of theology. Up to this time the Arminian Baptists had been the stronger in New England, and the colonies of New York and New Jersey, and it was at one time probable that they would control the development of the denomination. It was the Philadelphia Association that turned the tide, and decided the course of American Baptist history. The Association speedily became the leading body among American Baptists—a position it has not wholly lost to this day. Pretty much everything good in our history, from 1700 to 1850, may be traced to its initiative or active co-operation.

During this early period little progress was made in the founding of Baptist churches in the South. The story of the origin of the First Church of Charleston has already been told. In 1733 a schism in this church caused the organization of a General Baptist church— the original body being Calvinistic—and in 1736 a church was formed at Ashley River, which, while a symptom of growth, still further depleted the strength of the mother church. In 1737 some members of the Welsh Tract church went southward and established the Welsh Neck church. Here, then, was a promising little group of churches in one Southern colony.

The only other region where promise of growth had been manifest was in Virginia. There were probably some Baptists, certainly some people opposed to the baptism of infants, early in the history of the colony, for as early as 1661 the Assembly provided that a fine of two thousand pounds of tobacco should be imposed on parents who refused to have their children baptized. By 1714 there had come to be a number of this persuasion in the southeastern part of the State, probably English immigrants and probably General Baptists in their old home, since they appealed to this body in England for help. Two ministers were sent out to them from England, one of whom lived to reach the colony and founded a church at Burleigh. Another church is known to have existed before 1729 in Surrey County.

In the neighboring colony of North Carolina, a church was formed by Rev. Paul Palmer in 1727, consisting of thirty-two members, at a place called Perquimans, in Chowan County.

In all, therefore, there were forty-seven Baptist churches, of which we have certain knowledge, before the Great Awakening, of which all but seven were north of Mason and Dixon's line.

CHAPTER XX

DURING the first century of their history, American Baptists did not escape the effect of that spirit of worldliness which nearly paralyzed the churches of the Standing Order. They were firm in adherence to the true scriptural principle that the church should be composed of the regenerate only, but they lived in communities where it was hard even to get a hearing for this idea. The New England community was a theocracy, and the privileges of citizenship were enjoyed only by those who were members of the church. The theory of *imperium* and *sacerdotium* was not more firmly insisted on, and not half so consistently followed, in the relations between the medieval Church and the Holy Roman Empire, as in the connection of Church and State in New England. They were like the obverse and reverse of a coin, two aspects of one indivisible entity. The certain result of such a polity in modern Christianity, as in ancient Judaism, must be to corrupt the spiritual body—to destroy all distinction between regenerate and unregenerate.

The adoption of the Half-way Covenant, in 1662, was at once the natural result and an aggravation of the state of things that had come to pass. This covenant provided that those baptized in infancy were to be regarded as members of the church to which their parents belonged, although not to be admitted to the communion without evidence of regeneration. Such persons were allowed to offer their children for baptism, provided they publicly professed assent to the doctrine of faith, and were not scandalous in life. It was not long before ministers declared that sanctification was not a qualification for the Lord's Supper, but saw in it a converting ordinance and a means of regeneration. Consequently, persons who had been baptized in infancy, and were not charged with scandalous conduct or heresy, were regarded as entitled to full communion with the church.

Against this worldly condition of the church a reaction was certain to come. It manifested itself in the Great Awakening that began at Northampton, in 1734, under the preaching of Jonathan Edwards, and gradually extended throughout the towns of Massachusetts and Connecticut. The visit of Whitefield to this country, in 1739, gave a new impulse to this revival of true religion, extending it far beyond the bounds of New England. With this second revival began a new era in the spiritual life of American Christians. The leaven did not spread without opposition, and among Baptists two parties were formed—the " Regulars," who adhered to the old ways and disparaged revivals, and the " New Lights," or " Separates," who adopted the methods of Whitefield. The literature of the times is full of this controversy, and shows that the newer and more scriptural method of preaching did not win its way to its present general acceptance without bitter opposition.

Nevertheless, from this time the growth of Baptists became rapid. In Massachusetts, for example, there had been only eight Baptist churches organized before the Great Awakening; between 1740 and 1775, when the war of the Revolution began, twenty-seven new churches had been formed, and in 1784 the total number had increased to seventy-three, with a membership of three thousand and seventy-three. Extension to the regions beyond was also begun.

The most active agent in this new advance was Hezekiah Smith. He was born on Long Island, in the town of Hempstead, in 1737, but while he was still young his parents removed to Morris County, N. J. Rev. John Gano, at that time pastor of the church at Morristown, preached at several stations near-by, and relates the following: "At one of these places there was a happy instance of a promising youth (by name Hezekiah Smith), who professed to be converted, and joined the church—who appeared to have an inclination for education, to which his parents objected. His eldest brother joined me in soliciting his father, who finally consented to his receiving an education." Young Smith became a pupil at the Hopewell Academy, the first educational institution established among American Baptists, of which Rev. Isaac Eaton was principal. He then went to Princeton College, where he took his bachelor's degree in 1762.

Directly after graduation he made an evangelistic tour through the Southern States—possibly with something of a young man's desire to see the world, but still more to try and improve his gifts in preaching. During this fifteen months he traveled on horseback four thousand two hundred and thirty-five miles, and preached one hundred and seventy-three sermons. It must be admitted that he was not idly traveling for pleasure. He returned North to find that the Philadelphia Association had resolved to found an institution of higher learning; and had selected Rhode Island as the most eligible location for a college, and James Manning, Smith's classmate at Princeton, as the head of the new institution. Smith threw himself into this project with all the enthusiasm and energy of his nature, and he was energetic and enthusiastic beyond most men, while cool-headed and judicious at the same time. He was successful in winning the support of many who might otherwise have held aloof, and was at all times the right-hand man of President Manning in his laborious and difficult task.

Smith had been ordained to the ministry at Charleston, during his Southern tour, but had accepted no pastoral charge there, and for some years he held none in the North. He rather itinerated among the churches of New England, preaching with much acceptance wherever he went. During his journeys he visited the town of Haverhill, Mass., and the pulpit of the Congregational church being vacant, he was asked to preach. He remained some weeks, and the people would gladly have had him for their pastor, but he was too stanch a Baptist for that. After he left, he was solicited to return by people in the town, and when he did so a Baptist church was organized, of which he was recognized as pastor in 1766. It was the only pastorate of his life, and at his death, in 1805, the church had become one of the strongest in New England, and is now the oldest surviving Baptist church north of Boston.

He was more than the faithful pastor of this church; he was a missionary to the regions beyond. At that time there was a great religious destitution in the newer towns of New Hampshire and Maine, and the few Baptists scattered here and there were as sheep without a shepherd. Up to the outbreak of the Revolution, Mr. Smith made many horseback tours through these regions, preaching the gospel and gathering converts; and it is said that at least thirteen of the churches organized in those States owed their existence to his labors and counsels. In his later years, as well as his strength permitted, he was equally earnest and effective as an evangelist. At this time there were no missionary organizations among Baptists, and what evangelizing was done was carried on in this independent way. Hezekiah Smith was a whole State mission society in himself, and doubtless his labors had no little to do with the organizing of the first society of that kind, the Massachusetts Baptist Missionary Society. He was one of the most active agents in forming this organization two years before his death.

We have still to consider one of the most honorable episodes in Mr. Smith's history. On the outbreak of the Revolution, he offered his services and was appointed brigade-chaplain, with the pay and rations of a colonel. Six of the twenty-one brigade-chaplains in the service are known to have been Baptists; and we have it on the authority of Washington himself that Baptists were "throughout America, uniformly and almost unanimously, the firm friends to civil liberty, and the persevering promoters of our glorious Revolution." Mr. Smith was in service with the army of Gates during the Burgoyne campaign, and was afterward stationed at various points along the Hudson with the army of Washington. He gained the confidence and esteem of his general, as is abundantly shown by the fact that Washington corresponded with him after the war. He was not a fighting chaplain, but he repeatedly exposed his life in order to give help and consolation to the wounded and dying. His service in keeping up the *morale* of the army was equal to that of any officer, and was so esteemed by all military authorities.

Returning to Haverhill and resuming his pastoral duties, revivals followed in the community that increased the membership of the church to nearly two hundred. There were then but three larger churches in New England. No preacher was in more demand for services of all kinds, and none was more influential in denominational councils. Mr. Smith took a leading part in the organization of the Warren Association, the first union of Baptist churches in New England, in the rehabilitation of the Rhode Island College (soon to be known as Brown

University), and all other denominational enterprises. He was cut off by paralysis in the midst of his usefulness, having preached with unusual power on the preceding Sunday, leaving behind him the memory of a man who had been faithful in all things, stainless in character, and foremost in all good works.

Though there had been churches formed earlier in New Hampshire (Newton, in 1750, and Medbury, in 1768), they had proved short-lived, and Hezekiah Smith established the first enduring organization in 1771 at Brentwood. Other churches sprang up rapidly, and by 1784 there were twenty-five churches and four hundred and seventy-six members. The church at Berwick, Me., was organized in July, 1768, of members whom Mr. Smith had baptized into the fellowship of his church at Haverhill, and who had been dismissed to form the new body.

The earliest churches in Vermont seem to have owed their origin in part to people from the other New England colonies, and in part to people from New York. The oldest church now existing is Wallingford, formed February 10, 1780. An older church, the Shaftesbury (1768), was disbanded in 1844. By the close of the century there were thirty-two churches and the membership had reached one thousand six hundred. In 1784, the entire strength of New England Baptists was one hundred and fifty-one churches and four thousand seven hundred and eighty-three members. Of course, these figures are only approximate, though as to the number of churches they are probably very nearly accurate.

The Revolution interrupted for a time the rapid progress that Baptists began to make after the Great Awakening. The results were most disastrous, as might be expected, where the British occupation was longest—in and about New York and Philadelphia, and through

" the Jerseys." The Baptists as a whole were patriots, and many of their preachers served as chaplains with the American troops, as the work in their churches could not be carried on with regularity. There was, however, one noted exception: Scholarly, laborious, warm-hearted, eccentric, choleric Morgan Edwards, one of the most interesting of the early Baptist ministers of our country and one of those most deserving of honor. His very faults had a leaning toward virtue's side, and in good works he was exceeded by none of his day, if indeed by any of any day.

Edwards was born in Wales in 1722, and received his training for the ministry at the Baptist college at Bristol, England, after which he began to preach at Boston, Lincolnshire. Seven years he ministered to a little flock there, and then went to Cork, Ireland, where he was ordained in 1757. He remained there nine years, and then returned to England. While preaching there the Baptist church in Philadelphia sent to their English brethren a request for a pastor. By advice of his brethren, Morgan Edwards responded to this appeal, made the voyage to America, visited the Philadelphia church, and became its pastor for nine years (1761-1770). He was an able preacher and a good man, but not always an easy man to get on with. He had a trait characteristic of Welsh people (and some others), which they call firmness and others sometimes call obstinacy, and at various stages of his career this trait got him into trouble with people who were also " firm."

Before he had been in the country much more than a year, Morgan Edwards induced the Philadelphia Association to do one of the things that most honor its history. Mention has already been made of the founding of Rhode Island College and the work of Manning and Smith in connection with that enterprise. The

pioneer in the movement was Edwards. He saw at once
on his arrival that the weakness of American Baptists
was their deficiency in educational advantages. They
would not have been reduced to send to England for
him if they had had schools of their own. Others
agreed with him; and when he proposed the founding of
a college, at the meeting of the Philadelphia Association
in 1762, his resolution was carried without difficulty. He
took hold of the project with his usual ardor, and the
success of the project was no less due to him than to
Manning and Smith. He was most influential of the
three in enlisting the sympathies of Baptists generally
in favor of the college and obtaining funds for its endowment. He made a voyage to England for the purpose
and brought back a large sum of money. He interested
his Welsh Baptist brethren especially, and one of them,
Doctor Richards, bequeathed to the college his library of
one thousand three hundred volumes. Brown University
has to-day, in consequence, probably the finest collection
of books in the Welsh language to be found in America.
Moreover, Edwards traveled all over the States, through
many years, preaching and collecting for the college.

These labors were interrupted by the war of the Revolution, and thereby hangs a tale that is to us amusing
but was most vexatious to his contemporaries. You have
to get at some distance from things sometimes to see
their funny side, and this is one of those cases. Edwards,
it will be remembered, had not been " caught young ";
he was nearly forty when he came to this country, and
the troubles that led to the Revolution were already
begun. He had not been here long enough to be really
Americanized when Lexington and Bunker Hill gave the
signal for a general rebellion against King George and
his tyranny, and his sympathies were naturally with the
country and flag of his birth rather than with the land

of his late adoption. He was almost, if not quite, the only Tory among the Baptist clergy during the Revolution, and so found himself isolated among his brethren. Not only so, but as he did not hesitate to express his sentiments with his usual freedom and vigor, he soon found himself the object of suspicion, not to say hostility. Finally his brethren in the ministry took the matter up with vigor on their side, and others joined them; and Edwards was finally persuaded or intimidated into signing a " retraction," in which he admitted that he had spoken unadvisedly, asked the forgiveness of the public, and promised to avoid like offense in future. The promise is said to have been ill kept, however; the Welsh fire would break out from time to time in spite of all promises or efforts to repress it.

Such loyalty to king and country did honor to the heart, if not to the head, of Edwards; and after the independence of the colonies was achieved, he seems to have seen a great light and became as loyal to the new country as he had been to the old. He then resumed his journeyings and labors, continuing them until his death in 1795.

These journeyings had another object besides preaching the gospel and collecting funds for Rhode Island College. Edwards was a born antiquarian, and soon after coming to this country began to collect memorials of the past, especially facts relating to Baptist history. In his goings up and down the land—he visited pretty nearly every one of the thirteen colonies—he made researches among contemporary records and gathered up facts from living men who recollected Baptist beginnings, and little by little collected his Materials toward a History of the Baptists. Two volumes were printed during his lifetime, and slight portions have been printed since; but a large part still remains in MS.

The first Calvinistic Baptist church in the colony of New York was formed about 1740, at Fishkill, Dutchess County, and from 1753 a small company of Baptists held meetings in a private house. Not strong enough to form a church, they became members of the church at Scotch Plains, N. J., and were not constituted a separate church until 1762. By this time they had become twenty-seven in number, had built themselves a small house of worship in Gold Street, and had called the Rev. John Gano to be their pastor. Other churches were formed in the Dutchess region and its vicinity, to the number of ten in all, prior to 1780. From this time onward progress was quite rapid in the eastern and central counties of the State. For a time most of these churches sought and obtained membership in the Philadelphia Association, and it was not until 1791 that they felt themselves strong enough to form an Association of their own.

In the Southern colonies, while progress was greatly interrupted by the Revolution, there was less actual disintegration of the churches, since most of these were in more rural communities and were less affected by the fortunes of war. After the conclusion of peace, moreover, the most rapid growth of Baptists was in this region. Along the Atlantic coast as far as Charleston, many Baptist churches were founded by missionaries of the Philadelphia Association, and were for a time members of that body. Four churches thus constituted—Opekon (1743, reconstituted in 1752), Ketokton (1751), Smith's Creek (1756), Broad Run (1762)—formed the Ketokton Association in 1766, with the full approval of the mother body. A year earlier the Kehukee Association had been organized by several General Baptist churches in Virginia and North Carolina, but they soon adopted a modified form of the Calvinistic faith.

In 1754 a company of settlers from New England

settled in Virginia and began to propagate their views with vigor and great success. They were " New Lights," or adherents of Whitefield and his evangelistic methods. Prominent among them were two preachers of unusual gifts, Shubael Stearns and Daniel Marshall. The churches founded by them became known as Separate Baptists, and they grew like Jonah's gourd. The earliest of all, the Sandy Creek Church, in seventeen years was instrumental in establishing forty-two others, from which one hundred and twenty-five preachers were sent forth. Others were only less prolific; no wonder then that Baptists increased greatly in the Southern States. Their growth was much promoted by the healing of their divisions in 1787, Regulars and Separates uniting, on the basis of the Philadelphia Confession, to form " the United Baptist Churches of Christ in Virginia."

We can no longer trace the history of churches; we can only mark the progress of the body now by the formation of new groups of churches into Associations; and soon these too became too numerous to be followed in detail. The Philadelphia, as we have seen, is the venerable mother of all such bodies, but her first four daughters were born in the South—the Charleston (1751), Sandy Creek (1758), Kehukee (1765), and Ketokton (1766).[1] The New England Associations began with the Warren (1767), followed by the Stonington (1772), and Shaftesbury (1780). The formation of Associations went rapidly on, until by 1800 there were forty-eight, of which thirty were in the Southern States, and eight beyond the Alleghenies—six of these last being in Kentucky.[2]

[1] This is leaving out of account a " yearly meeting " of the Arminian Baptists of New England, begun previous to 1729, and afterwards developing into an Association.

[2] At the beginning of the Revolution American Baptists numbered less than 10,000, but even approximate figures are lacking. In 1792, according

If the figures given below are substantially accurate, and for good reasons they are believed to be, the period of greatest actual and relative advance among American Baptists was the last quarter of the eighteenth century. Several causes contributed to this result, chief among them being the granting of religious liberty in all the States, the missionary activity of the pioneer preachers, and the harmony between the democratic spirit of the people and the congregational polity of the Baptist churches. Though subsequent growth has not reached these unexampled figures, it has continually exceeded the rate at which population increases, and that in spite of the immense influx of foreign peoples, on many of whom Baptists have not yet succeeded in making any perceptible impression.

With the attainment of civil liberty came a spirit that made men see in religious persecution the tyranny and shame that it was. Virginia led the way, as became the colony that first made persecuting laws, and had equaled all others in the bitterness of her intolerance, if indeed she had not surpassed all. In 1629 the Assembly forbade any minister lacking Episcopal ordination to officiate in the colony, and this rule was enforced by severe penalties up to the Revolution. Baptists were also taxed for the support of the Episcopal Church and their property was seized and sold to pay such taxes. At length, however, they found champions in such men as Thomas Jefferson and Patrick Henry; the latter, though a mem‧ ber of the Established Church, being too genuine a lover of liberty to have any part in persecution. The first

to Dr. Rufus Babcock, there were 471 churches, 424 ministers, and 35,101 members. By 1800 they had increased to an estimated number of 100,000. In 1850 the numbers had risen to 815,212, of whom 686,807 were " Regular " Baptists. In other words, in 1776 Baptists were about 1 to 264 of the population; in 1800 they were 1 to 53, and in 1850 they had become 1 in 29.

patriot legislature, which met in 1776, repealed the penal laws, and taxes for the support of the clergy were repealed in 1779. It was not until January, 1786, that the legislature passed an " Act for establishing religious freedom," drawn by Jefferson and powerfully advocated by James Madison.

The other States more or less rapidly followed the lead of Virginia. The spirit of intolerance lingered longest in New England, and it was not until 1833 that the last remnant of proscriptive laws was swept from the statute book of Massachusetts. And even so good and wise and great a man as Lyman Beecher thought the bottom had dropped out of things when his State (Connecticut) no longer compelled his unwilling Baptist neighbor to contribute to his support.

The disabilities removed, the Baptist churches grew apace. The secret of this growth was incessant evangelization. There were no missionary societies, national, State, or even local. Some of the Associations did a work of this kind. Thus, soon after the organization of the South Carolina Association, they sent North for a missionary preacher, and secured the Rev. John Gano, afterward pastor of the First Baptist Church of New York, and a man of note in his day. His labors in the interior of the State resulted in the establishment of several churches and the organization of the Congaree Association. But for the most part this evangelization was the work of men who were not sent forth, but went forth to preach in obedience to a divine call. Many Baptist preachers spent at least a part of their lives, if not the whole of them, as itinerant preachers; and to their labors was due the growth of Baptist churches in the closing quarter of the eighteenth century.

As the population extended over the Alleghenies into the new regions of the great West, the missionary zeal of the churches kept step with the colonizing enterprise of the people. Without societies or other means of organizing their scanty resources of men and money, they pushed out boldly into the regions beyond. Many Baptists from North Carolina and Virginia were among the first settlers of Kentucky and Tennessee, and in the latter State their churches were organized as early as 1765. By 1790 there were eighteen churches and eight hundred and eighty-nine members in the State. In 1782, Baptist churches were formed in Kentucky; and in 1790 there were forty-two churches and three thousand and ninety-five members. Baptists were among the first to enter Ohio as settlers and religious workers, a church having been organized at Columbia (five miles above Cincinnati) in 1790,[1] and the Miami Association being formed by four churches in 1797. In Illinois, Baptists from Virginia were the first Protestants to enter and possess the land, a number settling there not later than 1786. In the following year a Kentucky pastor preached there, but the first church was not formed until May, 1796, at New Design, St. Clair County. The first sermon on the site of what is now the great city of Chicago was preached October 5, 1825, by the Rev. Isaac McCoy, then a Baptist missionary to the Indians of Michigan.

Many men of God went forth into this wilderness not knowing where they should find a night's lodging or their next meal, willing to suffer untold privations if they might only point some to the Lamb of God. It is impossible to estimate too highly or to praise too warmly the services of these men of strong faith and good works. Their hardships were such as we of the present day can hardly imagine. They traveled from little settlement to settlement on horseback, with no road save an Indian

[1] This church changed its place of worship in 1808, and was thenceforth known as the Duck Creek Church.

trail or blazed trees, fording streams over which no bridges had been built, exposed to storms, frequently sleeping where night found them, often prostrated by fevers or wasted by malaria, but indomitable still. If they did not wander " in sheepskins and goatskins," like ancient heroes of faith, they wore deerskins; and homespun took the place of sackcloth. Their dwelling was " all out o' doors." Living in the plainest manner, sharing all the hardships of a pioneer people, the circuit preacher labored in a parish that, as one of them said, " took in one-half of creation, for it had no boundary on the west." One of them writes in 1805: " Every day I travel I have to swim through creeks or swamps, and I am wet from head to feet, and some days from morning to night I am dripping with water. . . I have rheumatism in all my joints. . . What I have suffered in body and mind my pen is not able to communicate to you. But this I can say: While my body is wet with water and chilled with cold my soul is filled with heavenly fire, and I can say with St. Paul: ' But none of these things move me, neither count I my life dear unto myself, so that I might finish my course with joy.' "

In general, the preacher was kindly received, often with tears of joy. The people who were running a neck-and-neck race with death by starvation or freezing had not much to give the itinerant minister. Even to offer him food and shelter meant sacrifice, but in nearly every case he was welcome to his share of whatever comforts the pioneer family possessed. In the wilderness, like Paul, he passed through perils many—perils by the way, perils from savage beasts, perils from the savage Indians, perils from godless and degraded men hardly less savage than either beast or Indian. But God, who closed the mouths of the lions, was with his servant, the pioneer preacher. Many died prematurely of privation and disease in this hard life, but there is no record of one who died of violence.

The houses of worship in which these preachers held their services were generally God's own temples—the woods and prairies. Their libraries consisted of a Bible and a hymn-book, carried in their saddle-bags. They did not read polished essays from a manuscript, as their degenerate successors so often do. The rough backwoodsman had no use, as he phrased it, " for a preacher who couldn't shoot without a rest." The preaching was of a rough-and-ready sort, not always scrupulous of the king's English, strongly tinged with the good, old doctrines of grace—eminently evangelistic, to use our modern phrase, and was richly blessed of God to the conversion of their hearers. These men, uncouth as they would seem now, unwelcome as they would be to the pulpit of any fashionable Baptist church in our cities, led multitudes to the cross of Christ, founded churches in all the new communities of the West, laid the foundations of denominational institutions, on which a magnificent superstructure has since been built. Let us honor as he deserves the pioneer preacher of the West. We who have entered into the labors of such men are noble indeed if we are worthy to unloose the latchet of their shoes. Time would fail to tell of such men as Ebenezer Loomis, the Michigan evangelist; of James Delaney, the Wisconsin pioneer; of Amory Gale, who preached over one hundred thousand miles of Minnesota; of " Father " Taggart, of Nebraska; and of scores of others equally worthy of undying honor. Their record is on high; their names are written in the book of God's remembrance. " And they shall be mine, saith the Lord of hosts, in that day when I make up my jewels."

But a still greater opportunity was before American Baptists. When Thomas Jefferson became president, in

1801, the United States included an area of eight hundred and twenty-seven thousand eight hundred and forty-four square miles, all to the east of the Mississippi River. In 1803, Jefferson, with noble inconsistency setting aside all his past record as a strict constructionist of the Constitution, bought from France for fifteen million dollars a strip of territory that more than doubled the area of his country. This Louisiana purchase, as it was called, added to the national domain one million one hundred and seventy-one thousand nine hundred and thirty-one square miles. From this territory were afterward formed the States of Louisiana, Arkansas, Missouri, Iowa, Kansas, Nebraska, Wyoming, the two Dakotas, Montana, the Indian Territory, and Oklahoma, besides a considerable part of the States of Minnesota and Colorado.

Settlement of this new region necessarily proceeded very slowly for some time. The Indians were hostile and threatening on the north, and the possession of the southern part was menaced by the British. The energies of the country were too much absorbed by the war of 1812, the struggle to preserve the independence so hard won in the Revolution, to have much surplus energy for colonization. At the battle of Tippecanoe, in 1811, General Harrison broke the power of the Indians, who were never formidable again east of the Mississippi; while " Old Hickory," by his defeat of the British at New Orleans in 1815, forever assured the integrity of our possessions against any foreign attack. Peace soon came to crown these victories, and then the great westward movement of population began. In a half-century the face of this continent was transformed as no similar expanse on the earth's surface was ever transformed in so short a time.

The unsystematic system that had been so undoubtedly effective for a time was outgrown; something else must be devised. Highly privileged is the man who becomes an agent of God's providence in the founding of a great and beneficent institution. There were many men who had an honorable part in the founding of the American Baptist Home Mission Society; but if one must be chosen from them who was preeminent, that one can be no other than John M. Peck. He was born in Litchfield, Conn., in 1789, was converted at the age of eighteen, and joined the Congregational church. In 1811 he removed with his wife to Windham, N. Y., and there a careful study of the Bible made him a Baptist. He was almost immediately licensed to preach, and was ordained to the ministry at Catskill in 1812.

From the first he was a missionary, his only pastorate being of not much over a year's duration, at Amenia, N. Y. Becoming acquainted with Luther Rice, when the latter was telling abroad the story of Judson and the work in India, effectually determined his bent in that direction; only it was home missions, not foreign, that appealed most strongly to him. In 1817 the Triennial Convention commissioned him as a missionary to the region west of the Mississippi, and the rest of his life was spent in that work. It was a journey of one thousand two hundred miles to an unknown country, almost as heathen as Burma and far less civilized, that he and his then took. Let us make no mistake, John M. Peck was quite as heroic as Judson or Boardman.

From his arrival at St. Louis he became the apostle of the West. His labors were incredible in extent and variety, and though he had a constitution of iron, they made an old man of him by the time he was fifty. During his first three years he had organized several churches, secured the establishment of fifty schools, introduced a system of itinerant missions, projected a college, and undertaken part of the support of Rev. Isaac McCoy, missionary to the Indians. It was bad enough to contend with poverty, ignorance, and irreligion, but in Peck's case perils from false brethren were added to all the other perils of the wilderness. Anti-mission Baptists were strong at that time in Kentucky, and began to make their way into Missouri and Illinois—old high-and-dry Calvinists like those with whom Carey had to contend, who held that it was flying in the face of Divine Providence to plead with men to come to Jesus, and such new-fangled things as missionary societies were of the devil. To the everlasting shame of the Triennial Convention, it permitted itself to be influenced by the complaints that came to it from such sources, and in 1820, or soon after, all support was withdrawn from this Western enterprise. No appeals or remonstrances served to secure a reconsideration of the question, and Peck was compelled to look elsewhere for help. He could not think in any case of deserting the work to which God had called him—a work whose importance became more clear to him each year.

Had it not been for this unfaithfulness to its duty on the part of the Triennial Convention, this disgraceful desertion of a true and tried man, the Home Mission Society would doubtless never have been formed. Peck turned first to the Massachusetts Baptist Missionary Society, which made him its missionary at the munificent salary of five dollars a week—no doubt all that it had to give at the time. He resumed his work with fresh courage and was unwearied in it, traveling all over the States of Illinois, Indiana, and Missouri. Then he took a brief—not *rest,* but change of labor, by making a tour of the Eastern States to interest them in Western missions, returning with over one thousand dollars pledged for a seminary at Rock Spring, Ill., which forthwith began, with him as professor of theology. Then he added to his other enterprises the publication of a newspaper, *The Pioneer,* in 1829. No wonder that his health quite broke down in 1831, and he was compelled to rest from his labors for a time.

Even then he was not idle—such a man could not be idle. He could think and plan, if he could not actively work. At just this time Elder Jonathan Going was sent West by the Massachusetts Baptists to look over the field and report on its needs; for three months he and Peck traveled over the new States of the West, and before they separated, so an entry in Peck's journal informs us, they had agreed on the plan of the American Baptist Home Mission Society. These two were the founders of that organization. For the practical execution of the plan, Going was the very man, and it was not more than six months after his return before the Society was an assured fact. On April 27, 1832, the new Society was formed in New York, where its headquarters have since remained. The motto selected for the Society was an assurance that no local interests should be permitted to circumscribe its sympathies or activities.

Its first work was in the Mississippi Valley. This was the far West of that day; the outposts of civilization were just beginning to push beyond that barrier of nature. Here a great battle was to be fought. The population of the Louisiana purchase was almost exclusively Roman Catholic. We can see now that the question of the supremacy of this continent, for which the Protestant Saxon race and the Catholic French race long contended, was fought out and settled on the plains of Abraham, in 1759, when Wolfe defeated Montcalm and captured the stronghold of Quebec. But this was not so clear at the time. Rome is an antagonist that does not know when she is beaten. She recognized, indeed, that she had received a severe check in the New World, but could not believe it a final defeat. She dreamed that in the valley of the Mississippi, with the great advantage she already had, not only all her losses might be regained, but a victory might be won far surpassing her apparent defeat. And who shall say that this was all dream? As we look back it seems a not unreasonable forecast, from the realization of which only a merciful Providence saved us. The fruits of Wolfe's victory might have been lost but for the fact that just at the critical hour God raised up such missionary and evangelizing agencies as the American Baptist Home Mission Society.

During its earliest years, Elder Peck was the Home Mission Society in the West—its visible embodiment, its chief adviser, and local executive. Time and space would fail to tell of the variety and extent of his labors. He was foremost in organizing the Illinois Educational Society, in founding and endowing Alton Seminary and Shurtleff College; the churches, educational institutions, societies of all kinds, that owe their life to him—their name is legion. And he was not merely active; he was wise, far-seeing, shrewd. He made few mistakes, and his previsions of the greatness that would come to these Western communities failed only in being far short of the reality, daring as they seemed to his contemporaries, The Baptist cause in the Middle West owes what it is to-day to the work of John M. Peck more than to any other score of men that can be named.

In 1856 he died, a man worn out by his labors before his due time; for though he had reached the age of sixty-six—a good length of years for many men—his constitution should have made him good for twenty years more. But if other men have lived longer, few have lived lives more useful or that have left greater results. If we adopt Napoleon's test of greatness—what has he done?— there has been no greater man in the history of American Baptists than John M. Peck.

Into the New West of the "thirties" the new Society moved, at first with but slender resources, yet with a dauntless spirit. It became the great pioneer agency of the denomination. One of its first missionaries was the Rev. Allen B. Freeman, who in 1833 gathered the First Baptist Church of Chicago—the first church of the denomination to be established in what was then the Northwest. Call the roll of the great cities of the West— St. Paul, Minneapolis, Omaha, Denver, Los Angeles, San Francisco, Portland—what would the Baptist cause have been in them but for this Society? In nearly all of these cities, not only was the first Baptist church established by this organization, but most of the Baptist churches existing in them to-day owe their birth and continued existence to its fostering care. Call the roll of our great Western commonwealths—Illinois, Wisconsin, Iowa, Minnesota, Texas, Colorado, Nebraska, Kansas, Dakota, Wyoming, Utah, Idaho, Montana, California, Oregon, Washington—in every one of these this Society has been the pioneer agency of the denomination by from two to twenty years.

In 1845 the Society began the evangelization of the far West by the sending of Rev. Ezra Fisher and Rev. Hezekiah Johnson from Iowa to Oregon. Their hardships on the way were great, but they reached their destination safely, and the foundations of Baptist churches were speedily laid in that State. In 1848, before the discovery of gold in California was announced in the East, Rev. O. C. Wheeler was sent to San Francisco, via the Isthmus of Panama; and later Rev. H. W. Read was sent overland to the same destination; but on reaching New Mexico he was so impressed with the importance and destitution of that field that he asked and obtained the consent of the Board to remain there. In the other States, mission work was begun as fast as men and means could be found to extend operations westward. In Kansas the Society had a missionary as early as 1854, and one was sent into Nebraska in 1856. The troublous times just before and during the Civil War brought this advance to a temporary standstill, but in 1864 it was again resumed, entrance having been made in that year into two States —Dakota and Colorado. In 1870 Washington and Wyoming were occupied, and in 1871 Montana and Utah.

What have been the results on the denominational growth? They are difficult to compute. In the year 1832, when the Home Mission Society was organized, there were in its peculiar field—the West—nine hundred churches, a large part of them feeble and pastorless, since there were but six hundred ministers, and the total membership was but thirty-two thousand. In 1896 the Baptist denomination in that field, and in the farther West that is still more distinctively missionary territory, had seven thousand four hundred and seventy churches and five hundred and eighty-one thousand members.

Though the work of home missions was thus first in point of time and in pressing necessity, it was not the first to be organized on a permanent basis. Long before this had come about, a clear providential summons had come to Baptists to fulfil the Great Commission, and preach the gospel to every creature. This was accomplished through Adoniram Judson, the son of a Congregational minister of Massachusetts, who was educated at Brown University and Andover Theological Seminary. Through the influence of Judson and some other students at Andover, the American Board of Commissioners for Foreign Missions was organized; and in 1812 several missionaries were sent out to India, among whom were Adoniram Judson and his wife, Ann Hasseltine Judson. Their destination was Calcutta, where they knew some English Baptist missionaries to be laboring. It seemed probable to the Judsons that they would be called upon to defend their own doctrines and practice in the matter of baptism against these Baptists, and Mr. Judson began to study the question on shipboard with his usual ardor.

The more he sought to find in the Scriptures authority for the baptism of infants and for sprinkling as baptism, the more convinced was he that neither could be found there. Mrs. Judson also became much troubled. After landing at Calcutta they sought out the English Baptist missionaries, and continued their study with the help of other books procured. Finally both were convinced that the Baptist position was right, that they had never been baptized, and that duty to Christ demanded that they should be baptized. Accordingly, they were immersed in the Baptist chapel at Calcutta by Rev. William Ward, September 6, 1813. Shortly after, Luther Rice, another appointee of the same Board, who had sailed by another ship, landed at Calcutta, having undergone a precisely similar experience. He too was baptized. The question then arose, what were they to do? By this act, though they had obeyed Christ, they had cut themselves off from connection with the Board that had sent them forth, and were strangers in a strange land, without means of future support. It was resolved that Mr. Rice should return to America, tell the Baptists there what had happened, and throw the new mission upon them—for of abandoning the work of preaching the gospel to the heathen, to which they felt that God had called them, the Judsons seem never to have thought.

Mr. Rice reached Boston in September, 1813 and told his story. The Baptists of Boston and vicinity at once became responsible for the support of the Judsons, but they saw that the finger of Providence pointed to a larger undertaking than this. They advised Mr. Rice to visit the Baptist churches at large and try to interest them in this work. To their honor be it written, the Baptists of that day did not hesitate for an instant. They were poor and scattered, and the country was just beginning its second struggle for independence. No time could have been less propitious for the launching of a new enterprise, especially one projected on so large a scale as this. But our fathers were men of faith and prayer and good works; they obeyed the voice of God and went forward. With great enthusiasm they responded to the appeals of Mr. Rice; considering their relative poverty, the contributions were liberal; missionary societies sprang up all over the land; the denomination for the first time had a common cause, and became conscious of its unity and its power.

The need was at once felt of some one central organization that would unite these forces in the missionary cause, and after mutual counsel among the officers of several existing bodies, a meeting was called for the organization of a national society. This meeting was held at Philadelphia in May, 1814, and resulted in the formation of " The General Convention of the Baptist Denomination in the United States for Foreign Missions." The constitution declared the object to be to direct " the energies of the whole denomination in one sacred effort for sending the glad tidings of salvation to the heathen, and to nations destitute of pure gospel light." From the circumstance of its meeting once in three years, this body was popularly known as the " Triennial Convention," though that was never its official title. It continued to be the organ of the denomination for its foreign work until 1845.

The Baptist churches of the entire country were represented in its organization and conduct and support. Its first president was Richard Furman, of South Carolina. There was, however, considerable opposition, not by any means confined to any one section, to this new missionary movement. Many Baptist churches held a form of Calvinistic doctrine that was paralyzing to all evangelical effort. Their doctrine of the divine decrees was practically fatalism: when God was ready to convert the heathen, he would do so without human intervention; and to send out missionaries for this purpose was an irreverent meddling with the divine purposes, as reprehensible as Uzzah's rash staying of the ark of God when it seemed about to fall. Consequently, from this time onward the Baptists of the United States became divided into two parties, missionary Baptists and anti-missionary Baptists. The latter were at first equal, if not superior, in numbers to the former; in some districts the anti-mission Baptists were largely in the majority. But a doctrine and practice so discouraging of practical effort for the salvation of men produced its legitimate results in a generation or two, by reducing the number of anti-mission Baptists to nearly or quite the vanishing point in the greater part of the United States. Remnants of the sect still survive, and in a few Southern States the churches are still quite strong. Their total number has for years been given at about forty thousand in denominational statistics, but the census of 1890 states their total membership as one hundred and twenty-one thousand three hundred and forty-seven. Though they long since practically disappeared from the Northern States, they have a few churches in almost every State of the Union, except the newer ones beyond the Mississippi.

The first mission established by the General Convention was in Burma, whither the Judsons went in 1813, because the intolerance of the British East India Company denied them the privilege of laboring in India, the land of their first choice. The work began at Rangoon in

July, 1813, but it was not until July, 1819, that the first convert, Moung Nau, was baptized. The war between England and Burma broke out just as the work began to prosper, and for three years Judson and his devoted wife suffered incredible tortures of body and spirit. After the war the mission came under British protection and prospered. Doctor Judson continued to preach and teach until his death, and gave the Burmans the Scriptures in their native tongue.

The work in Burma has not been so prosperous among the Burmans as among the Karens, a people living in the hill districts. Among them the gospel has made great progress from the establishment of the mission by Rev. George Dana Boardman, in 1828. A mission in Arracan was established in 1835, and one in Siam in 1833. In 1834 Rev. William Dean began a mission at Bangkok among the Chinese of that city. In 1842 Mr. Dean left on account of his health, and began a mission in Hong Kong. A mission was established in Assam in 1836, and in 1821 two Negro missionaries were sent out to Liberia. These were practically all of the missions among the heathen begun and carried on during the history of the General Convention. Several European missions, however, belong to this period—the missions to France, Germany, Denmark, and Greece. Of these, something more will be said in another chapter.

These beginnings of foreign missionary work by American Baptists were largely blessed in the extension of the work among the heathen; but it may be doubted whether the reflex blessing on the Baptist churches of this country was not the larger blessing of the two. Never was the Scripture better illustrated than in the history of Baptists in the United States: " There is that scattereth and yet increaseth; there is that withholdeth more than is meet, but it tendeth to poverty."

CHAPTER XXI

THE DAYS OF CONTROVERSY

PAUL the apostle enumerates "perils among false brethren" as not the least of the trials that befell him in preaching the gospel. So Baptists found it in the first half of the nineteenth century. One controversy fraught with peril to their churches began in New England before the century opened. It was, indeed, the natural, almost the necessary, result of the Great Awakening. Just as the Reformation of Luther produced the counter-reformation of Loyola, so the Edwards-Whitefield revival produced the Unitarian reaction—produced in the sense of precipitating, not in that of original causation. Unitarianism had, for some time, been in solution in New England, and the revival caused it to crystallize into visible form. What had been a tendency became a movement; a mode of thinking became a propaganda; the esoteric doctrines of a few became the openly avowed basis of a sect. We can only glance at this interesting topic as we pass by, its place in this survey of Baptist history being justified merely by the fact that the New England Baptists stood as a chief bulwark against the heresy. In 1800 two of the six orthodox churches left in Boston were Baptist, while eight Congregational churches and one Episcopal church had gone over bodily to Unitarianism. Samuel Stillman and Thomas Baldwin were the pastors of these two churches during these troublous times, and no two men did more than they to resist false doctrines by preaching the truth. Indeed, throughout New England it is said that not one

Baptist church forsook the faith, and not one Baptist minister of note became a Unitarian. This stanch orthodoxy of the Baptists had a profound effect on the history of American Christianity, as will be pointed out in another connection.

A controversy more serious in its results upon the denomination was that which grew out of the question of the circulation of the Scriptures. In the year 1816, the American Bible Society was formed by delegates representing seven denominations of Christians. There had been local Bible Societies previous to this time. This organization was intended to be a national society, in which all American Christians might co-operate. Its formation was due to the success of the British and Foreign Bible Society, the organization of which in 1804 was directly owing to the agency of Rev. Joseph Hughes, an English Baptist. The Baptists of America were active in the work of the Society from the first, and contributed generously to its treasury. The object of the Society was avowed, at the time of its organization, to be "the dissemination of the Scriptures in the received versions where they exist, and in the most faithful where they are required." In accordance with this principle, for the first eighteen years of its existence the Society appropriated money from its funds for the printing and circulation of versions of the Scriptures in many languages, made by missionaries of various denominations.

Perhaps Doctor Judson's greatest service in the cause of missions was the translation of the entire Bible into the Burmese language. It was his life-work, and remains to this day the only version of the Scriptures in that tongue.[1] All competent witnesses have borne testimony

[1] It is true that in recent years copies of the Scriptures have been put in circulation in Burma in which *baptizo* and its cognates are transliterated or mistranslated; but these are not independent versions, only Pedobaptist revisions of the Judson Bible.

from the first to the faithfulness and elegance of his translation. The New Testament was printed at Moulmein in 1832, and the Old Testament two years later. Appropriations for this purpose were made by the American Bible Society. It was well understood on all hands, through official communications and otherwise, that the missionaries sent out by the American Baptists, in all their versions of the Scriptures endeavored to ascertain the precise meaning of the original text and to express that meaning as exactly as possible, transferring no words into the vernacular for which a proper equivalent could be found. In accordance with this principle, Doctor Judson's version rendered *baptizo* and its cognates by a Burman word meaning to immerse, or dip. During this same period appropriations were voted for the circulation of other missionary versions, made by other than Baptist missionaries, yet made on the same principle of translation, though they did not agree with Judson as to the meaning of *baptizo*. In 1835 the propriety of this course was for the first time questioned. In that year application was made to the Society for an appropriation to aid in printing and circulating a version of the Scriptures in Bengali, made on the principle of Doctor Judson.

This application was discussed in committee and in the full Board for many months. The Baptist members of the Board vainly urged that the Society had already appropriated eighteen thousand dollars for the circulation of Doctor Judson's version, with full knowledge of its nature; that this was the only version in Burmese in existence, and that the alternative was either to circulate this or deprive the Burmese of the gospel; and that the adoption of another rule introduced a new and necessarily divisive principle into the Society's policy. At length, by a vote of twenty to fourteen, the managers rejected the application and formulated for the guidance of the Society a new rule regarding versions—that they would " encourage only such versions as conformed in the principle of their translation to the common English version, at least, so far that all the religious denominations represented in this Society can consistently use and circulate said versions in their several schools and communities." At its next annual meeting in May, 1836, the Society approved the action of the managers.

Of course this decision made it impossible for Baptists to co-operate with the Society except at the sacrifice of their self-respect. In April, 1837, a convention was held in Philadelphia, composed of three hundred and ninety delegates from twenty-three States, and the American and Foreign Bible Society was organized, Doctor Cone being elected president. Dr. Charles G. Sommers, of New York, was the first corresponding secretary, and William Colgate the first treasurer. From the first there was difference of opinion among the supporters of this Society on one question, namely, the making of a new version of the Scriptures in English. Baptists were practically a unit in maintaining that all new versions into foreign languages should faithfully render every word of the original by the corresponding word of the vernacular. But many Baptists doubted the expediency, and still more questioned the necessity, of making a new version in our own tongue. The discussion of this question went on until May, 1850, when, after long and warm debate, the Society voted to circulate only received versions in English, without note or comment.

In the following June the American Bible Union was organized. Its object was declared to be " to procure and circulate the most faithful versions of the Scriptures in all languages throughout the world." The principle of translation adopted by the Union was to render every word of the original Scriptures into the vernacular word which would most nearly represent its meaning as determined by the best modern scholarship. This work was prosecuted with much energy, and revised versions of the Scriptures were printed and circulated in Spanish and Italian, Chinese, Siamese, and Karen. The Union also issued a version of the New Testament in English, in 1865, which has since passed through several careful revisions and is a most faithful, accurate, and idiomatic translation. It may still be had of the American Baptist Publication Society, and every Baptist should possess a copy; for, however much the King James' version may commend itself for use in public and private devotions, this more literal rendering is of the greatest service to one who would understand exactly what the New Testament teaches. From time to time parts of the Old Testament also have been published, and eminent scholars are now completing a translation, with notes, of the remaining books, under the auspices of the American Baptist Publication Society.[1]

Fierce denominational conflicts resulted from this division of effort among Baptists regarding the Bible work. Many continued from the first to co-operate with the American Bible Society, especially in the circulation of the received English versions. The remainder who took any interest in Bible work were divided in their affections between two organizations, and the participants of each waged a hot warfare against the others. At every denominational gathering the strife broke out. The newspapers of the denomination were full of it, and in time the churches became heartily tired and showed their sentiments by discontinuing their contributions. As the receipts dwindled and the work contracted, efforts were

[1] The work at this time (1906) is being pushed forward, and it is hoped that another year will witness its completion.

made from time to time toward a reunion of the American and Foreign Bible Society and the American Bible Union, and one or both Societies tried to effect a union with the American Baptist Publication Society. These efforts, which continued from 1869 to 1880, and even afterward, proved complete failures.

Finally, the whole question of Bible work, as done by the Baptists, was referred to a Bible convention, in which the denomination at large should be represented; and such a convention was held at Saratoga in May, 1883. It was unanimously decided to recommend both the existing Bible Societies practically to disband, and to commit the Bible work on the home field to the American Baptist Publication Society, while that on the foreign field should be done by the American Baptist Missionary Union. This was felt on all hands to be a happy decision of the vexed question, and since that time the denomination has enjoyed a season of peace, at least as regards the question of its Bible work.

To one reviewing the controversy after this interval of time it seems tolerably plain that while the course taken in 1836 was the only one that could have been expected under all the circumstances, it would have been better for the peace of the denomination and the effectiveness of its Bible work in the long run if a separate denominational Bible society had never been undertaken. There is not sufficient interest among Baptists in the translation and circulation of the Scriptures—probably there is not in any single denomination—to sustain a society that exists for that sole purpose. The project of circulating a denominational version of the Scriptures in English has been tested once for all and proved to be a disastrous failure. The version was successfully made and possesses many merits, but it could not be circulated; Baptists could neither be forced nor coaxed to use it.

They were greatly the losers and are still by reason of this apathy, but we must take the facts of human nature as we find them; and one fact now unquestioned is that the attachment of English-speaking Christians to the version of the Scriptures endeared to them by long use and tender association has proved to be too strong for the successful substitution of any other.

No controversy was more disastrous to the Baptist churches of the Middle States than the anti-Masonic struggle between the years 1826 and 1840. One William Morgan, a Mason, who had published a book purporting to expose the secrets of the order, suddenly disappeared in 1826, and was believed to have been foully dealt with. A body was discovered and identified as his, though the identification has always been regarded as doubtful. Excitement against the Masons, and secret fraternities generally, rose high, until the dispute became a political issue in State and even national elections, and the churches took the matter up. In a large number of Baptist churches the majority opposed secret fraternities, declaring them to be unscriptural and dangerous to the peace and liberties of the Commonwealth. In many cases the minority were disfellowshiped, and not a few flourishing churches were crippled, or even extinguished, while the growth of all was much retarded. The lessons of that period have taught American Baptists to be chary of interfering through church discipline with questions not strictly religious, and to beware of attempting to settle by an authoritative rule questions of conduct which it is the right and duty of each Christian man to decide for himself. Thus, while at the present time, the majority of Baptists strongly favor total abstinence as a rule of personal conduct, and prohibition as a practical policy, in very few churches is either made a test of fellowship.

The Baptist churches of the South and West were

much disturbed during the second quarter of this century by the agitation that culminated in the establishment of the Disciples as a separate body. Up to that time the churches of these regions, to a considerable extent, held a hyper-Calvinistic, almost antinomian, theology. The preaching was largely doctrinal, and was not edifying to the majority of the hearers, however much it might be enjoyed by a few. Since the revival of 1800, religious experiences in this region had been attended with much emotional disturbance. Christians professed to see visions, to hear heavenly voices, and to experience great extremes of grief and joy. Undue importance came to be attached to experiences of this type, and the relation of a series of vivid and emotional phenomena approaching the miraculous was considered an almost indispensable requisite before the acceptance of a candidate for baptism.

About the year 1815 certain preachers in Western Pennsylvania, Ohio, and Kentucky began to preach what they called a reformation. The professed object was to return to the simplicity of the New Testament faith and practice. The Scriptures alone were to be the authority in this reformation, whose motto was, " Where the Scriptures speak, we speak; where they are silent, we are silent." All human creeds were rejected, candidates for baptism were not required to relate any experience, but merely to profess faith in Christ, a faith that was little, if anything, more than a mere assent of the intellect to the facts narrated in the Scriptures concerning the historic Christ. On such profession the candidate was baptized " for remission of sins," the teaching being that only in such baptism could he receive the assurance that his sins had been pardoned.

The foremost leader in promoting this reformation was Alexander Campbell, of Scotch ancestry and training, at first a Presbyterian of the Seceder sect, who had been baptized on profession of faith by a Baptist minister in 1812, and from that time onward maintained for some years a nominal connection with the Baptist denomination. Very early, however, he manifested marked differences of opinion from the views then and since held by the majority of Baptists; and it soon became evident either that the faith and practice of the denomination must undergo a remarkable change, or Mr. Campbell and those who agreed with him must withdraw.

When in 1827, through the influence of Rev. Walter Scott, the practice of baptism " unto remission of sins " became a recognized feature in the reformation, Baptists who saw in this nothing but the old heresy of baptismal regeneration, promptly bore testimony against it. The Mahoning Association, of Ohio, was so deeply permeated by the new teaching that it disbanded, and the churches followed Messrs. Campbell and Scott almost in a body. The Redstone Association, of Western Pennsylvania, withdrew fellowship from Mr. Campbell and his followers in 1827. Two years later the Beaver Association, of the same region, issued a warning to all Baptist churches against the errors taught under the guise of a reformation, and in 1832 the Dover Association, of Virginia, advised Baptist churches to separate from their communion " all such persons as are promoting controversy and discord under the specious name of reformers." This advice was given on the ground that the doctrines taught were " not according to godliness, but subversive of the true spirit of the gospel of Jesus Christ, disorganizing and demoralizing in their tendency, and therefore ought to be disavowed and resisted by all the lovers of sound truth and piety." Twenty years after, Rev. Jeremiah B. Jeter, one of the ablest Baptist opponents of the Disciple movement, and one of the authors of this resolution, published it as his belief that the report adopted by the Dover Association contained " some unguarded, unnecessarily harsh expressions," and particularly acknowledged that this characterization of the doctrines of Campbell as " demoralizing in their tendency " was unjust. After the action of the Dover Association those who sympathized with Mr. Campbell either voluntarily withdrew from the Baptists or were disfellowshiped by them, and in a decade the separation was complete.

The effect of this separation was very great. The new reformation had been started, ostensibly at least, with the desire of uniting all Christian denominations. Its practical result was the addition of another to the already long list of sects. The Baptist churches in the West and Southwest were rent in twain by the schism. Large numbers of Baptist churches went over to the reformation in a body. Many others were divided. A period of heated and bitter controversy followed, the results of which have not yet passed away. The Baptist churches succeeded in separating themselves from what they rgarded as dangerous heresy, but at a tremendous cost; and in our own day the Baptists and the Disciples (as the followers of Mr. Campbell prefer to be called) have so nearly approached agreement that the sons of the men who fought hardest on either side are already discussing the question whether terms of reunion are not possible, without either party sacrificing any real principle.[1]

But perhaps the most bitter controversy of all, certainly that which left behind it the deepest scars and most permanent alienations, was that which arose over the question of slavery. This was not an experience

[1] It must be said, however, that thus far the discussion of this question has thrown no great light upon the possibility of a reunion, and that the immediate occurrence of such an event cannot be predicted with hopefulness.

peculiar to Baptists; nearly every religious body in America was rent by the same contentions, and in most cases permanent schisms were the result.

When the General Convention was organized, this was by no means a burning question. Slavery had been originally common to all the colonies, and the people of New England had done their full share toward introducing and perpetuating the system. Perhaps the eyes of Northern people were more readily opened to the iniquities of slavery because the system never proved profitable in the North. Whether owing to this or other causes, an anti-slavery sentiment spread through the Northern States to an extent sufficient to induce them to emancipate their slaves early in the nineteenth century. About the year 1825 the new anti-slavery sentiment in the North, demanding immediate emancipation, became prominent, and from January 1, 1831, when William Lloyd Garrison issued his first number of the " Liberator," this sentiment rapidly spread. It met with much opposition, and soon the Garrisonian anti-slavery agitation placed itself in direct antagonism to the Christian churches of the North. Nevertheless, there was a growing sentiment among the churches, and especially among the Baptist churches, that a Christian man ought not to be a holder of slaves. This agitation became the cause of division even among the Baptist churches of the Northern States, and naturally threatened the peace and unity of the denomination as a whole.

Differences of opinion regarding the slavery question appear in the minutes of the General Convention for several years before the final break. These appeared to reach the culminating point in the year 1844. The question of the relation to slavery of Baptist churches represented in the Convention came up during the meeting of that year for thorough discussion, and after careful consideration the Convention almost unanimously adopted the following:

Resolved, That in co-operating together as members in this Convention in the work of foreign missions, we disclaim all sanctions either expressed or implied, whether of slavery or anti-slavery; but as individuals we are free to express and to promote elsewhere our views on these subjects in a Christian manner and spirit.

This certainly was the only possible method of treating the question if denominational unity was to be preserved. Had the terms of that resolution been fairly adhered to, it is possible that the peace and unity of the Baptist churches might have been preserved, at least until the outbreak of the Civil War. But its terms were not respected. Up to this time the rule for the appointment of missionaries by the Board of the Convention was to approve " such persons only as are in full communion with some church in our denomination, and who furnish satisfactory evidence of genuine piety, good talents, and fervent zeal for the Redeemer's cause." This was certainly the only proper rule to be adopted by an institution representing all the Baptist churches of the United States—the only rule under which all those churches could unite in its support. The Executive Board had received a mandate from the Convention in 1844 to preserve this attitude of neutrality. Nevertheless, in the following December, in response to a question addressed to it by a Southern body, the Executive Board made the following reply, which was, in fact, the adoption of a new rule: " If any one who should offer himself for a missionary, having slaves, should insist on retaining them as his property, we could not appoint him. One thing is certain, we can never be a party to an arrangement which would imply approbation of slavery."

No doubt the Board was actuated by conscientious motives in making such a reply, but it is easy now to see that they misjudged their duties as Christian men. They were the agents of the body that appointed them, and were under moral obligation to obey its commands. In making this rule they flagrantly disobeyed. If they felt as Christian men that obedience to the higher law of God forbade them to carry out their instructions, their honorable course was to resign. There is no adequate defense of their conduct in thus disobeying the plain mandate they had received from the Convention only a few months before. At its meeting in April, 1845, the American Baptist Home Mission Society, moved by a similar conflict of sentiment and the majority of its attendants being Northern men, adopted resolutions declaring it to be " expedient that the members now forming the Society should hereafter act in separate organizations at the South and at the North in promoting the objects which were originally contemplated by the Society." These two acts on the part of Northern Baptists rendered the maintenance of denominational unity impossible.

In May, 1845, in response to the call issued by the Virginia Foreign Mission Society, three hundred and ten delegates from the Southern churches met at Augusta, Ga., and organized the Southern Baptist Convention. Its constitution was precisely that of the original General Baptist Convention: " For eliciting, combining, and directing the energies of the whole denomination in one sacred effort for the propagation of the gospel." It established two Boards, one for foreign missions, located in Richmond, and one for domestic missions, at Marion, Ala. Since that time the Southern Baptist churches have done their missionary work through this organization. During the Civil War the need was greatly felt of some means of effectually prosecuting Sunday-school work and a Sunday-school Board was established at Greenville, S. C. In 1872 this was consolidated with the Home Mission Board.

The division thus caused has remained until the present time. There have been occasional propositions for a reunion between Northern and Southern Baptists, but they have met with little favor either North or South. The opinion has been general that more and better work is accomplished between the two organizations than could be accomplished by a single Baptist Convention for the whole United States. But Northern and Southern Baptists are not, as some apparently delight to say, two separate denominations. The churches, both North and South, hold substantially one system of doctrine, agree in all important points of practice, receive and dismiss members from each other without question, and are in full, unrestricted, uninterrupted intercommunion. The old cause of bitterness and disunion, the question of property in slaves, has disappeared. The generation that caused the breach of denominational unity has nearly disappeared. Those who are now the leaders of the Baptist hosts, both North and South, are largely men who have been born since the Civil War or were too young to have a vivid recollection of it, and they have little part in or sympathy with the ante-bellum controversies, misunderstandings, and bitterness. Such causes of estrangement as still remain are diminishing with every year, and if separate organizations are maintained or shall hereafter be formed for any kind of denominational work, it will be not because of mutual hostility and narrow sectional feeling, but because, in the judgment of cool-headed and judicious men, the work of our Lord may be more advantageously and efficiently accomplished by such division of labor.

After the Southern Baptists withdrew from the General Convention, acts of legislature were obtained in Pennsylvania and Massachusetts, authorizing the changing of its name to the American Baptist Missionary Union, and fixing its headquarters at Boston. The Union is now composed of delegates appointed by the churches on a fixed basis. The most important business is transacted by a Board of Managers (of whom one-third are elected at each annual meeting), and an Executive Committee chosen by this Board.

CHAPTER XXII

EVANGELISM AND EDUCATION

A S was pointed out before, the line of demarcation between the periods of American Baptist history is uncertain, and dates cannot be positively fixed. Overlapping the period of rapid growth and missionary extension, ending at the latest about the year 1850, is a movement of another sort, manifesting itself in the spiritual quickening and edification of the churches. For nearly a half-century after the Great Awakening there had been no marked revivals of religion. Then a great revival wave, beginning in New England about the year 1790, swept over the whole country within the next ten years. In the Southwest it was marked by a fanaticism and a series of remarkable physical phenomena that tended to bring revivals into disfavor with the sober-minded and judicious. Thereupon ensued another period of inaction, lasting about a generation. It was broken by the revivals of Finney, through whose agency in the ten years following 1825 there were added fully one hundred thousand persons to the Northern Presbyterian churches. The year 1857 saw an even more remarkable wave of revival, from the influence of which no part of the country was exempt, and a half-million are said to have been converted in a single year.

Since then the norm of church life seems changed. No longer do we have periodic waves of intense religious excitement, with intervening periods of coolness and indifference, but a slowly rising tide of spiritual power. Progress is no longer by occasional leaps, but by a steady advance. Evangelism is not less genuine now than in the days when a Finney or a Knapp stirred whole communities as they never were stirred before, but now an evangelist preaches weekly from nearly every pulpit. The type of preaching has changed; it is simple and direct; it aims more consciously at the conversion of men. It is more intelligently adapted to reach the will through the intellect and affection, and to produce an immediate decision for or against Christ. Whether the change is permanent it would be rash to pronounce. The names of Moody and Sam Jones, unfitting as it is in other ways for them to be pronounced together, testify to the fact that both at the North and at the South it is still possible to interest great crowds in religion, and that occasional revivals may be expected rivaling all that we read of in past years.

The large place filled by local and State work during the past fifty years should be by no means overlooked, for it is one of the chief factors in Baptist progress. The State Conventions or general Associations now organized in every State are missionary bodies, whose usefulness it would be difficult to overrate. In the Baptist Missionary Convention of the State of New York, one of the oldest and most active of these bodies, will be found a good type of all. The object of this Convention is declared in its constitution to be " To promote the preaching of the gospel, and the establishment and maintenance of Baptist churches in the State of New York; to encourage the common educational interests of the denomination within the State, the general care and encouragement of denominational Sunday-school work, to promote denominational acquaintance, fellowship, and growth." Forty-three local Associations are found in the territory of this Convention. Many of the local Associations—which in the oldest States usually follow county lines—do a similar work, and often on a scale not inferior to that of the State organization, though in a field more circumscribed. Of these the Southern New York Association is a good type. Organized for " The cultivation of fraternal sympathy, the promotion of each other's spiritual welfare, and the establishment and strengthening of Baptist churches within its bounds," its churches have long maintained efficient city mission work in the metropolis, to which is largely due the past and present growth of the New York Baptists.

Another chief distinguishing feature of American Baptist history is the remarkable development of educational work. Almost from the first, Baptists felt the necessity of a better education for their children, and especially for the rising ministry. An academy was established by the Rev. Isaac Eaton, at Hopewell, N. J., in 1756, and continued its work for eleven years. It even obtained a small endowment through the aid of the Philadelphia and Charleston Associations, which was, however, lost during the Revolution through the depreciation of Continental money. During the continuance of its work, one of its pupils was James Manning; his conversion occurred while he was at the academy, and is to be ascribed under God to his teacher. If the Hopewell Academy had done nothing more than give the world James Manning, it would be entitled to the gratitude of Baptists for all time. But it also gave us a man only less distinguished and useful than he, Hezekiah Smith, and many other eminent ministers and laymen were among its pupils. Similar private schools of a like grade were established in other places by Baptists; among them one at Lower Dublin (now in Philadelphia) by Dr. Samuel Jones, one in New York by Doctor Stanford, and one at Bordentown, N. J. by Dr. Burgess Allison.

About 1750 some Baptists in the Philadelphia Associa·

tion began to consider seriously the project of founding a higher institution of learning. Few Baptist students could avail themselves of the advantages offered by the existing colleges, which were besides strongly anti-Baptist in sentiment and often in teaching. For various reasons it was difficult to obtain a charter for such an institution from the legislatures of New York, New Jersey, or Pennsylvania. Consequently, though the project for the new college originated in the Philadelphia Association, the eyes of the brethren were turned toward Rhode Island as the State most likely to grant the Baptists a liberal charter for a college. They looked about for a suitable head of such an institution, and found it in James Manning, who had gone in 1758 from Hopewell Academy to Princeton College, and was graduated four years later with the second honors of his class. Shortly after his graduation he married Margaret Stites, the daughter of a ruling elder of the Presbyterian church in Elizabethtown, who proved " an help meet for him " indeed. A year was spent in travel through the country, and when Manning returned he found his life-work ready for him.

Manning was a young man to take the lead in such an enterprise, it is true, but was greatly esteemed for his prudence and good sense, of fine presence and good repute as a scholar, in every way fitted to be an educational leader. He met the Baptists of Rhode Island, or some of their representative men, at Newport, in July, 1763. He unfolded his plan, and it met with their acceptance. A charter was drafted, and after some legislative pitfalls were successfully avoided, it was enacted in February, 1764. It provided that the president, twenty-two trustees, and eight fellows were forever to be Baptists, but the remaining trustees of the thirty-six were to be of the different denominations then represented in the State:

while four fellows were to be elected " indifferently of any or of all denominations." To all positions in the faculty save that of president, and to all other honors and advantages, persons of all religious denominations were to be freely admitted. Such a charter, while it gave to the denomination that founded the institution perpetual control of it (as was but right), was in perfect harmony with the spirit of religious liberty that had characterized the colony of Rhode Island from the first.

The college began giving instruction in Warren in 1766, Mr. Manning being president and professor of languages; and that year the institution had one student. The college celebrated its first commencement September 7, 1769, when the degree of bachelor of arts was conferred on seven young men. In 1770 the people of Providence subscribed four thousand two hundred dollars for the erection of University Hall, and the college was removed to that city. In 1776 the capture of the city by the British made necessary the suspension of instruction, which was not resumed until 1780, the college building being used much of the time by the British as a barracks. Doctor Manning continued his labors as president until his death, in 1791. During the greater portion of the time he was also pastor of the First Baptist Church of Providence. In 1804 the name of the institution (at first Rhode Island College) was changed to Brown University, in honor of Nicholas Brown, its generous benefactor. This, the oldest and best-known Baptist institution of learning, has a long and distinguished roll of alumni and a property valued at two and a half million dollars, besides an endowment of nearly three millions.

Very soon the need of more distinctively theological education was felt, but for some time nothing was done. The Newton Theological Institution owes its origin to a meeting of ministers and laymen held in Boston, 1825. Its early years were marked by difficulties and debt, but at length a permanent endowment was secured. It has graduated or instructed over eight hundred students, and among its alumni are many of the most useful and distinguished preachers and teachers of the denomination. Another New England institution is Waterville College, Maine, which was founded in 1818 by the Rev. Jeremiah Chaplin, as the outcome of a private school maintained by him at Danvers. The collegiate charter was granted in 1820. The early history of the institution was one of continual struggle with adversity, but of late years it has found generous friends. In recognition of the benefactions of one of these, Gardner Colby, the name was changed, in 1867, to Colby University; and still later the ambitious name of university was changed into the more modest and truthful title, college.

New England Baptists have been wiser in their day than those of most other sections, by providing liberally for secondary or academic education. Thus Colby has three Maine academies closely connected with it as feeders, while New Hampshire and Vermont have each a flourishing academy. Worcester Academy, in Massachusetts, and the Suffield Literary Institute, in Connecticut, care for the Baptist youth of those States, and are among the principal sources whence Brown University derives students. The educational system of New England Baptists therefore stands on a solid foundation; they have not committed the error of resting the pyramid on its apex.

In the Middle and Western States, and to some extent in the South, there has not been this unity of action in educational matters. Early in the present century a new development of interest in education was manifest among the Baptists which took form in the organization of

education societies. One of the first of these was formed
at Hamilton, N. Y., in 1817, and the following year
Jonathan Wade was admitted a student of the new institution. President Garfield said once that his idea of
a college was Mark Hopkins at one end of a log and a
young man at the other. That was about how the Hamilton Literary and Theological Institution began; at one
end was Daniel Hascall, at the other Jonathan Wade.
The second student to join this infant institution was
Eugenio Kincaid. Soon others came, and in 1820 the
institution was opened to the public and formal instruction
began.

Another institution that belongs to this early period
is the Columbian College, at Washington. It owes its
origin, like so many of our best denominational agencies,
to the Philadelphia Association. As far back as 1807,
Dr. William Staughton began to receive students into his
household. He continued this work for a series of years,
partly on his own account, partly as an appointed " tutor "
of the Baptist Education Society of the Middle States.
Finally, at the instance of the Rev. Luther Rice, the
General Convention took the matter up, and undertook
the establishment of a higher institution of learning, especially for the training of ministers. This movement
resulted in the chartering of the Columbian College (now
University) in 1821, and the removal of Dr. Staughton's
school to Washington as the " theological department "
of the new college. The hope of establishing a school
at Washington for the training of ministers proved futile,
and this theological department was finally transferred
to Newton, at its establishment in 1825.

The school at Hamilton, in 1834, developed into the
Hamilton Literary and Theological Institution. In 1846,
the literary department was chartered as a university,
its name being changed to Madison University, the

theological seminary being maintained as a separate institution, but in harmony with the college. The village of
Hamilton was thought by many Baptists to be an unsuitable site for a denominational school, and in 1847 an
effort was made to remove it to a better location.

The city of Rochester offered special inducements, and
was decided upon as the new site. But a party rallied
to the defense of the old site, discussions grew warm,
passionate feelings were excited, and the end was a division—part of the faculty and supporters going to found
a new institution, since known as the University of
Rochester. The new institution opened its doors to students in 1850. April 6, 1853, Martin Brewer Anderson
was chosen president, and filled the office with conspicu-
ous ability until 1888. David J. Hill, then president of
Bucknell University, was elected his successor, and
resigned in 1895. After an interregnum of several years,
Prof. Rush Rhees, of the Newton Theological Institution,
was chosen president, and assumed his duties in 1900.

The Rochester Theological Seminary was an outgrowth
of the same movement, but had a separate existence from
the first, though for a time it had quarters in the University buildings, and some men taught in both faculties.
The Seminary was founded in 1850 by the New York
Baptist Union for Ministerial Education, and in 1853,
Dr. Ezekiel G. Robinson was elected president. At his
resignation, in 1872, Rev. Augustus Hopkins Strong was
chosen to be his successor. A German department was
organized in 1854, and has ever since been maintained.

In the meantime the friends of the institution at Hamilton rallied to its support and gradually increased its
endowment. The family of William Colgate have repeatedly been its munificent benefactors, and in honor of
them the institution was named Colgate University in
1890. Thus, out of seeming misfortune has come some

good. Still this division of the New York institution has been marked by a corresponding division among the churches, part of which have supported the one and part the other. The old bitterness has somewhat subsided of late years, but it is in the highest degree unfortunate that the present generation should seem willing to perpetuate divisions caused by the unwisdom and contentiousness of their fathers.

This experience has been duplicated in several Western States, and rival institutions have been founded in excess of educational needs, with the result of making all poor and inefficient, where a single strong institution might have been established. So serious had become the lack of unity, and the consequent waste of money and labor, that there was organized at Washington, in May, 1888, an American Baptist Education Society, under whose leadership it is to be hoped that the mistakes of the past may be avoided. Its great achievements thus far have been assisting the Southern and Western institutions to add to their endowments, and the founding of the new University of Chicago, through the liberality of Mr. John D. Rockefeller. Though established so recently as 1890, this university has already property amounting to nearly or quite ten millions and an endowment of nearly equal amount. This accomplishment in so short a period may be justly termed phenomenal.

We can do little more than name the principal schools of learning founded by Baptists during the last half-century; if it were attempted to give even a brief sketch of the career of each, these chapters would stretch out to quite unwieldy proportions. The following should at least be named: Baptist Union Theological Seminary, Morgan Park, Ill. (1867);[1] Crozer Theological Seminary, Upland, Pa. (1868); Southern Baptist Theological

[1] Since 1890 the Divinity School of the University of Chicago.

Seminary, Louisville, Ky. (1858); Bucknell University, Lewisburg, Pa. (1846); Columbian University, Washington, D. C. (1821); Richmond College, Richmond, Va. (1832); Denison University, Granville, Ohio (1832). Vassar College, founded in 1861, at Poughkeepsie, N. Y., by the beneficence of Matthew Vassar, is the best endowed college for women in the world. The omission of other names does not imply that institutions equally worthy and doing excellent work do not exist in many parts of our land.

One of the most striking things in the recent religious history of America has been the development of work among and for the young. The Sunday-school was established as a department of church work early in the present century, and from about the year 1860 societies for young people began to be formed almost simultaneously in most of the evangelical churches. There was nothing like a concerted movement, however, for another twenty years.

In the Williston Congregational Church, of Portland, Me., a society was formed February 2, 1881, to which the name was given of " The Society of Christian Endeavor." It attempted to organize the young people in a closer relation to the church than had been general, and to train them for Christian service. The idea was catching, and societies of this kind were rapidly organized in many localities and among various denominations.

Not a few Baptist pastors desired a society that should be more distinctively denominational in character, and have a denominational name; and for a time there was much discussion and even prospect of serious trouble in the denomination. In October, 1889, at the meeting of the Nebraska State Convention, the Nebraska Convention of Baptist Young People was organized, and all societies of Baptist young people in the State were invited to affiliate with it, without giving up the name or form of organization that they preferred. At the instance of the American Baptist Publication Society a conference of friends of the work was held in Philadelphia, April 22, 1891, as a result of which this policy was commended to the Baptist churches at large. Accordingly, at Chicago, on July 8 of the same year, the Baptist Young People's Union of America was organized on a basis so broad that any society of young people in a Baptist church, or the young people of a Baptist church who have no organization, are entitled to all its privileges.

The distinctive work of this organization is educational. In its organ, " Service," it publishes every year three courses of study on the Bible, missions, and denominational teachings and history. These Christian Culture Courses are now pursued by many thousands of young Baptists, the number of students increasing every year, and several of the courses of study have been published in permanent book form. It is the hope and expectation that the coming generation of Baptists will be, as a result of this educational work, more intelligent, consistent, and loyal Baptists, and not less catholic Christians. Several other denominations have watched this work with growing interest, and are planning something of a similar nature for their own young people.

Chief among the educational institutions of the denomination may be reckoned the American Baptist Publication Society. Beginning at Washington, D. C., in 1824, as the Baptist General Tract Society, its transfer to Philadelphia was voted in November, 1826. In 1840 its name was changed to the American Baptist Publication and Sunday-school Society (the word Sunday-school being dropped in 1844), and the purposes of the organization were enlarged, being now defined as " to promote evangelical religion by means of the printing-press, colportage, and the Sunday-school." In 1856 the Society acquired by purchase the " Young Reaper," and from that time added other Sunday-school periodicals to its list, until it has reached its present proportions and immense circulation. In the earlier years of the Society, its work of publication was necessarily confined in the main to books and papers for Sunday-schools; but it was never a part of its plan thus to restrict the field of its operations. As early as 1844, the publication of books for the denomination at large was begun by the issue of an American edition of the writings of Andrew Fuller, the first of a long list of books of the highest value and of many varieties. Contrary to a general impression for many years, the bulk of the Society's issues has been in this field of general literature, not in Sunday-school publications. With the increase of capital and the gathering of a corps of authors, the Society has come to take an honorable and prominent place among the great publishing houses of the United States, as estimated by the size and value of its annual literary output; while the enlargement and improvement of its mechanical facilities has enabled it to vie with the foremost of American publishers in all that constitutes good book-making. The query, " Who reads a Baptist book? " has become as obsolete as that other question, once so provocative of wrath, " Who reads an American book? " Besides its colportage work in this country, the Society has from time to time engaged in foreign colportage, men like Oncken, Wiberg, and Bickel having been aided in this way to carry on missionary work in Europe. Since 1862 this work has been conducted by a missionary department, with separate offices and separate accounts.

CHAPTER XXIII

THE LAST FIFTY YEARS

IN order to appreciate the Baptist history of the past fifty years, we must first of all gain as vivid and accurate a picture as we may of the state of the Baptist churches of America at the middle of the nineteenth century. Naturally our first resort is to statistics, but we speedily discover that no really trustworthy figures are accessible.[1] The only statistics of the denomination for the year 1850 are taken from the Baptist Almanac for the following year, and are as follows:

	CHURCHES	MINISTERS	MEMBERS
Northern	3,557	2,665	296,614
Southern	4,849	2,477	390,807
Total	8,406	5,142	687,421

These figures are open to much suspicion. In a table, many times republished, which first appeared in the Baptist Year-Book for 1872, the following totals are given for the year 1851: Churches, nine thousand five hundred and fifty-two; ministers, seven thousand three hundred and ninety-three; members, seven hundred and seventy thousand eight hundred and thirty-nine. So great an increase in a single year as is shown by a comparison of these figures, particularly in the number of churches and ministers, appears quite improbable. We may, how-

[1] Until 1868, when the American Baptist Publication Society began issuing the " Year Book," nothing like official denominational statistics were known, and it is only in an accommodated sense that the " Year Book " figures since that date may be called " official."

ever, take seven hundred thousand as approximately the number of Baptists in the United States in 1850. The census of that year returned the total population as twenty-three million one hundred and ninety-one thousand eight hundred and seventy-six. There was at that time, therefore, one Baptist to about thirty-two persons in the population—reckoning only those in full denominational fellowship. If we had included all the varieties of Baptists in our computation, the total number would become not fewer than eight hundred thousand (the Baptist Almanac gives eight hundred and fifteen thousand two hundred and twelve), and the proportion would be about one in twenty-nine of the population. This was a very marked increase from the year 1800, when the proportion is supposed to have been one Baptist to every fifty-three persons, or thereabouts. It is further to be noted that in making these comparisons, only actual reported members of Baptist churches are included. If we computed " adherents," at the rate of three for each member, it would probably be true that in 1850 one person in each eleven of the population was a Baptist *in esse* or *in posse*.

But even if one could trust these numerical results as precisely accurate, they would give us a most inadequate idea of the condition of Baptists in 1850. We need to know many facts besides mere numbers. What was the measure of the piety and intelligence of these people? How did they compare in evangelistic and missionary zeal with other Christian bodies? Were they united in their efforts or disorganized by heresy and faction? The answer to such questions as these will go further to decide the strength of a denomination than an array of figures, however imposing. This is what some have meant by saying that a denomination must not only be counted, but weighed.

Perhaps the most striking fact, as we survey the denomination in 1850, is that it had just emerged from a period of prolonged and bitter controversies, which had resulted ir a number of schisms. In spite of these contests, Baptists had continued to increase with wonderful rapidity, far outstripping the growth of population, and surpassed in numerical increase by the Methodists alone of all American Christians. This growth was not due to immigration, as in the case of many religious bodies; nor to proselytism, as in the case of certain others; but to the making of converts among the native population.

As to the state of piety and intelligence among Baptists in 1850, it is not easy to speak in general terms that will be at once accurate and just. In intelligence, they may be conceded to have been inferior to some other denominations, notably to the Presbyterians, inferior to the standard that now obtains among themselves. It would be shame to them if it were not so. If all the educational advantages enjoyed by this generation have not set them above their fathers, then those fathers toiled and sacrificed in vain for unworthy children. The standard of piety was high among the Baptist churches of 1850. The fathers believed heartily in the fundamental Baptist principle of a regenerate church; and candidates for membership were subjected to a thorough and searching examination of the grounds of their belief that they had been born again. And in most cases, the fathers insisted strenuously that a profession of regeneration should be avouched by a godly walk and conversation. Discipline was not one of the lost arts among Baptist churches in the " fifties."

Most important of all—at any rate, most striking of all things that may be said of the Baptists of 1850—is the fact that they had unconsciously come to the beginning of a new order of things. Up to this time, or near it, Baptists had been the sect everywhere spoken against —the Ishmael among denominations, every man's hand against it, and to a certain extent its hand against every man. Before this, Baptists had everywhere been few in numbers, composed chiefly of what are contemptuously called "the common people," often persecuted, always despised, frequently unlearned. Now they had become the largest Protestant body but one in the United States; they surpassed most other bodies in the scope and effectiveness of their missionary operations; they were rapidly increasing in wealth, intelligence, and social consequence. In a word, it was actually becoming respectable to be a Baptist. Only those who have carefully studied the beginnings of the denomination, in our own country and elsewhere, can fully comprehend how much that means. Some can remember communities where, since 1850, it was not *quite* respectable to be a Baptist— where to be a member of that denomination was to incur a social stigma of which most who live to-day have had no personal experience.

Fifty years of history—what have they brought forth for the Baptists of America? We are to consider the half-century most wonderful for the rapidity of its material development in the history of mankind, and the country in which this development has been unmatched elsewhere on the globe. To these five decades belongs almost wholly the growth of the mighty West, with its fourteen new Commonwealths containing a greater population to-day than the whole United States could boast in 1810. Nor is the religious development of this vast region one whit less wonderful. How far have Baptists kept pace with both?

Again let us have recourse to statistics, as a beginning. The actual population of the United States in 1900 was seventy-four million six hundred and ten thousand

five hundred and twenty-three, or, including all the
Territories, seventy-six million three hundred and three
thousand three hundred and eighty-seven. The denominational statistics show that four million one hundred
and eighty-one thousand six hundred and eighty-six persons were members of regular Baptist churches—or one
Baptist to every eighteen of the population. If we add
those churches which, though not in full fellowship, may
be fairly said to hold and practise Baptist principles, the
proportion is about one in sixteen. If we add " adherents "—those connected with Baptist families, congregations, Sunday-schools—one person in every seven or
eight of the entire population may be reckoned a Baptist
in sentiment.

In the way of numerical increase, what could be more
gratifying to a religious body? The population has increased about three and one-third fold during the last
half-century, while, in the same time, Baptists have increased in numbers almost sixfold—nearly twice as fast
as the population.

This is the counting; now for the weighing. Has the
increase in piety, in intelligence, in wealth, in missionary
zeal, kept pace with this growth of numbers? In many of
these particulars, if not in all, it is possible to answer
the question with an emphatic " yes." It is, in truth,
speaking soberly, to say that the numerical increase of
Baptists during the last fifty years is the least striking
feature of their history. To present the subject with any
approach to adequate fulness would require a volume;
but it is possible, even within the limits of this chapter,
to indicate the facts that warrant this assertion.

Consider then, in the first place, the progress in education made by the denomination in fifty years. In 1850
Baptists had in the East five institutions of collegiate
grade: Brown University (1764), Waterville College,

now Colby (1818), Madison University, now Colgate (chartered in 1846, but really founded in 1819), Columbian University (1821), and Lewisburg University, now Bucknell (1846). Most of these names were prophecies, which have not yet been fulfilled; there was not then, anywhere in the United States, an institution that deserved the name university. The combined buildings and endowments of the five institutions named would be considered in these days not too large a "plant" for one good academy. There were, in addition, two theological seminaries—that at Hamilton (1817), and the Newton Theological Institution (1825). In the West and South there were sixteen other institutions [1] of nominally collegiate grade (several of which were not in reality above academic), all struggling to keep the breath of life within them, all practically unendowed. Possibly I have overlooked some institution that then had a name to live, but had little else, and soon ceased to have even that. There are no statistics of these schools, but it is hazarding little to say that the total invested funds of all would not have exceeded five hundred thousand dollars. There was at this time no theological institution in the West, but a theological department was maintained at several of the colleges for the instruction of candidates for the Baptist ministry.[2]

The provision for academic education was even more scanty in 1850. It is true that of existing Baptist academies, nine were established prior to that year, and that an unknown number had been begun and had come to an

[1] These are: Baylor College and Baylor University (both 1845), Denison (1831), Franklin (1834), Georgetown (1829), Howard (1841), Kalamazoo (1833), Limestone (S. C., 1845), Mercer (1837), Richmond (1832), Shurtleff (1827), Southern Female College (two of same name, both Ala., 1842, 1843), Southwestern Baptist University (Tenn., 1845), Wake Forest (1843), William Jewell (1849).

[2] These have all been discontinued except the one at Shurtleff, but a new one has been lately established at Baylor.

untimely end before that date, but in their beginnings at least most of these academies were private schools, and are not at the middle of the century to be reckoned among denominational facilities for education.

The year 1850 marks the beginning of a really great work in the foundation and equipment of schools of learning by Baptists. The following decade saw the establishment of twenty-three colleges and two theological seminaries, beginning with the two institutions at Rochester. In the "sixties" three more seminaries were founded, thus completing the denominational provision for theological education, but only eight colleges were added, three of which were schools for the freedmen, established after the close of the Civil War. The last three decades have been the period of most rapid increase in educational facilities. The "seventies" saw the addition of fourteen colleges, of which six were for the freedmen; in the "eighties" twelve colleges were established, only one of which was for the Negro race; and fifteen colleges have been added during the last ten years, including the greatest of all Baptist institutions—the University of Chicago.

But here again weighing is no less necessary than counting, for the mere multiplying of institutions is not necessarily educational progress. It is not needful to deny, rather would one affirm, that good judgment has not always been characteristic of those who brought these schools into being. But whatever lack of wisdom Baptists have shown in the founding of denominational colleges, the one thing that is not shown is lack of appreciation of the value of higher education. And therefore, on the whole, a Baptist has no reason to be ashamed of the record. The zeal to found has in most cases been followed by the zeal to endow. Of the ninety-two schools of collegiate grade now existing, it is true that fifty-three are wholly without endowment; but on examination it proves that these are mainly of three classes: schools very recently founded, schools for the Freedmen, and Southern schools for young women—which last have always depended for support on the tuition fees received from their patrons, like the "seminaries" for young women in the North. All but about half a dozen of the unendowed colleges come under one of these heads.

But it is still true that the movement to secure adequate endowment for these institutions has been comparatively recent. The earliest educational statistics are found in the Baptist Year-Book for 1872. According to this table, there were then nine theological schools (two of them departments in colleges), with endowments amounting to one million sixty-nine thousand dollars (an average of over one hundred and fifty thousand dollars each for the seminaries proper), and other property worth eight hundred and twenty-three thousand dollars. There were twenty-eight colleges, with a total endowment of two million three hundred and seventeen thousand nine hundred and fifty-four dollars (an average of less than one hundred thousand dollars each), and other property valued at two million six hundred and sixty-four thousand dollars. There is no report of academic institutions, but such a report appears the following year (1873). Thirty-one institutions are named (some of which have since been transferred to the collegiate list), of which three had endowments aggregating but sixty-five thousand dollars, and the rest were utterly unendowed; the whole number reporting property valued at one million two hundred and three thousand seven hundred dollars.

The statistics for 1880 show an advance that is highly gratifying, but hardly surprising. There are now reported eight theological schools. with endowments of one million three hundred and thirty-seven thousand eight hundred and twenty-six dollars, and property amounting to one million seven hundred and fifty-one thousand two hundred and four dollars; thirty-one colleges, with three million two hundred and forty-three thousand six hundred and forty dollars in endowments, and other property valued at seven million three hundred and thirty-six thousand and seventy-four dollars; forty-nine schools of academic grade, with four hundred and twenty-two thousand two hundred and thirty-five dollars endowment, and two million five hundred and seventy thousand one hundred dollars in other property. In the next decade the advance is yet more notable. In 1890 the tables show seven seminaries with endowments almost double those of 1872 (two million sixty-nine thousand eight hundred and one dollars), while the other property very little exceeded that reported in 1872 (nine hundred and forty-six thousand one hundred and thirty-four dollars). This last rather surprising item proves, on analysis, to be due to more conservative estimates of the value of the property. For example, Newton reported buildings and other property to the value of four hundred thousand dollars in 1872, but in 1890 these are set down at only one hundred and twenty-six thousand three hundred dollars. There are also tabulated returns from thirty-one colleges, with endowments of five million five hundred and ninety-six thousand seven hundred and seventy-one dollars, and other property worth four million eight hundred and thirty-one thousand eight hundred dollars; thirty-two schools for women only, having six hundred and sixty-eight thousand five hundred and seventy-seven dollars in endowment, and two million seventy-one thousand and thirty-eight dollars in general property; forty-six academies with seven hundred and fifty-eight thousand six hundred dollars endowments and one million eight hundred and sixty thousand nine hundred and eighteen dollars in property; besides seventeen schools for the Freedmen and Indians, with only nominal endowments, amounting in all to fifty-four thousand six hundred dollars, and other property valued at eight hundred and two thousand three hundred and twenty-five dollars.

But it is in the last ten years that the really surprising progress has been made. The endowment of the seminaries has reached two million five hundred and eighty-six thousand and sixty-five dollars, and their other property is valued at two million two hundred and forty-four thousand and fifty-one dollars. Here the greatest increase has been in providing adequate material facilities, in buildings, libraries, etc. The universities and colleges now report endowments of fourteen million four hundred and forty-two thousand eight hundred and seven dollars, and other property to the amount of fifteen million two hundred and forty-nine thousand and fifty-eight dollars. Even subtracting the large sums credited to the University of Chicago, it is found that both endowments and other property have been just about doubled during the past decade. The academies now have endowments of one million four hundred and fourteen thousand four hundred and seventy-three dollars, and other equipment worth three million four hundred and fourteen thousand four hundred and seventy-three dollars—sums inadequate, it is true, but marking an immense advance.

It would be less than just not to point out that a chief factor in this progress has been the agency of the American Baptist Education Society, organized in 1888, and the grants made through this society by a single Baptist, Mr. John D. Rockefeller. What he has given personally, and what his gifts have impelled others to contribute, together constitute the major part of the increased endowments of the past decade.

Altogether, American Baptists have to-day invested in their educational institutions the enormous sum of forty-four million dollars, of which fully half is in productive endowments, and almost the whole of which is the accumulation of the last fifty years. But not only has there been this great material development, the standard of education has also risen proportionately; educational ideals and educational methods are far higher than a generation ago—so much higher that work that made a man a valedictorian when some of us were students would not insure his graduation to-day. In all that constitutes a liberal education, as well as professional and technical, Brown University in the East and the University of Chicago in the West must now be reckoned as standing among the very first American universities. And Baptist colleges, attempting the less ambitious task of giving to young men only that course in the arts and sciences that is crowned by the baccalaureate degree, are to-day, as they have been from the first, fully abreast of the more famous institutions. Man for man, these colleges have always sent out graduates in every way as well equipped as those that have gone from the most renowned halls of learning; and in the hard push of life it has not often been their alumni who have gone to the wall.

How far have the people taken advantage of these facilities? This may be quickly answered. In 1872 there were in all Baptist schools two thousand four hundred and fifty-seven students; in 1873 there were also four thousand two hundred and forty-seven academic students —making a total of six thousand seven hundred and four. In 1880 there were nine thousand five hundred and twenty-four; in 1890 the number had risen to twenty thousand five hundred and forty-one, while in 1900 it is reported as thirty-eight thousand and twenty. Nothing can be more gratifying than to see the eagerness of the youth of our denomination, and outside of it, to take advantage of the increased facilities for education that have been provided. If so much space has been given to educational development, it is because this is really the most impressive thing in the Baptist history of the past fifty years.

It is time to give our attention to the advance in missionary zeal that has marked the same period. Let us first consider the progress of foreign missions, so far as it is marked by definite results. In 1850 there were in Baptist Asiatic missions sixty-nine churches, with seven thousand five hundred and twenty-one members; by 1860 they had increased to two hundred and seventy-eight churches, with fifteen thousand six hundred and fourteen members; in 1870 these had become three hundred and seventy-two churches, and eighteen thousand seven hundred and forty members; in 1890 there were seven hundred and forty-three churches and seventy-five thousand eight hundred and forty-four members—a rate of increase seldom, if ever, paralleled in the history of the denomination; and for 1900 the figures are: churches, eight hundred and forty-four; members, one hundred and fifteen thousand nine hundred and twenty-nine. In recent years African missions have been added, with twelve churches and one thousand nine hundred and twenty-five members. This survey does not include missions to the nominally Christion lands of Europe. In 1850 there were in such missions fifty-nine churches and three thousand and thirty-eight members, of which number two thousand eight hundred were in Germany, where ten times that number of Baptists are now reported—viz., twenty-eight thousand six hundred and forty-one. Since that time there have been many fluctuations in the fortunes of these missions, some having been abandoned altogether, others pursued fitfully, so that comparison by decades would be misleading without elaborate explanation of the figures. Suffice it to say, that in 1900 there are reported in connection with European Baptist missions nine hundred and fifty-one churches and one hundred and five thousand one hundred and seventeen members.

If we consider the advance in the annual gifts of the denomination for this work, as a practical mark of increase in zeal, results are not greatly different. In 1850 the total receipts of the A. B. M. U. were eighty-seven thousand five hundred and thirty-seven dollars; in 1860 they had risen to one hundred and thirty-two thousand four hundred and twenty-six dollars; in 1870 they were one hundred and ninety-six thousand eight hundred and ninety-seven dollars; and in 1880, two hundred and fifty-two thousand six hundred and seventy-seven dollars. Then there was a great leap to four hundred and fifteen thousand one hundred and forty-four dollars in 1890, which has become six hundred and twenty-six thousand eight hundred and forty-four dollars in 1900.

In five decades, therefore, the members of these missionary churches have doubled nearly four times, and the income of the Society has doubled three times. In the same period the supporters of the Society have hardly doubled twice. The growth of the denomination in missionary zeal, and in the fruitfulness of its work, has far outstripped its progress in mere numbers. It is doubtless true that much more might have been accomplished, but the bitter reproaches of their denomination in which writers and speakers sometimes indulge might well be softened in view of these facts.

If now we turn to home missions, we meet the initial difficulty that it is not possible to compute numerically the results of this work on the growth of the denomination, because the churches established by the agency of this Society have soon taken their places in the regular statistical column of the denomination, and have no longer been reckoned separately. We can for the most part only apply the financial tests, and assume a fairly constant rate of fruitfulness. In 1850 the total income of the American Baptist Home Mission Society was twenty-five thousand two hundred and one dollars; by 1860 it had nearly doubled—forty-four thousand six hundred and seventy-eight dollars; but after the Civil War a great advance was made, largely on account of the new interest felt in the freedmen's work, and the income became one hundred and forty-four thousand and thirty-two dollars. Since then a constant and large rate of increase has been maintained: in 1880 the income rose to two hundred and seventeen thousand and ninety-three dollars; by 1890 it became three hundred and seventy-five thousand two hundred and fifty-four dollars, and in 1900 it is returned at four hundred and sixty-one thousand eight hundred and one dollars. In 1850 there were one hundred and ten laborers employed, a number that has gradually risen to one thousand and ninety-two. In the fifty years just closed, four thousand six hundred and five churches have been organized by the agents of this Society—nearly one-tenth of the net increase of Baptist churches in the whole United States during that period.

The special work of Baptist women for missions has been a development of the last thirty years. In 1871 the Women's Baptist Foreign Missionary Societies were organized, one for the East, with headquarters at Boston; one for the West, with headquarters at Chicago. Both societies have sustained auxiliary relations with the Missionary Union—the women nominating missionaries and designating funds, the Union appointing the missionaries and disbursing the funds. Similar relations to the Home Mission Society are sustained by the Women's Baptist Home Mission Society of the East, formed in

1877, with headquarters at Boston; but the like society for the West, formed the same year, and having its headquarters at Chicago, has from the first maintained a complete independence, making its own appointments and managing its own affairs. This last society maintains a missionary training school. It was prophesied that the formation of these separate societies for women would divide missionary interest and divert funds from the older societies. Experience shows that whatever may be accomplished in this direction finds ample compensation in the general increase of intelligent interest in missions, and the consequent growth of contributions to all causes.

Thus far facts have been given relating only to the operations of our Northern societies. Similar facts are not accessible regarding the work done by the Southern Baptist Convention. No statistics regarding foreign missions have been discovered prior to 1890, in which year there were one thousand three hundred and thirty-eight members reported, which have increased in a single decade to five thousand three hundred and forty-seven. The receipts of the Foreign Mission Board regularly increased up to 1890, when they reached one hundred and forty-nine thousand five hundred and eighty-four dollars; since then there has been a decided falling off every year (one hundred and nine thousand two hundred and sixty-seven dollars reported in 1900). The Home Mission Board reported contributions of sixteen thousand two hundred dollars in 1880, sixty-nine thousand three hundred and ninety-eight dollars in 1890, and sixty-one thousand two hundred dollars in 1900. Inasmuch as the work only began in 1850, and was not vigorously prosecuted before 1880, the ratio of increase in the missionary operations of the Southern churches shows an excess over that of the Northern societies.

This has been a period also of expansion, in many

directions, in the Society's work. In 1852 the church edifice department was established, at first with the object of making loans exclusively to churches in the West, but since 1881, gifts outright have been made in the larger number of cases. By the close of the century, over two thousand churches had been aided, about seventeen hundred of these within the past twenty years. The growth of educational work among the freedmen since the Civil War has already been described. The eleven schools controlled by the Society have buildings and equipment valued at over a million dollars, and productive endowment amounting to over two hundred and eighty-six thousand dollars. Missions have been established and are maintained among our various foreign-born citizens, those especially flourishing being among the French of New England, the Germans, Scandinavians, Italians, and Spanish. A mission to Mexico was begun in 1870, which has hàd a fair degree of success and promises to accomplish much more. The acquisition of Porto Rico and our intimate relations with Cuba opened new and interesting fields just as the century closed, which the twentieth century will see occupied and developed.

Though the American Baptist Publication Society was founded as a tract society as early as 1824, and reorganized as a general publishing house in 1840, almost the whole of its labors belong to the period under consideration. The active history of the Society begins with its acquisition of a building in Arch Street, Philadelphia, in 1850, and the election of Benjamin Griffith as secretary in 1857 marks a further step forward. Thenceforward progress was rapid. In 1869 the prosperity of the business warranted the establishment of branches in the principal cities, to which others have since been added. Other events of great importance were the beginning of the chapel-car work in 1891, the erection of the new printing

house in 1896, and the completion of the fine main building in 1898.[1] There have been over two thousand eight
hundred publications issued by the Society, of which
eight hundred and twelve million copies have been
printed. From the profits of the business, two hundred
and fifty thousand dollars has been paid to the missionary
department, which has received and expended altogether
three million three hundred and forty-three thousand dollars. The colporters and missionaries thus employed
have been instrumental in the organizing of eleven thousand five hundred and sixty-one Sunday-schools and one
thousand three hundred and fifteen churches. The total
assets of the Society have increased during the fifty years
from almost nothing to a million and a half, and its annual transactions amount to little short of a million
dollars.

Has the denomination increased in wealth as rapidly as
in numbers during the half-century? We have inadequate means of answering this question with the definite-
ness desirable, since facts of the sort required were not
recorded until a comparatively late day. The first attempt to gather and tabulate the general financial statistics
of the denomination was made in the Year-Book for
1880. A good measure of the increase of denominational
wealth is the valuation of church property. In 1885 this
was twenty-six million six hundred and eighty-five thousand nine hundred and fifty-nine dollars; in 1890 the
figures rose to fifty-eight million one hundred and sixty-
two thousand three hundred and sixty-seven dollars—part
of which increase was doubtless due to the better gathering of the facts. In 1900 there is reported eighty-
six million six hundred and forty-eight thousand nine

---

[1] This building has since been sold, at a large profit to the Society, and
a new structure will be erected in the near future, still better adapted to
the business and missionary needs of the Society.

hundred and eighty-two dollars. Another fair measure is the annual expenditure in maintaining public worship. This in 1885 was four million seven hundred and two thousand three hundred and eighty-one dollars; in 1890 it was six million nine hundred thousand two hundred and sixty-six dollars; and for 1900 the figures are nine million six hundred and twenty-two thousand and sixty-six dollars. Another measure of wealth, as well as of zeal, is the total contributions for missionary purposes: in 1885, six hundred and sixty-one thousand one hundred and sixty-six dollars; in 1890, one million ninety-two thousand five hundred and seventy-one dollars; and in 1900, one million one hundred and twenty-three thousand eight hundred and thirty-nine dollars. The totals of contributions for all purposes will be regarded by many as the most satisfactory test of relative ability to give. In 1885 these were six million five hundred and seventy-nine thousand eight hundred and seventy-two dollars; in 1890, ten million one hundred and ninety-nine thousand two hundred and fifty-nine dollars; and in 1900, twelve million three hundred and forty-eight thousand five hundred and twenty-seven dollars. Allowing for the imperfect gathering of facts at first, it would appear that the property of the denomination has tripled within fifteen years, while its annual contributions for all purposes have more than doubled. In the same time the membership has increased about sixty per cent. Applying every practicable test, we come to the conclusion that the denomination has increased in wealth fully twice as fast as in numbers.

The close of this half-century sees Baptists not only greater, richer, wiser, better organized, but more united, than at any previous time in their history. It sees them also enjoying greatly improved relations with other denominations—convictions respected, distinctive principles better understood, and in cases not a few, tacitly admitted or even accepted. Controversy has nearly disappeared, jealousy is less frequently manifested. Mutual respect, comity, co-operation, are the rule; and if the organic union of all Christians, of which some have prophesied, must be regarded by the sober-minded as " such stuff as dreams are made on," some form of federation in evangelistic and missionary effort is certainly one of the possibilities of the present century.

Certain counter-currents ought not to be overlooked in this study of Baptist progress. The unity of the denomination in its doctrinal and practical teaching has been the boast of its members and the wonder of others. Apparently a rope of sand, each church independent of every other in theory, and to a great extent in practice, it has not been the inferior in coherence of bodies that have a strong centralized government. The reason of this is not far to seek: it has been the close adherence of the Baptist churches to their understanding of the teaching of the Scriptures, and their loyal acceptance of this teaching as the supreme authority in all matters of religion. It is not putting it too strongly to say that Baptists from the beginning of their separate history have been fully conscious that they had no justification for a separate existence except this loyalty to what they believed the Scriptures to teach, and their conviction that the teaching of the Scriptures must be followed at all cost. But the last decades of the closing century have seen a very considerable weakening among them of this conviction, some important modifications of their understanding of what the Scriptures are and what they teach. If this weakening should become general, there cannot fail to be a great denominational disintegration. The historian can only record what has been and what is; to tell what shall be is the office of the prophet.

As has already been implied, there has been a decline

in the discipline maintained among Baptist churches, as serious as it is great. In the majority of churches in the cities, exclusions are practically unknown except for some notorious wickedness. Even in cases of notorious wickedness, there is often complete immunity for the offender. Little serious attempt is made to exercise oversight of the lives of members, and to hold them to accountability for departures from even a moderate standard of Christian ethics. The place of exclusion has been taken by a new practice, called " dropping," by which is meant the simple erasure of a name from the roll of membership, no stigma of any kind attaching to the person so dropped, with no inquiry, no charges, and of course no examination or trial. This growing practice threatens to become universal in much less than another half-century, with results on the spiritual efficiency of the churches and the personal piety of their members that cannot fail to be most disastrous. Nothing can explain such disuse of discipline but a general weakening of moral fiber. This is an alarming phenomenon, and goes far to offset all that has been recorded of material and spiritual progress.

There has been a notable change in the character of preaching, and in the methods of church work, during the past fifty years. In these things, however, Baptists are in no way peculiar; they have but shared in the change that has come over American Christianity as a whole, and it is only the conservative that views all change with alarm who will see necessary evil in this change. One important result is, however, worthy of specific mention. Owing to the increasing infrequency of revivals, and the decline of the older evangelism, the majority of the converts are now received into the churches through the Sunday-school and the young people's society; the conversion of adults becomes with every decade increasingly rare. It is yet too soon to measure the effects of this great change upon denominational life and character.

Another striking result of the past fifty years has been the great development of the denominational societies. These, nominally the creatures and servants of the churches, have become in fact great independent corporations that control the churches, so far as their united efforts in missionary and educational enterprises are concerned. The annual meetings of these societies are in theory composed of delegations from the supporting churches; in fact, they are mass meetings composed of any who care to attend. The officials seldom have any trouble in directing such a meeting into any channel agreeable to them. The officials are men of high character and practical wisdom, and the affairs of the corporations have been most wisely managed; but the inevitable result of the system has been a growing estrangement of the churches from the societies and the work that they represent. Year by year the difficulty becomes greater, and just how it is to be surmounted is the greatest problem the Baptist denomination has at present to solve. A sentiment is growing in favor of the unification of Baptist societies into something resembling the old Triennial Convention, and the making of this Convention a strictly delegated body, so that all the denominational enterprises shall be once more, in fact and not in theory only, subordinated to the churches. Whether this sentiment will prevail is one of the questions that the twentieth century must be left to decide.

What manner of men ought they to be who have entered upon the great opportunities of the twentieth century, the inheritors of such a history? What boundless possibilities of growth, of achievement, lie before them! How much Baptists may and should do to hasten the coming of the kingdom of God! How great will be their condemnation if, having this wealth of opportunity in their hands, they squander it selfishly, or slothfully fail to make of the ten talents intrusted to them other ten that they may present with joy to their Lord at his coming!

CHAPTER XXIV

THUS far we have considered only the "Regular"
Baptists in the United States. There are numerous
other bodies that agree with these "Regular" Baptists
in their fundamental doctrine of the constitution of the
church and the nature of baptism. Any Christian body
that practises believers' baptism—meaning by "baptism"
immersion, and by "believer" one who gives credible
evidence of regeneration—is fundamentally Baptist, by
whatever name it may be called, or whatever may be its
oddities of doctrine or practice in other respects.

The earliest of the irregular Baptist bodies—and the
term "irregular" is used simply as a distinguishing
epithet, with no idea of disparagement—are various organizations that differ somewhat among themselves, but
agree in holding an Arminian theology. The first of
these to become definitely organized were the Six-principle Baptists. They have existed in Rhode Island from
1639, some of the original members of the church founded
at Providence by Roger Williams seemingly having been
of that persuasion. From 1670 they have held a definite
standing, and, as we have seen, their yearly meeting in
New England was the second organization of the kind
to be formed. A second yearly meeting or Association
was afterward formed in Pennsylvania, where it still exists, with a membership of five churches. In all, this
body has but eighteen churches and not a thousand
members.

In 1729 a number of Baptist churches in North Carolina that held Arminian notions joined in an Association. Some of these afterward became " Regular," and the rest were popularly known as " Freewillers." This name was accepted after a time as a fitting one, and still later, to distinguish themselves from other bodies of like name, they called themselves Original Freewill Baptists. Their Confession of Faith is distinctly Arminian, not merely in asserting that Christ tasted death for every man, but that all men, at one time or another, are found in such capacity as that, through the grace of God, they may be eternally saved. They also hold that God has not decreed the salvation or condemnation of any " out of respect or mere choice," but has appointed the godly unto life and the ungodly who die in sin unto death. They practise the washing of the saints' feet and the anointing of the sick with oil, as perpetual ordinances of the gospel. A plural eldership is also a feature of their churches. There are three annual conferences, which have more power than the regular Association, since they can try and " silence " preachers and settle difficulties between the churches. They had in 1890 in the two Carolinas one hundred and sixty-seven churches and eleven thousand eight hundred and sixty-four members.

The body better known as Freewill Baptists dates, as a separate organization, from 1780, when Benjamin Randall organized the first church of this order at New Durham, N. H. He had been converted under the preaching of Whitefield, and was at first a Congregationalist, but adopted Baptist views and joined a Regular Baptist church. Before this he had begun to preach the gospel with much acceptance and power. In his preaching he declared that God was not willing that any should perish, that a full atonement had been made for the sins of all, and that every man might, if he would, come to Christ—

such doctrine as every successful evangelist has preached.
But the Baptists of his time and region were of the
straitest sect of Calvinism and would have none of this
theology. In a brief time Mr. Randall found himself
practically disfellowshiped, though he was never formally
excluded by his church. In 1780 he was ordained by two
Baptist ministers who shared his views, and the new denomination began. It rapidly extended in New England, and in 1841 the Free-communion Baptists of New
York united with this body. Before this, in 1827, a General Conference had been organized, which formerly met
triennially, but of late years holds biennial meetings.

During the anti-slavery agitation the Freewill Baptists
took strong ground in favor of abolition, and declined
overtures for union made by about twelve thousand Baptists of Kentucky, because the latter favored slavery.
The Freewill Baptist Foreign Mission Society was organized in 1833, and has a vigorous mission in India.
A Home Mission Society was formed in 1834, and an
Education Society in 1840. The denomination sustains
Hillsdale College, in Michigan; Bates College, in Maine;
besides numerous schools of academic grade. It also has
a publishing house, formerly located at Dover, N. H.,
but now at Boston, Mass. The official name of the body
was changed some years ago to Free Baptists, though
they are still usually called by the old and better-known
name. Their numbers are now under ninety thousand.
The old asperities of theological difference have been
greatly softened, and many suggestions have been made
in recent years for the union of the Free and " Regular "
Baptists. Thus far possibly the chief barrier against
such union has been the teaching of the Free Baptists
that participation in the Lord's Supper is the " privilege
and duty of all who have spiritual union with Christ,"
and " no man has a right to forbid these tokens to the

least of his disciples." No other Christian body has, in
its official confessions, declared that the unbaptized have
either right or duty to participate in the Lord's Supper.

The rise of the Separate Baptists, in connection with
the Whitefield revivals, has already been told. They
were also known as Free-communion Baptists. In the
Northern States they have been largely absorbed by the
Free Baptists, and in the South most of them reunited
after a time with the Regular Baptists. Two Associations in the South, which still retain the name Separate,
are counted with the Regular Baptists, but a single Association in Indiana still refuses any fellowship with the
Regular Baptist churches. There are twenty-four
churches in this Association, which had one thousand
five hundred and ninety-nine members in 1890. When
the " Separates " and " Old Lights " united in the South
they assumed the name of United Baptists at first. For
the most part this name was gradually dropped, and the
United Baptists became simply Baptists and are reckoned
with the " Regulars." But in a number of States (Alabama, Arkansas, Kentucky, Missouri, Tennessee) there
are still churches and Associations that retain the name
United and hold aloof from all other organizations. In
1890 there were two hundred and four churches of this
order and thirteen thousand two hundred and nine members. The terms of the union provided that the teaching
of a general atonement should be no bar to communion,
but most of the United Baptists are Calvinistic in theology. They hold that feet-washing should be practised
by all believers.

In 1824 an Association called the Liberty was organized in Kentucky, composed of churches holding Arminian views, but practising strict communion. In 1830
they adopted the practice of open communion, and in
1845 so revised their articles of faith as to make them

more unmistakably Arminian. Churches of this order were rapidly organized in the neighboring States, especially Indiana, Illinois, and Missouri, and everywhere bore the name of General Baptists. The connection of this body with those of the same name in England is shadowy, if not impossible to trace. In 1870 a General Association was formed that represents three hundred and ninety-nine churches in seven Western and Southern States, with a membership of twenty-one thousand three hundred and sixty-two.

There are also a number of Calvinistic Baptist bodies that for one reason or another decline fellowship with the Regular Baptists. A considerable number of Baptists in the early part of this century separated from the other churches on account of doctrinal and practical differences. Holding a hyper-Calvinistic theology, they were opposed to missions, Sunday-schools, and all " contrivances which seem to make the salvation of men depend on human effort." These differences may have been latent from an earlier time, but they first began to manifest themselves actively about 1830, and from 1835 onward they produced schisms in many churches and Associations. They call themselves Primitive Baptists, and have been called by others " Antimission," " Old School," and " Hard-shell " Baptists. Their Associations decline fellowship with any church that supports any " missionary, Bible, tract, or Sunday-school union society or advocates State Conventions or theological schools." Washing of the saints' feet they hold to be an ordinance of the gospel to be continued until Christ's second coming. They have churches in twenty-eight States, and are strong in the country districts of Georgia, Alabama, North Carolina, Kentucky, and Tennessee. There has been an impression until late years that they had become a feeble body, rapidly on the way to extinction. Such is undoubtedly the case in the North, but in the South they seem to be not merely holding their own, but increasing. In 1890 they had three thousand two hundred and twenty-two churches and one hundred and twenty-one thousand three hundred and forty-seven members.

Even more fiercely Calvinistic are the Old Two-seed-in-the-Spirit Predestinarian Baptists, who are said to owe their origin to the curious theology of Elder Daniel Parker, a Baptist minister who labored in the States of Tennessee and Illinois from 1806 to 1836. Parker taught that part of Eve's offspring were the seed of God and elect to eternal life; part were the seed of Satan and fore-ordained to the kingdom of eternal darkness. By the divine decree all events whatever, from the creation to the final consummation, were foreordained, so that nothing can interfere with or change his plans. Many of these Baptists object to a paid ministry, and they agree with the Primitive Baptists in reprobation of all " modern insti-tutions," including theological schools. They practise feet-washing. In 1890 they had four hundred and sev-enty-three churches and twelve thousand eight hundred and fifty-one members, distributed through twenty-four States. They are strongest in Kentucky, Arkansas, and Texas.

The Baptist Church of Christ seems to have originated in Tennessee, where the oldest organizations were formed in 1808, and where more than half the membership is still found. From this center they have spread to six other States, and in 1890 had one hundred and fifty-two churches and eight thousand two hundred and fifty-four members. They are mildly Calvinistic and practise feet-washing.

The Seventh-day Baptists had their origin in Rhode Island, a church being founded at Newport in 1671 by

Stephen Mumford, who had been a Sabbatarian Baptist in England. A General Conference was organized early in the present century, which has met triennially since 1846. They formed a foreign missionary society in 1842, and support a tract and publishing house. Their headquarters are at Alfred Center, N. Y. Here they maintain a college, while another is located at Milton, Wis. They have one hundred and twelve churches, and over nine thousand members. German immigrants, settling at what is now Germantown, Pa., in 1723, formed the first German Seventh-day Baptist church. According to the census of 1890, there were then one hundred and six churches of this order in twenty-four States, and nine thousand one hundred and forty-three members. The Seventh-day Baptists are strongest in New York, one-fourth of the churches and one-third of the members being found in that State.

Thus far all of the irregular Baptist bodies that we have considered embody the word Baptist in their official titles. There are a number of other bodies, called by various names, that accept the fundamental principle of believers' baptism. The most important of these is a body that calls itself simply " The Brethren," but is usually called Dunkards, sometimes Tunkers, and occasionally " German Baptists "; but they are not to be confounded with the regular German Baptists. The Dunkards originated in Schwartzenau, Germany, about 1708. To escape persecution they emigrated to Pennsylvania, where they settled in considerable numbers from 1719 to 1730, and have prospered greatly in numbers and wealth. They hold in the main the same doctrines as the " Regular " Baptists, but add some peculiarities of practice, chief among which is trine immersion. The candidate kneels in the water, and is immersed forwards at the naming of each person of the Trinity in the baptismal formula.

They have an ordained ministry, but pay ministers no salary, regarding even the receiving of fees with great disfavor. They oppose Sunday-schools and secret societies; practise feet-washing as a religious ordinance; interpreting literally the words of the apostle in 1 Cor. 16 : 20, they " greet one another with a holy kiss." They bore consistent testimony against slavery, and are now active advocates of total abstinence. They were for a time inclined to regard higher education as conforming to the world, but they have now several colleges and high schools in which co-education is practised. They still oppose the establishment of theological schools and seminaries, but some of their ministers are educated in other institutions. Owing to differences of various kinds, chiefly about matters of discipline, they have become broken into four separate bodies, one of which observes the seventh day. In 1890 there were nine hundred and eighty-nine churches.

The Winebrennerians, or " Church of God," owe their origin to the labors of Rev. John Winebrenner, who in the year 1820 was settled as pastor of the German Reformed Church at Harrisburg, Pa. A great revival of religion began among his people, and the work aroused much opposition in the church, which looked unfavorably upon such manifestations of abnormal excitement (as they viewed revivals). After five years of conflict, Mr. Winebrenner and his people separated from the German Reformed Church and formed an independent congregation. About this time similar revivals occurred in the surrounding towns, and resulted in the organization of new churches. In the meantime, Mr. Winebrenner had been studying the Scriptures, and came to the conclusion that neither in doctrine nor in discipline did the German Reformed Church correspond to the apostolic model, which he now conceived to be independent churches, composed only of believers, and without any human creed or laws, the Scriptures alone being accepted as the rule of faith and practice. In October, 1830, a meeting was held at Harrisburg, at which a regular system of co-operation was adopted by the churches sympathizing with these views, and Mr. Winebrenner was elected speaker of the Conference. This body now meets annually, and fourteen other Conferences or annual elderships have since been organized, besides a general eldership that meets triennially. The Church of God has an itinerant ministry, the appointments being made by the respective elderships; they practise feet-washing as a religious ordinance, recognize only immersion of believers as baptism, and hold that the Lord's Supper should be administered to Christians only, in a sitting posture, and always in the evening. The church has a publishing house at Harrisburg, an academy at Bosheyville, Pa., and a college at Findlay, Ohio. In 1890 they had four hundred and seventy-nine churches and twenty-two thousand five hundred and eleven members, and were represented in fifteen States.

The River Brethren, probably of Mennonite origin, settled in eastern Pennsylvania, near the Susquehanna River, about 1750; from their baptizing in that river they gained their name. They practise trine immersion and feet-washing; and in the doctrines of non-resistance and non-conformity to the world they resemble the Friends as well as the Mennonites. There are now three divisions of the River Brethren. In 1890 there were one hundred and eleven churches and three thousand four hundred and twenty-seven members, and they have spread from Pennsylvania into eight other States.

Several other bodies practise adult immersion, though they are not in all cases scrupulous about requiring evidence of regeneration. The Adventists arose from the teachings of William Miller, before described, and are already broken into six sects or groups, with a total strength of over sixty thousand. The Christadelphians have some affinity with Adventists, but reject the doctrine of the Trinity, though believing Christ to be the Son of God. They are a small body of about twelve hundred members. The Christians or Christian Connection originated about 1806, in several independent movements, and are very like the Disciples of Christ in doctrine and practice. They have no formal creeds, but practise immersion of believers only; and while no one type of theology prevails among them, their teachers nearly all oppose Calvinism. Their polity is mainly congregational, though they have annual Conferences, composed of ministers and lay delegates, which receive and ordain their preachers. A General Convention, meeting every four years, has charge of their missionary and educational work. In 1890 there were seventy-five conferences, one thousand two hundred and eighty-one churches, and ninety thousand seven hundred and eighteen members. The Social Brethren is a body that originated in Arkansas and Illinois about 1867, from Baptist and Methodist churches, and partakes of the peculiarities of both denominations. These Brethren reject infant baptism, but agree with the Methodists in permitting a candidate to choose between immersion, pouring, and sprinkling. It is said that immersion is chosen in the majority of cases. In 1890 they had twenty churches and nine hundred and thirteen members. These last-named bodies are mentioned, less because they have genuine affinity with Baptists than to answer questions continually coming to the author from readers of this history, about the doctrines and practices of these denominations.

CHAPTER XXV

BAPTISTS IN OTHER COUNTRIES

MEN still living can remember the beginning of a new Baptist history in Europe. In 1832 the Triennial Convention established a mission in France, under the direction of Prof. Irah Chase, of the Newton Theological Institution. A Baptist chapel was opened in Paris by Rev. J. C. Rostan, a Frenchman who had for some years been a resident of the United States. He died of cholera the following year, and Rev. Isaac Willmarth, a recent graduate of Newton Theological Institution, was sent out to take charge of the work. Before the coming of these men, there were a few earnest persons who had learned the truth from the New Testament and sought to follow its teachings, ignorant that any people in the world held similar views. A church was organized in 1835, of six members, and the following year the first native pastor, Rev. Joseph Thieffry, was ordained. He labored in the north of France until his death, at an advanced age, choosing that field of labor because there were in existence there churches holding substantially the principles of Baptists, though often defective in organization, and holding various errors of doctrine. By 1838 there were seven churches and one hundred and forty-two members connected with the mission.

When the mission was begun, the opportunity was thought to be especially favorable. The revolution that had placed Louis Philippe on the throne had done much to lessen the hold of the Church of Rome on the French people, it was believed. But it soon turned out that

394

the " citizen king " was as thoroughly priestridden as any Bourbon, and the Baptists met with continued and bitter persecution. At Genlis, where a member had built a church on his own estate, the magistrate would not permit it to be opened for eleven years. Every preacher or colporter was liable to arrest, and punishment by fine or imprisonment; and against many of them the law was rigorously enforced. The legislative chambers made it a penal offense for any association of more than twenty persons to meet for religious worship without the consent of the government, and punished any one who permitted his house to be used for such an assemblage, by a fine of sixteen to two hundred francs. Wealthy friends in New York paid these fines, and for several years it was found expedient to print reports from the mission with blank spaces for names and places, to spare these brethren persecution. The revolution of 1848 drove Louis Philippe from the throne and established a republic. The new constitution declared religious liberty, though this principle was qualified by the proviso that such liberty could be allowed only to organizations recognized by law. Toleration, however, speedily became an accomplished fact, and serious persecution has never since been known.

The church first formed in Paris was scattered during these times of civil turmoil and religious persecution. It was reorganized by Rev. T. T. Devan in 1850 with four members, and in spite of many obstacles, continued to grow until, in 1863, it numbered eighty-four members. In 1872 the church built, with generous assistance from England and America, a neat and commodious chapel. Mr. Devan also organized a church in Lyons, in 1852, and other churches were gradually added. The establishment of the McAll mission in France greatly helped the growth of the Baptist churches, and at length one of the best workers of that mission, Rev. Reuben Saillens, withdrew and devoted himself to the Baptist ministry. The second church in Paris was founded by him, and his evangelistic labors in many parts of the country have been and still are very fruitful.

The only American workers since 1856 have been those connected with the establishment of the theological school in Paris, which was begun in 1879 by Rev. Edward C. Mitchell, and continued after 1883 by Rev. Henri Andru. Quite a number of the younger French Baptist ministers are graduates of this school, and their labors should be of the greatest aid in the future growth of the Baptists of France. In the last report available there are said to be forty-five churches, with thirty-five ordained ministers, and two thousand and forty-eight members; and two hundred and eighty were baptized during the year.

The name Baptist has been an epithet of scorn and contempt in Germany for centuries. The German people have never been able or willing to forget the disorders at Mülhausen and Münster during the sixteenth century, the blame for which was unjustly laid upon the Anabaptists of that period. For a man to profess himself a Baptist in that country is, therefore, to suggest that he is likely to believe in propagating the kingdom of Christ by the sword, in communism, polygamy, and various other horrifying things. In spite of this deep-seated prejudice, Germany is precisely the country of Europe where Baptists have during the past century made their most rapid, most healthful, and most permanent advances. This is because the movement originated on German soil and with German people—not by the agency of a foreign missionary.

The leader in this work was Johann Gerhardt Oncken, who was born at Varel, in Oldenburg, in 1800.

In his fourteenth year a Scottish merchant took him to Great Britain, and there he was converted, after which he joined a Congregational church. The Continental Society was founded in London in 1819, for the propagation of evangelical religion in Europe. Mr. Oncken had a great desire to preach the gospel among his own people, and in 1823 he was sent to Germany as a missionary of this Society. He began to preach the gospel in Hamburg and Bremen with great success. Many were converted, but the bitter hostility of the State Church was aroused against him and his work.

After some years of this work, Mr. Oncken, by a faithful study of the Scriptures, became convinced that the baptism of believers only is taught in the New Testament or was practised in apostolic times, and that the only baptism known to the Scriptures is immersion. Concerning this experience he has himself said the following:

It was about this time [1828] that I became fully convinced from the study of the Scriptures (for I was entirely unacquainted with the sentiments of the Baptists) of the truth of believers' baptism and the nature of a Christian church. I and a few of the converts who had also seen the same truth now only waited for some one who, having himself followed the Lord in his ordinance, should be qualified to baptize us and form us into a church. But for this we had to wait five long years, though we applied to both England and Scotland. . . In 1834 [April 22] a little company of seven believers were rowed across our beautiful Elbe, in the dead hour of night, to a little island, and there descending into the waters, were buried with Christ in baptism. . . The next day we were formed into a church, of which I was appointed the pastor.[1]

The man who was led by divine providence to the performing of this service was the Rev. Barnas Sears, then professor in the Hamilton Literary Institution, who was

[1] From " Triumphs of the Gospel," a tract by Oncken, published at Hamburg (no date).

spending some time in Germany in study and had become known to Mr. Oncken as an American Baptist. This was the first Baptist church on German soil in modern times. Two helpers were soon won to the cause. The first, Julius Köbner, a Danish Jew, formerly an engraver, became the poet and hymn-writer of the German Baptists, as well as an ardent preacher. Gottfried Wilhelm Lehmann was the second co-worker; he and five others were baptized by Oncken at Berlin, May 13, 1837, and so the second church was constituted. The memory of this trio of preachers—they have all now gone to their reward—will always be precious to German Baptists, among whom they are known as " the clover-leaf."

In the following September the Triennial Convention employed Mr. Oncken as a missionary, and the Baptist cause began to make steady, and at times rapid, progress in Germany. He also became agent for the Edinburgh Bible Society, and his colporters went throughout Germany selling Bibles and preaching the truth. By 1838 the Hamburg church had grown to seventy-five members, and three other churches had been established. This success aroused the ire of the Lutheran clergy, and they complained to the Hamburg Senate, who directed the police to suppress the Baptist meetings. For a time German Baptists suffered severe persecution. Mr. Oncken was several times imprisoned and fined. In May, 1840, he was imprisoned four weeks, and on his release all his household goods were sold to pay his fine and costs. He was forbidden to hold religious services at which any except members of his own household attended! Members of Baptist churches were required by law to bring their children to Lutheran ministers for so-called baptism, on pain of imprisonment or fine. Their property was liable to confiscation, and in general they were treated as men who had no rights that others were bound to respect.

These cruelties provoked many indignant remonstrances from England and America, and such expressions of enlightened Christian sentiment were not without their effect on the Hamburg Senate. A great fire in 1844 destroyed a great part of the city, and the efforts of the Baptists to relieve the distress of the suffering caused a great change in public opinion and official action. From this time Oncken and his church were unmolested, but in other parts of Germany the Baptists were less fortunate. The revolution of 1848 brought about changes for the better in most of the German States. The new constitution adopted in Prussia in 1850 provides, in article 12: " Freedom of religious confession, of meeting in religious societies, and of the common exercise of religion in private and public is guaranteed." It was not until 1858, however, that the Hamburg church was recognized by the State as a religious corporation. Even yet the Baptists do not enjoy complete toleration throughout Germany, though interference with them becomes more rare with each successive decade.

In spite of all difficulties, remarkable progress was made from the first. Baptist churches sprang up in all the principal cities, while in the smaller towns they spread even more rapidly. They organized themselves into Associations, after the American plan, and in 1849 the five Associations then existing formed a general Triennial Conference, which since 1855 has been known as the German Baptist Union, and has held annual meetings. Another great advance was taken when Dr. Philip Bickel, a German by birth, who had been educated in the United States, went to Hamburg in 1878 to take charge of the publication house, begun in 1838 by Mr. Oncken as a private enterprise, and turned over to the German Baptist Union. This has since been removed to Cassel. The jubilee of the German mission and the death of its

founder both fell in the year 1884. The seven members
with which it began fifty years before had grown into
nearly thirty-two thousand, and have since increased to
about fifty thousand. These are not all in Germany
proper; the German Baptists have been mindful of
the Great Commission, and have sent out missionaries
to Denmark, Finland, Poland, Holland, Switzerland, Russia, Hungary, Bulgaria, and Africa. Some twenty-three
thousand of the members they now report have been
gathered as the result of these missionary operations.
Their most important enterprise of recent years has been
the establishment, in 1880, of a theological school at Hamburg, in part by the aid of American Baptists. In 1888
a new and commodious building was dedicated, that had
been erected for the use of the seminary in a suburb of
Hamburg. The course of study occupies four years, and
the institution is doing much for the training of the
German Baptist ministry.

The Baptists of Sweden, in a sense, owe their origin
to American Baptists, yet no American Baptist has been
directly concerned in the work. A Swedish sailor, Gustaf
W. Schroeder, who had been converted in some Methodist meetings at New Orleans in April, 1844, a few months
later found his way into the Mariners' Baptist Church,
New York, and on the third of November of that year
was baptized in the East River, at the site of the present
Corlear's Hook Park. The following year he met Frederick O. Nilsson, also a Swedish sailor, who had been
converted in New York in 1834, and then was a colporter. Led by Captain Schroeder to inquire into the
subject of baptism, Nilsson was brought to a knowledge of the truth, and was baptized in August, 1847, by
Oncken in the Elbe, near Hamburg. In September of the
following year the first five Swedes who were baptized
were, with Mr. Nilsson, constituted a church with the

aid of Rev. Mr. Forster, a Danish Baptist minister, and the following year Nilsson was ordained in Hamburg, and began to preach in Sweden. His success was marked, but the persecution that followed was bitter; and in 1851 he was banished from the country. After a short stay at Copenhagen, he headed a colony of emigrants to this country, who settled in the State of Minnesota. This is not to be confounded with another colony, sent to this country in 1870 by Captain Schroeder, which went across the State of Maine, " poled in canoes " up the upper St. John, and planted a Baptist church at a place which they named New Sweden, in Aroostook County.

A successor to Nilsson was found in Andreas Wiberg, a Lutheran minister, educated at the University of Upsala who, in 1849, became unable to remain longer with good conscience in the Lutheran Church, where he was obliged to administer the communion to converted and unconverted alike. Meeting Mr. Oncken, and being led to the study of the New Testament anew, he embraced Baptist views. At this time he fell dangerously ill, and partly for the recovery of his health, partly in hope of enlisting the aid of American Baptists, ·he decided to make a voyage to the United States. The vessel was detained for two days at Copenhagen, and Wiberg sought out Nilsson and was baptized in the Baltic Sea, July 23, 1852. His visit to the United States was successful; much interest in the cause in Sweden was aroused, and he returned to his native land as a colporter of the American Baptist Publication Society, in 1855. From this time onward the work progressed rapidly. The press was free in Sweden, and much was done for the spread of the truth by the circulation of books and tracts.

In 1861, Captain Schroeder returned to Sweden and soon after bought a lot and built at his own expense a house of worship for the Baptist church at Gothenburg—

the first edifice of the kind in the country. Baptists had been accused of doing their works in holes and corners, so Captain Schroeder had a large signboard put along the front of the house, with the legend, " Baptist Meeting Hall." The pastor of this church was Rev. F. O. Nilsson, who by royal grace had been permitted to return from his banishment. Both he and Captain Schroeder were summoned, at the instigation of Bishop Bjorck, to appear at the police court, after the first public service, and the Captain was fined a sum that with costs finally amounted to fifty dollars. The shame and disgrace of the trial, however, so reacted on the prosecutors that the church was molested no further.

In other places, however, the Baptists were less fortunate. Fines and imprisonments and distraint of property were common. Babes were forcibly taken from their parents and baptized in Lutheran churches. One of their ministers was summoned before the courts sixteen times, was imprisoned six times, and once was shackled for many days and compelled to pay a large fine. These persecutions, in most cases instigated by the State clergy, and in all cases approved by them, aroused much sympathy and indignation in Sweden itself, and also in other countries. Strong representations were made by the Evangelical Alliance; petitions for liberty of worship poured in upon the government; remonstrances were formally made by representatives of England and the United States, and gradually these severities were relaxed. Such persecutions were the more intolerable, in that they were wholly illegal. The Constitution of Sweden, adopted in 1809, declares: " The king shall not coerce anybody's conscience or allow it to be coerced, but protect every one in the free exercise of his religion, provided the peace of the community is not disturbed or general scandal caused thereby." In the midst of the persecutions, King Oscar I. declared, in his opening speech to the Diet, October 17, 1856: "Toleration, founded on individual, immovable conviction, and respect for the religious faith of others, belongs to the essence of the Protestant Church, and ought to be accepted among a people whose heroic king, Gustavus Adolphus, by brilliant victories and the sacrifice of his life, laid the foundation of freedom of thought in Central Europe. Those laws, therefore, which hinder religious liberty and freedom of worship ought to be abolished, and the general law be brought into agreement with the sixteenth section of the constitution" [already quoted above]. These were brave words, yet both the king and his courts went on in the work of persecution, though the king frequently used his royal authority to soften its bitterness. Baptists do not yet enjoy complete toleration. A law was made in behalf of Dissenters in 1860 and amended in 1873; but the provisions of this law are so obnoxious and offer so slight advantages that few Baptist churches have ever availed themselves of it. For the most part they continue to be nominally members of the State Church. As such they are conceded the right to meet together, so long as they do not teach anything that may be considered as leading to separation. The enforcement of this restriction has been dropped by general consent.

For ten years the work in Sweden went on under the direction of the Publication Society, and then it was transferred to the Missionary Union. From nine churches in 1855 they grew by the end of the century to five hundred and sixty-four, and from four hundred and seventy-six members to forty thousand seven hundred and fifty-nine—a truly wonderful increase, which takes no account of their missionary growth. In 1867 they began to preach the truth in Norway, where a church was organized the following year. Progress has been slow in comparison with the work in Sweden, but the century closed with thirty-two Baptist churches and two thousand six hundred and seventy one members in that country. A mission in Finland was begun in 1868, as a result of which thirty-one churches and two thousand and thirty members greeted the twentieth century.

The Conference of Swedish churches was formed in 1857, and has done much to promote Baptist progress. It has greatly stimulated the missionary spirit. Throughout their history the Swedish Baptists have been in the forefront of all Christian enterprise. They were the first to establish Sunday-schools in that country, not one being known in 1855, while in 1857 Mr. Wiberg reported eight among the Baptists, with three hundred and thirty-nine scholars. The first Christian Endeavor Society in Sweden was organized in the Baptist church at Orebo, and in work for the young people Baptists are in advance of all other Christians.

In October, 1866, the Bethel Theological Seminary was established in Stockholm, under the care of Rev. Knut O. Broady, D. D., and has since been doing a work of great importance in the education of the Swedish ministry. In 1883 it entered a commodious building erected for its use in Stockholm, and has been more prosperous and useful since that date than before. Baptists have done much to sustain this, as well as the German mission, in the way of contributions of money from time to time; but they have received their reward already. It is said, and doubtless with truth, that ten per cent. of the converts made by Baptists in Sweden go to swell the membership of Baptist churches in this country, and that an equal proportion of the graduates of their seminary become pastors of Swedish churches in America.

The Baptist cause in Denmark, as has already been said, is the result, not of anything done by American

Baptists, but of the missionary enthusiasm of our German brethren. A Baptist church was organized in Copenhagen near the close of the year 1839, eleven being then baptized by Mr. Oncken, and ten in July of the following year, when P. C. Moenster was ordained as pastor of the church. Another church of eight members was formed by Mr. Oncken in September, 1840, at Langeland; and in the following October a third church of ten members was formed at Aalberg by Moenster. Rigorous persecutions were almost immediately begun by the government, then an absolute monarchy. King Christian V. promulgated the following law: " That religion alone shall be allowed in the king's lands and realms which agrees with the Holy Scriptures, the Apostolic and Nicene creeds, the Athanasian creed, and the Augsburg Confession, and with Luther's Minor Catechism." Pastor Moenster was imprisoned from about the first of December, 1840, until November of the following year. His brother, Adolph, who took his place, shared his fate in May, 1841. In 1842 Moenster was imprisoned a second time, from January to July. Drs. Horatio B. Hackett and Thomas J. Conant, acting in behalf of American Baptists, visited the Denmark brethren in 1843, and attempted to alleviate their condition. High Danish officials, both in Church and in State, bore witness to the blameless character of these persecuted Baptists, and gradually the severities practised against them were relaxed.

It was, however, not before 1850 that they began to enjoy much toleration; and added to this difficulty they lost many of their members by emigration to a land of greater liberty. They began to form Associations of their churches in 1849, and in 1887 withdrew from the German Baptist Union and formed a union of their own. They had not been unmindful of missionary obligations, and have missionaries on the Congo field. The Danish Baptists now number over four thousand.

One of the most interesting of the German Baptist missions is that in Russia. There were already Mennonites in the southern region who were virtually Baptists, while the Stundists and other native sects have close affiliation with Baptist beliefs and practices. But the planting of Baptist churches has gone on steadily for quite a generation. The work began among the numerous German colonies, but has extended among the Russians themselves. There are now some twenty-five thousand members of Baptist churches in Russia proper, and the number would have been greatly increased but for the severe persecutions they have experienced, in common with all dissenters from the State church. Russia professes to grant complete religious liberty, the imperial decree reading as follows: " All the subjects of the Russian empire not belonging to the Established Church, both native Russians and those from abroad who are in the service of the State, are permitted at all times openly to confess their faith and practise their services in accordance with the rite. This freedom of faith is assured not only to Christians of foreign confessions, but also to the Jews, Mohammedans, and heathen, so that all the peoples in Russia may worship God, the Almighty, with different tongues, according to the laws and confessions of their fathers so that they may bless the government of the Russian tsar, and pray for his welfare to the Creator of the world." This seems like a very liberal provision for freedom of conscience, but most of the concession is interpreted away by other acts. Liberty of worship is secured to men in the faith of their fathers, but they have no liberty to change their religion except by adopting that established by law. Nobody must persuade an orthodox Russian to join another church. He who does so is guilty of a high crime and misdemeanor, forfeits all his legal and civil rights, and is punishable by banishment to Siberia. Thousands of our Baptist brethren are said to have suffered this penalty—in some cases whole churches and their pastors having been deported. Any Russian who leaves the orthodox communion to become a Baptist may be put under the jurisdiction of the ecclesiastical courts. This means that guardians will be appointed for his children, and an administrator for his estates, until his return to the orthodox faith; his obstinate refusal to return makes these penalties permanent. In spite of such laws and their rigid enforcement, the Baptist cause has continued to prosper in Russia.

A mission to Greece was begun in 1836 by the American Baptist Missionary Union, but very small results followed many years of hard labor. The chief convert of the mission became its leading minister, Rev. Demetrius Z. Sakellarios. The mission was suspended in 1856, but was resumed in 1871, and finally discontinued in 1886. A recent historian of our missions sums up the history of the mission thus: " While the Greeks are of high intelligence and have great interest in religious subjects, they are not open to that influence of religious truth which will enable them to endure separation from their own people and church for the sake of a purer gospel and a more living faith." [1]

A Baptist mission founded in Spain by Rev. W. I. Knapp, has had a history but little more encouraging. At one time it was nearly extinct, but it was revived by the sending of a missionary from this country. There are now several vigorous Baptist churches and active pastors, and it is possible that the Baptist cause in Spain has a future more encouraging than its past.

[1] Merriam, " History of American Baptist Missions," p. 201.

The Southern Baptist Convention has maintained a mission in Italy, with varying success, since the year 1870. An independent mission was also for a time maintained in Rome by Rev. W. C. Van Meter, with the help of Baptists and others, but the Missionary Union has never established an Italian mission. Rev. George B. Taylor, D. D., was the efficient superintendent of the Southern Baptist missionary operations for many years. Thirty years of labor have established sixty-four Baptist churches in the kingdom, from the Alps to the island of Sicily, with one thousand four hundred and thirty members. There has been a good deal of sentimentalism connected with this mission; the idea of having a Baptist church under the very shadow of the Vatican has been most captivating to many minds. As was said at Balaklava, " It is magnificent, but it is not war." That sort of thing may gratify the remnant of the old Adam in us, but it is not evangelizing the world.

The only cases in which our European work has proved prosperous, or even had the capacity of permanent life, are those in which there has been a self-originating body of Baptists, whom their American brethren have simply aided by counsel and money. Where we have sent out missionaries from this country, or where the work has not been from the first carried on mainly by native Baptists, there has been a succession of mortifying failures. Nor is it difficult to see why this should be the case. Europe is not a pagan country. Its people already have the religion of Christ—in a perverted form, it is true; yet not so perverted but that multitudes find in it the way of salvation. It is inevitable that such people should look with coldness upon foreigners who come to teach them, not a different religion, but what they have been bred to consider a heretical form of their own.

The belief has therefore become of late years very

general that it is unadvisable for American Baptists to maintain missions in European countries by direct support of missionaries or pastors. So soon as churches are formed it is believed to be best that they support their own pastors. Help may well be given from this country for the education of a native ministry, and occasionally for other exceptional forms of work. Whatever is done beyond that, experience seems to show, does not tend to the ultimate stability of the churches or the permanent growth of the cause. Churches, like men, are the better for being self-reliant, and early learning to stand alone. It is an open question whether aiding churches in our own country has not too frequently resulted, like indiscriminate giving to beggars, in pauperizing a large number of bodies that if properly stimulated to self-help might long since have become robust. But this is to leave the domain of the historian and enter that of the social philosopher.

CHAPTER XXVI

A S we have seen, the number of Baptists at the end of the nineteenth century had come to be more than five millions. But a denomination that has nothing better upon which to congratulate itself than mere numbers is to be pitied. Numbers alone are not strength. Before our worth to the world can be duly estimated, it becomes necessary to ask and answer the question, What have Baptists contributed to the religious thought and life of the world, and what is the value of that contribution?

It may be sufficient to reply to this question that the value of Baptist contribution to Christian life and thought is sufficiently proved by the fact that nearly all the principles for which Baptists have contended are now the common property of Christendom. This may seem a sweeping if not a rash statement. Let us proceed to justify it in detail.

The chief of these distinctive principles of Baptists, as has been set forth in a previous chapter, relates to the nature of the church. Baptists have always contended that the church is not a worldly, but a spiritual body—spiritual, not in the sense of lacking a local organization or visible identity, but because organized on the basis of spiritual life. In other words, the church should consist of the regenerate only—that is, of persons who have given credible evidence to the world that they have been born again of the Spirit of God. This principle of Baptists, which was scouted at first and for centuries, has now won its way to general acceptance among nearly all

Protestant denominations, such bodies as call themselves evangelical. In Europe, where State churches still exist, the principle has, it is true, made comparatively little progress. Where citizenship and church-membership are practically identical terms, it is evident that the church cannot insist upon regeneration as a condition of membership. Every one who is born into the State and upon whom some form of so-called baptism has been practised, must be presumed to be regenerate, and therefore to be a fitting person for all the privileges of church-fellowship, unless by a notoriously immoral and profligate life he negatives the assumption and warrants the State-supported minister or priest in refusing him communion. In many of the New England towns during the early period, church-membership was essential to the full enjoyment of the rights of citizenship, the State being in fact and almost in form a theocracy. It was natural, therefore, that persons who lacked spiritual qualifications for church-membership should yet desire a formal membership, in order to avail themselves of the accompanying civil privilege. How this pressure brought about the " Half-way Covenant," with its disastrous effects on the churches, has already been told. It was for vehemently protesting against these evils that Jonathan Edwards was driven from his pastorate at Northampton, and sent forth like Abraham, " not knowing whither the Lord should lead him."

The Baptist churches, as we have seen, through insistence upon a regenerate membership, were a bulwark against the rising tide of anti-scriptural doctrine that for a time threatened to overwhelm evangelical religion in New England. The influence of these facts was potent, not only among the Congregationalists, but among Presbyterians and other Protestant bodies. The necessity was clearly seen of a reform that should separate the worldly from the spiritual elements in the church. Gradually but surely, without outward change in their formularies or an avowed alteration of practice, these bodies came virtually to adopt the Baptist principle of a regenerate membership. They still to a certain extent vitiate the principle by maintaining the unscriptural practice of infant baptism, but they are quite rigid in the requirement that those thus baptized in unconscious infancy shall, on reaching years of maturity, make a public and personal profession of religion before they are received into full membership. And in many churches, Congregational, Presbyterian, Methodist, if not in all, this profession is not a mere form of words, but care is taken by the officers of the church to secure credible evidence of regeneration before the candidate is received. In many cases the examination is quite as careful and searching as that to which candidates for baptism are subjected in Baptist churches. While, therefore, we regret that our evangelical brethren of other faiths do not see the truth as we see it and that they are yet, as we believe, rendering an imperfect obedience to the commands of Christ, we have reason to rejoice that Baptist example has so far borne fruit that these brethren have in so large measure adopted, as their rule of church order, the cardinal distinctive principle of Baptists.

We may note as a second contribution of Baptists to Christian thought the fact that what is known as the baptismal controversy is now practically at an end. The issue has been decided and the verdict of scholarship is rendered. It is true that there are some Pedobaptists who imagine that the war is still going on, just as there are said to be mountaineers in Tennessee who still imagine that Andrew Jackson is a candidate for the presidency. But Andrew Jackson is not more unmistakably dead and buried than the baptismal controversy. No scholar of world-wide repute would risk his fame by denying that the primitive baptism was immersion, and immersion only. Not more than one or two Greek lexicons ever printed give any other meaning for the word *baptizo* than " immerse " or " dip " or their equivalents in other languages.[1] No exegete of the first rank attributes any other meaning than this to the word wherever it occurs in the New Testament. No church historian of the first rank has put his name to any other statement than that in apostolic times baptism was always the immersion of a believer. The admissions to this effect from Pedobaptist scholars of all countries during the last three centuries are numbered by scores, even by hundreds. There is no voice to the contrary except from men of scant scholarship, and the question is no longer disputed by anybody who is worth the attention of a serious person.

The candid Pedobaptists have entirely changed their ground. They no longer engage in pettifogging about the meaning of *baptizo* and the force of certain Greek prepositions; they boldly acknowledge, with Dean Stanley, that " there can be no question that the original form of baptism—the very meaning of the word—was complete immersion in the deep baptismal waters," but that such immersion is " peculiarly unsuitable to the tastes, the convenience, and the feelings of the countries of the North and West." This argument ignores, to be sure, the historical fact that sprinkling originated in the warm South, and immersion lingered longest in a cold country like England; but never mind that. The triumphant conclusion is fine—this quite unauthorized substitution of sprinkling for immersion, though it " has set aside the larger part of the apostolic language regarding baptism,

[1] The secondary meaning, " to dye," recognized in most lexicons, cannot be called another meaning, since it expresses a mere modification of the root signification of the word—the *dyeing* is performed by *dipping*.

and has altered the very meaning of the word," is nevertheless to be regarded as "a striking example of the triumph of common sense and convenience over the bondage of form and custom."

To meet their opponents on this changed ground, Baptists have but to stand by their cardinal principle that the authority of the Lord Jesus Christ, as expressed to us through the Scriptures, is paramount with a true follower of Christ. When he says, Do this, whatever it may be, his loyal follower has no choice but to obey. And he cannot long persuade himself or persuade the world that it is obedience to do something quite different, under the plea that "it will do just as well." Nothing will do as well as unquestioning, exact, glad obedience to Christ's lightest word.

It would be flattering to denominational pride to say that a third Baptist contribution to Christian thought is the doctrine as to the place of the Lord's Supper among the ordinances of Christ; but to say this would not be true. The Baptist doctrine in this respect has never been peculiar, though opponents have sometimes made strenuous efforts to represent it as such. There is not—there never has been—a Christian body whose standards authorized its clergy to administer the communion to the unbaptized. Individual ministers have stretched church law to cover their own wrong practice in this regard. It is not uncommon, for example, for Episcopal clergymen to admit to the communion practically all who present themselves and are not known to them to be persons of immoral life, and they sometimes invite people whom they know to be Christians not in fellowship with their church.

These things are, however, done in spite of the rubric, which says, "And there shall none be admitted to the Holy Communion until such time as he be confirmed or be ready and desirous to be confirmed." If Episcopal ministers here and there violate the well-established rule of their own church, that cannot be regarded as altering the rule. This principle applies equally to pastors of Presbyterian, Methodist, and Congregational churches that on their own authority invite to the Lord's table other than baptized Christians. Their church formularies authorize no such invitation.

Only the exceptionally ignorant or the exceptionally unscrupulous now reproach Baptists because of their " close " communion, since intelligent and candid Pedobaptists know and acknowledge that we stand precisely where all Christendom stands, and where all Christendom always has stood from the days of the apostles until now, with regard to the qualifications for communion. All that Baptists can claim to have done in this matter is to have cleared away the mass of sophistries with which opponents had beclouded this question, until no excuse for ignorance and no apology for misrepresentation are possible.

But if Baptists cannot properly claim the honor of contributing this principle to Christian thought, they can honestly claim to have added another principle, namely, that the union of Church and State is contrary to the word of God, contrary to natural justice, and destructive to both parties to the union. Next to a regenerate church-membership, this has been the principle for which Baptists have most strenuously contended and with which they have been most prominently identified. For this teaching they were from the time of the Reformation until a period within the memory of men now living, despised and rejected of men, loaded with opprobrium, reviled, persecuted, put to death. Toleration was a byword and a hissing among all parties of Christians, and religious liberty was an idea that apparently never entered men's minds until it was professed, defended, and exemplified by Baptists. It is difficult for Americans, living in an atmosphere of perfect religious liberty, where no law restrains any man from worshiping God in any way that his conscience dictates, or compels him to contribute of his substance to the support of any worship that he does not approve—it is hard for us even to imagine a state of society in which the majority determined what the community should believe, how men should worship God, and repressed all dissent with savage laws and penalties that did not stop short of the stake and the scaffold.

The once despised teaching of a few Baptists has become a commonplace of thought in our country, a fundamental principle of law, and he would be laughed at who should propose its overthrow or even its modification. But to appreciate what change has been wrought by this idea in American religious and civil life, an American must study the institutions of Europe, where there is no State that has not its established church, where dissent from the established religion is punished more or less severely by civil and social disabilities, if not by imprisonment and fines ; and where, even if unmolested, those who dissent from the established religion are, nevertheless, heavily taxed for its support. This was the principle that prevailed during the colonial period in our own land. This would be the system under which we should now be living had not this despised principle of the Baptists become incorporated into the very spiritual and moral fiber of the American people.

There is still reason why Baptists should continue to bear their testimony in favor of this principle. It is generally acknowledged and professed, but not always obeyed. The separation of Church and State is not yet absolutely complete. Appropriations are made from Federal and State funds for the support of sectarian institutions on one plausible pretext or another; a certain denomination is recognized as having almost a monopoly of chaplain-ships in the army and navy, and its form of worship is generally maintained in both services; in some States inoffensive people who conscientiously observe the seventh day are prosecuted and punished by fines or imprison-ment for quietly laboring in the fields on the first day of the week. And it is a fair question for debate whether the exemption of church property from taxation is not a relic of the old idea of church establishments. Here are still opportunities for Baptists to lift up the voice in behalf of their cherished principle, to cry aloud and spare not, until it is not only acknowledged to be abstractly true, but is concretely obeyed.

The Baptist principle of the independence of each church has also won its way to a very considerable de-gree of acceptance among churches of all orders. Among the Presbyterian, Episcopalian, and Methodist churches, although in theory there is a more or less centralized and hierarchical government, the independence of the local church is practically unquestioned. The Methodist bishop still retains his theoretical power of ordering any man to any church, but it somehow happens that where a church desires a certain pastor, and the pastor desires to settle with that church, the bishop makes that identical ap-pointment. The Episcopal bishop has, in theory, large powers; in practice, every Episcopal church chooses its own rector as absolutely as though there were no bishop. In theory, no Presbyterian church can call a pastor, and no pastor can be dismissed, without the concurrence of presbytery; but where both parties have made up their minds, presbytery always concurs.

Baptists have also contributed their share to the world's advancement by their interest in missions, in education, in Sunday-schools, and in general philanthropic movements.

The facts that justify this claim have been given in detail in previous chapters of this history, and only this statement needs to be made here, by way of giving completeness to this brief summary. Though not, strictly speaking, pioneers in most of these forms of religious activity, our churches have helped to bear the heat and burden of the day.

Though Baptists have thus powerfully influenced other bodies of Christians, it would be a mistake to infer that they have themselves escaped modifications in belief and practice through the influence of other Christian brethren. Mr. Spurgeon was reported, some years ago, as proudly remarking that he had never changed an opinion, and that he then preached precisely what he did when he began his ministry. The remark is probably not authentic, and was certainly not true; and if it had been true, it would be a reflection on the intelligence of a man who could spend fifty years in the ministry without learning anything. Mr. Spurgeon's admirers, and their name is legion, cannot think so meanly of him. If a great preacher cannot live and labor a half-century without having his beliefs modified, still less can a large body, composed of many elements, some of them discordant, exposed to numerous hostile and disintegrating influences, and subject to those laws of development and growth that affect all social organisms. Change was inevitable, but change is not necessarily deterioration. Whether the modification is for the better may be left for the decision of theologians; the historian merely records the fact.

Modifications in Baptist faith and practice during the last two centuries may be noted (1) in the character of public worship, (2) in a less rigidly Calvinistic theology, (3) in a change of emphasis that marks the preaching of our day.

The feeling has gained ground among Baptist pastors

of late years that the public worship of our churches lacks elements of color and variety and richness that it should have, and that it has departed from the scriptural method in practically giving over the public worship of God to two hired functionaries—the minister and the choir. The introduction of congregational singing and the use of the Psalter, as well as certain ancient forms of devotion that are the common heritage of Christendom and not the property of any church, has followed close on the conviction. Something like a general tendency in this direction is now observable, but how far it will proceed it were vain to speculate.

That both Calvinism and Arminianism have been so modified as to bear little relation to the systems once passing under these names is so well understood, and so little likely to be questioned, that it is not worth while to waste space in more than a statement of the fact. Each has reacted on the other, and between the latest statements of the two opposing systems a critical student can discern little more than a difference of emphasis. Both assert the sovereign election and free grace of God as the ground of the sinner's salvation; both admit that the will of man, free as regards all external constraint, accepts God's proffered grace; the Calvinist laying the greater stress on the former idea, the Arminian on the latter.

This matter of a changed emphasis has not been confined to theological circles alone; it has affected every pulpit. Any one who will read the published discourses of a century ago and compare them with those of the present day must be struck by this fact. The same doctrines are professed and believed as then, but how different the mode of presentation. The eternity of future punishment is still an article of faith, but the preacher no longer threatens sinners with a hell of material fire.

Retribution is conceived as something at once more spiritual and more terrible than physical torture. The infinite love of God as shown in the redemption of a lost world; the atonement a satisfaction for its sins; salvation not a thing of the future life, but beginning here and now, not a mere rescue from hell, but the consecration of a life to God—these are the ideas that are most emphasized in the best preaching of to-day. To note the change is not to pronounce judgment on either the past or the present.

Another change is at present in progress among Baptists, but it is too soon to attempt to record its history. Two parties are in process of formation in the denomination, one who call themselves Progressives, another commonly called Conservatives. The names are not very happily chosen, but they are convenient, and their application is generally understood. These parties differ on questions of speculative theology, of history, of literary criticism, of denominational policy, of church order. At times there are symptoms that their opposition may break out into an open warfare; at times a peaceful issue seems not only hopeful, but certain.

In the judgment of men of other faiths, the most characteristic fact in the history of the Baptists during the last two centuries has been, not their rapid growth in numbers, but their marvelous continuity of belief, their orthodoxy of doctrine. It is the wonder of many members of other churches having elaborate written standards, and an ingenious system of checks and devices to prevent and punish heresy, that a denomination without a creed, without a government, with no central authority or other human device for preserving unity, with each local organization a law unto itself and responsible to none save Christ—that such a rope of sand should hold together at all, much less sustain a strain that the strongest bodies have borne none too well.

But one cause can be plausibly assigned for this phenomenon, and that is, Baptist loyalty to their fundamental principle, the word of God the only rule of faith and practice. The Scriptures are easily " understanded of the people," even the unlettered who approach them with open minds desiring to know the will of God. Such may not become great biblical scholars, but they will learn everything that it is important for them to know for their eternal salvation and daily guidance. They may not become profound theologians, but they will learn the cardinal truths of the Christian faith, and learn them more accurately in their right relations than the student of some human system is likely to learn them.

Loyalty to this principle has been the strength of Baptists in the past, and as they are loyal to it in future they may expect increase in numbers, in strength, and in unity.

INDEX